ECHOES

Beyond the Pages

ECHOES

Beyond the Pages

Exploring Marginality through Life Stories of African American Women Writers

Dr. Minu Kundi

EXCELLER BOOKS®
A GLOBAL PRESS

Echoes beyond the Pages

Exploring Marginality through Life Stories of African American Women Writers

Cover by Exceller Books using resources from Pixabay.com

ISBN: 978-93-48892-55-3

First published in India in 2025 by Exceller Books,
An imprint of GE Group,
G1, Dream Apartment, Degree College Road, Belgharia,
Kolkata, 700056, India
www.excellerbooks.com

EXCELLER BOOKS®
A GLOBAL PRESS

In loving memory of my mother, Smt. Surender Kaur Kundi - whose unwavering love, support, guidance and strength inspired this journey. Without you, this would not have been possible.

I extend my heartfelt gratitude to **Dr. Rekha Sharma***, my PhD guide, whose steadfast guidance, insightful advice, and constant encouragement made this work possible. Her mentorship has been invaluable throughout this journey.*

Contents

Chapter 1

An Overview of Southern Black Life in America: Introduction

There is no greater agony than bearing an untold story inside you.
– Maya Angelou

Representation has its origin in antiquity, from the times of Democritus, Plato, Aristotle, and political thinkers like Locke and Hegel, and psychologists like Freud, who have offered diverse interpretations of the relevance and necessity of representation. "Representation brings with it the problem of difference and identity, presence and absence, connection and disconnection" (Creech 12). According to Mitchell, representation began with the literary theories of Plato and Aristotle and has evolved into a significant component of language in Saussurian discourse. Aristotle has given three ways of representation: (1) The Object: the symbol being represented, (2) Manner: the way the symbol is represented, (3) Means: the material that is used to represent it. Literary representation is done via language.

Mitchell quotes Aristotle, stating that from childhood, man has an instinct for representation and in this respect, he differs from other animals, that is, he is more imitative and learns his lessons by representing. Man is the only living creature who has the power to create and manipulate ideas and uses signs to express ideas. Mitchell rightly avers, "Man is a representational animal, homo symbolicum, the creature whose distinctive character is the creation and manipulation of signs that 'stand for' or 'take the place of' something else" (qtd. in Lentricchia and McLaughlin 11). Representation, even purely aesthetic representation of fictional persons and events, can never be completely divorced from political and ideological questions. In fact, one may argue that representation is precisely the point where these questions are most likely to enter into a literary work.

"If literature is a 'representation of life,' then representation is exactly the place where 'life,' in all its social and subjective complexity, gets into the literary work" (Lentricchia and McLaughlin 15). Literature, through its representation of events, reflects multiple socio-cultural realities, including ideologies, cultural ethos, and power politics inherent in the dynamics of presenting reality. It is worth noting that representation is of substantial significance in literary analysis: "Representation is an essential part of the process by which meaning is produced and exchanged between members of a culture" (qtd. in Sharma 3). Representation underlines the reverberations of socio-economic realities along with culture and plays a decisive role in solving the conflicts owing to racio-cultural patterns of different communities.

Representation is a moot point in the present scenario, as it manifests itself to achieve one's subjective viewpoint: "Representation affects the ways in which actual individuals are perceived. Although some might view representations as harmless likeness, they undeniably do have a real effect on the world. They are meant to relay a message and influence opinion and action. Therefore, one needs to cross-examine the implicit ideological and political motivation for any representation, mainly because the image or idea formed in the mind has vast implications for real people in real contexts. Both the scarcity and the importance of minority representation yield what many have called 'the burden of representations'" (Dimri 66). Representation is thus an ideological tool, as it serves to reinforce systems of inequality and subordination, and as such, a great amount of effort and caution is required to dislodge dominant modes of representation so as to challenge the hegemonic forces of representation.

Jaiwanti Dimri opines, "Representations can be clear images, likeness, material reproduction, performances and simulations. Representation can also be defined as the act of stating facts in order to influence or affect the action of others.... Despite the fact of representation being the reproduction/representation of a likeness, these representations are most often thought to be somewhat realistic, a clear image of the represented object and this is why it becomes imperative to constantly question representations. If there is always an element of interpretation involved in representation, we must then note who may be doing the interpreting" (63–64). It can be defined as an act of placing and stating facts in order to influencc or affect an action. In contemporary times, these representations are reproduced in various forms of popular culture such as literary genres, novels, academic texts, journals, and magazines.

In representation, the marginal/oppressed group is rendered voiceless. This is largely due to the structural domination which is characterised by the international division of labour, as all forms of representation come from a privileged position of power, supported by educational opportunity, citizenship, class, race, gender, and location. Gayatri Chakravorty Spivak formulates the problem concisely: if the subaltern could speak – that is, speak in a way that really mattered to us – then they wouldn't be subalterns. Literature in the post-modernist era has emerged as a safety valve to give an outlet to repressive feelings. The representation of subalterns highlights their unique cultural features, their tragic exploitation, as well as their resistance to fight for their rightful claims.

The concept of "subalterns" was first used by Italian political activist Antonio Gramsci in *Notes on Italian History*, which later appeared as part of his seminal text *Prison Notebooks*, written between 1929 and 1935. He uses this term specifically to refer to "workers and peasants" who had been suffering under the hegemonic domination of the ruling class that denied them basic rights of participation in the making of local history and culture. He strongly feels that the citizens/subalterns must be united as a socio-politico-cultural force with awareness of its distinct consciousness. The subalterns have no independent space from which to articulate their voice because hegemony conditions them to believe in the dominant values. "Gramsci believed that the intellectual has the responsibility to search out subaltern initiative and class consciousness and effective political action" (Roy, Diss. South Florida Univ. 16). Epistemologically, the term "subaltern" is a British word which means someone of inferior rank. The term signifies those groups in society who are dominated by the hegemony of the ruling classes. Subaltern classes include women, tribals, peasants, and other groups denied access to hegemonic power. At present, the term "subaltern" is used to denote the entire people that are subordinate in terms of class, caste, age, gender, and office, or in any other way" (Abrams 237).

The notion of representation to subaltern subjects is based on the argument that the focus should now be shifted to the marginalized ones in society. The main motivation of this transaction is to centralize subalterns' marginal position in society. In the realm of literature, Gayatri Chakravorty Spivak heralded the subaltern discourse with the publication of her seminal essay, *"Can the Subaltern Speak?"* From Spivak's seminal question, which she answers with a qualified "no," to various literary representations of the subaltern in the texts that are part of an emergent canon, the subaltern as "other" is represented as a binary of the oppressed/oppressor. To the extent that the subaltern is made the central character, literary discourse complements the agenda of the Subaltern Studies Group. However, in addressing the subject, literary discourse takes on the side of the "intellectual" who speaks for the subaltern, granting him literary space but no voice. Consequently, representations of the subaltern function within the dichotomy of can/cannot speak. Within such a framework, there is no room for subaltern consciousness to be read as a complex negotiation of its own positional dilemmas and political importance, which is transformed even as it is transformative of its environment.

Spivak calls the subordinated people, particularly third-world women and so-called tribal people, "subaltern." She does not agree with intellectuals' idea of giving voice to the subalterns and concludes that the subaltern cannot speak—not in the sense that she does not attempt to articulate their feelings, desires, etc., but that one can never see this subaltern undistorted by power structures and discourses.

According to Spivak, subalterns are truly subjective, and they can never be homogeneous. "Though it takes a long time, the only possible way from Gramsci's perspective was to reach the state of freedom through a permanent victory which necessarily guarantees a dismantling of master/slave pattern" (Louai 5). The ideological weight of hierarchy and power, the problematic of subtly created spaces of binary oppositions, and the dynamics of superiority and inferiority traverse every realm of human experience and system of possibilities. Culture, societal relationships, and diverse institutions including family, education, religion, literature, and sexuality—all bear the imprint of hegemony and subjugation.

Language is one of the potent tools wielded by the dominant groups in society to create binary opposites. Prioritising one group naturally creates the "other." Pushing certain groups to the margin, to the periphery, away from the vitality and vivacity of the centre, necessarily involves the process of "cultural othering." The subaltern is thus created, burdened with the subordinated dimensions, always on the right side of the binary oppositions imbued with the negatives at all levels, be it social, cultural, sexual, or personal. The subaltern is the one who is denied an authentic presence, being bereft of voice or dignity—one who is a mere zero, a cipher with no essential meaning or sense of being.

It is a known fact that the dominant ones have used literature "as [a] potential instrument of manipulating, silencing or misrepresenting the oppressed. For the dispossessed victims, literary representation is the only empowering site to register their protest and contest oppressive hegemonies" (Prasad 14). Contemporary literature gives voice to the subaltern to expose the attitudes of society towards poverty, discrimination, and power politics. The oppressed are no longer inarticulate, as by telling their stories, by writing about their conditions and circumstances, the writers examine the materiality of the local and the present rather than the cultural legacy of the inherited past that poses questions about social stratification.

The gravity of the situation is intensified when the subaltern is a woman who is denied even subject position. Being at the precarious juncture, criss-crossed by multiple forces of oppression, she is the one who occupies the lowest position on the social ladder. Her presence is not even authenticated; if at all it is done, it is only to enforce the superiority of the male counterpart. She is the deviant, the deformant, signifying the lacks and voids. The predicament of the female subaltern is the worst of all oppressive beings. It is a lethal combination for the subaltern to be a woman: her life, dreams, hopes, and basic rights to a dignified survival are thwarted by numerous oppressive forces; she is a victim of racism, classism, and most importantly of the primarily subjugating patriarchy. The dream of transcending the threatening powers of oppression rather remains elusive for her. Even more pathetic is the fact that the dominant powers have so naturalised the subjugation of women that she often fails to recognize the pitfall she is in. She wails in that dungeon forever, often taking it as her ordained destiny to be erratic, aberrant, and abnormal.

In recent years, Subaltern Studies has established itself as an area of academic research of the marginalized, unrepresented, and misrepresented voices in literature that are now gaining centre stage. As a concept, it was first applied in a specific context of peasant insurgency with only repression as its main theme, but in the present context, "Subaltern Studies is primarily concerned with socio-cultural and historical aspects of the society incorporating the entire people that are subordinate in terms of class, caste, age, gender and profession. It is more psychological than physical. This lack and deprivation, loneliness and alienation, subjugation and subordination, the resignation and silence, the resilience and neglect, mark the lives of the subaltern. When they resist and rise up, they feel bounded and defeated by their subject positions" (Singh 1).

The literature of the oppressed sections of society is a reaction against the subjugation of the subaltern classes and the cultural imperialism that the dominant classes create by their dominant ideology. A shift in focus from core to periphery is one of the recent developments in literature at national and international levels. "Just as literature from marginalized areas like Africa, Canada and India is fast becoming a core subject of intense academic interest, various sub-groups and categories within these areas, hitherto relegated to the margins, are lending themselves to substantial literary investigation and critical research" (Chand 71). In literature, the subaltern voices are finding expression, as there is growing conviction that the "affective experience of social marginality transforms our critical strategies" (Bhabha 172). The importance of Subaltern Studies lies in the fact that it strives to subvert cultural politics, which suppress and oppress subalterns by providing them a platform to voice their versions. The primary aim of Subaltern Studies is to critique colonial historiography which supports the extreme "overt brutalities of colonization by creating categories of the 'other' which [were] used for subjugation and objectification of native societies to justify [the] imperialist process of discrimination, subordination and oppression" (Chakraborty PDF).

Subaltern literature has gained a wider connotation with time and is now used for the downtrodden, the neglected, the exploited, and the oppressed people living in poverty and miserable conditions. The need is to promote a literary tradition which represents the marginal viewpoint, to incorporate them into the mainstream literary discourse. Globally, there has been a revolution with regard to subaltern status, and the subalterns from all sections and sub-sections of society such as tribals and dalits, and rural and urban, are registering their voices. The purpose is to give realistic portrayal to the marginalized sections of society by giving them voice to assert their true concerns. Contemporary writers posit that subalterns are no longer meek, weak, or incapable of voicing their protest against injustice; they are men and women who can powerfully articulate their specific dilemmas and concerns.

Literature as a discipline necessarily involves representation, and the twentieth century has witnessed a spurt in the form of new literatures. This new trend questions the elitism and exclusiveness of literature to represent the powerful elite and advocates promoting the voice of the formerly oppressed "other." The inaudible and marginalized voice is brought to the forefront so that the earlier erasure and deliberate hegemonic mindset are subverted. Marginalization is a process by which certain people and certain ideas are privileged over others at any given point in time. It is a process by which, through shifts in position, any given group can be ignored, trivialized, rendered invisible and unheard, and perceived as the inconsequential, de-authorized "other," while others are valorized. To be marginalized is to be forced to occupy the sides or fringes and not be at the centre. It is a process wherein individuals or entire communities are denied rights, opportunities, and resources that are normally available to others.

The social, economic, political, and cultural factors work together to marginalize certain groups in society. The marginalized groups experience powerlessness in relation to the powerful dominant sections of society, which presents the overt actions or tendencies of human societies whereby those perceived as undesirable are removed or excluded. This means their exclusion from the prevalent systems of protection and integration, limiting their opportunities and means for survival. It lies at the core of social conflicting issues, where the marginalized ones have no choice but to accept their lot and suffer inevitably.

"Marginalization" exhibits powerlessness and exclusion experienced by a group, owing to inequality in society and, resultantly, being at the margins. This has a substantial effect on a person, for he is made to stand out and be different from the rest. The third-world nations, developing nations, and women comprise the various minority groups. African American women are triply marginalized on the basis of race, gender, and class. Bell hooks, in her preface to the first edition of *Feminist Theory: From Margin to Center*, explains the agony of living as part of the marginalized section of a larger American community: "To be in the margin is to be part of the whole but outside the main body" (xvi). African Americans are economically marginalized, for they have no means to earn or spend money, being slaves of the whites.

African Americans who were not baptized—a large majority of them—were forced to be slaves and work in mines and plantations or as house servants, and therefore, they did not have any control over their earnings and mostly worked without payment. African Americans did not have money to support themselves, and the whites made sure that they remained financially weak by denying them access to reading, writing, or owning property. The slaves could not choose or improve the quality of life, for the children of slaves had to be slaves and, as such, were incompetent to move up the social ladder. They were involuntarily separated from their families, culture, and religion. Their owners, usually whites, assaulted them and made them work hard for extended hours. They were considered the property of their owners and not human beings. African Americans were whipped and executed by their owners without redress. The women were sexually abused by the white owners; they either died while resisting or had permanent physical or psychological scars and often ended up being pregnant with no father figure to take care of the children. They lived in awful conditions, were starved and deprived of basic amenities, and were not allowed to leave the town. They were not considered American citizens, though many of them were born and brought up there, and as such, they were relegated to the lowest status.

As the marginalized "other," African Americans recount their identity struggles within a society where whiteness is an invisible norm. As white norms represent the yardstick for eligibility to survive in socio-politico-cultural spheres, the African American writer's psyche is inevitably disturbed by problems of "sameness" versus "difference," and "assimilation" versus "marginalization." In the last two hundred years, Black writers have contributed spirited and seminal works to American literature. These range from early narratives depicting slavery to modern works dealing with the lingering effects of apartheid, slavery, and racism.

For a long time, the world was the world, expressed and experienced by man; it was what man wanted it to be. Gradually, woman became aware of herself, and she asserted herself to find her place in the world. Black women in America are triply burdened and disadvantaged: they are Black, female, and economically underprivileged. This triple burden restricts them from a fuller and more meaningful participation in American society, mainly because they are confined to the narrow enclosures of race and sex. As a result, they suffer as Blacks amongst the Blacks and are forced to occupy a marginal place in American social life. Their Black identity and female self are denied by white men and also by their own people, particularly Black men. This renders them insignificant, faceless, subservient, and devoid of identity. The responsibility of attaining the denied humanity and worn womanhood falls on the shoulders of Black women.

Life writing is a fluid term for autobiographical fragments and other kinds of autobiographical-seeming texts. It includes the conventional genres of autobiography, biography, memoir, diary, letter, interview, testimony, autoethnography, personal essay, and, more recently, digital forms such as blogs and email. It is used for recording selves, memories, and experiences, whether one's own or another's. Though not as familiar as biography, autobiography, and memoir, life writing as a term has been in use since the 1700s and has gained widespread acceptance since the 1980s as a more inclusive and open reference that crosses challenges of genres, disciplines, and media. The study of life writing is now an established area of literary enquiry and is employed to describe all kinds of accounts of individual lives and life experiences.

Life writing is a form of autobiographical writing; sometimes "auto/biography" is used as an alternative term. According to Patti Millar, life writing is "non-fiction writing on subjects of personal experience and observation; it includes autobiography, biography, memoir, personal essay, and travel and sojourn writing" (Millar, web. 29 Aug. 2016). It is non-fictional writing which is done on the basis of observation and personal experience—a personal account of your life or another person's life. The genre of life writing uses memory to describe or narrate a story in a creative manner. Life writing is a powerful tool, as it has the ability to enhance the development and growth of a person. It facilitates an expression of feeling, a shift in personal thinking, and the development of self-control and self-identity.

Life writing underlines important issues, for it allows the problem to be dealt with in numerous ways. Herein, there is negotiation between two selves: a mature self-reflecting on a younger self, embracing personal lifestyle issues, as well as political and historical perspectives. Sidonie Smith and Julia Watson, co-authors of *Women, Autobiography, Theory*, define it as "a general term for writing of diverse kinds that takes a life as its subject. [That can be] novelistic, historical" (4). It provides an opportunity to explore one's history from a personal perspective, in relation to political and local happenings of the times, community events, academic experiences, and other occurrences that somehow impinge upon one's life. It facilitates sharing of one's culture and history with others. It articulates life story – personal narrative, autobiography, biography, or oral history – as a primary source for the study of history, society, and culture. It ascertains relations between the individual and the society, the local and the national, the past and the present, and the public and private experience. This involves grappling with theories of memory, power relationships, and self-representation, with potential for empowerment.

The creative endeavour is a therapeutic process for the writers. Of all the literary genres, life writing is the one that best lends itself to historical as well as literary approaches. It suggests the importance of time and place that have a pertinent bearing on the development of authors. The writers reinterpret 'self' for the reading of others: the historical self of the author is substantial for any life writing. Marlene Kadar, in *Essays on Life Writing: From Genre to Critical Practice*, discusses the genre of life writing "as genre of documents or fragments of documents written out of life, or unabashedly out of personal experience of the writer" (29). It comprises texts which are fictional and non-fictional, linked by "a thematic concern with a life or the self" (29). The readers are especially interested in the ways in which a sense of 'self' is constructed through narrative, the relationship between the self and the rest of society, the significance of ordinary lives, and authentic representation. The genre is also related to gender because of the "reconstruction of women's lives" (Kadar 29). In describing this genre, Kadar provides an explanation that it is practised by women who are interested in women's lives or ways of life (31).

Life writing takes into account how lives are written, encompassing everything from day-to-day life by embracing the lives of individuals, families, and groups. Writing of their own life opens up avenues for individuals to examine their formal education, cultural experiences, their impact on them, and how they perceive, react, and interact with each other. The sharing of insights gained from life writing allows others to have a better understanding of the writer. It is an excellent tool for the study and discovery of specific cultures, as it is considered to be a primary source for the scholarly investigation of people and cultures. It offers an insight into the attitudes and beliefs of the writer that provide a wealth of information about his or her cultural environment. The genre has gained currency owing to its multiple benefits. In 1975, psychologist Ira Progoff noticed that there are positive effects of life writing: it has the power to enhance an individual's thinking, develop feelings, and build confidence, especially in people with low self-esteem. Life writing inspires, explains, and exposes the world to locate oneself within the mix. Also, by recording memories, one can lower the risk of diseases such as dementia and Alzheimer's.

The history of African American literature is as old and varied as the United States itself, resonating with themes of combating racism, sexism, and classism, along with the search for identity and equality. Historically, African American literature portrays the whites oppressing the blacks and the blacks surviving and struggling to overcome that oppression (Anand 154). African American literature is viewed as a tool in the struggle for black cultural and political liberation. Black Americans have preferably employed the genre of life writing to pen their stories. The writing by black people in America originally took the form of slave narratives, which eventually helped black people, generations later, in defining their identities from the life stories of former slaves, which are brief encounters with their past in the words of ancestors.

The literary history of African American life writing is closely related to the rise and development of the genre of slave narratives in American literature. The personal narrative in African American literature is essentially a collective description of the racial memory of African Americans. Although contemporary African American life writing has dramatically moved away from the form and structure of the slave narrative, the notion of the collective memory continues to be an essential component of its didactic and thematic intent. In spite of the personal presentation of the African American author, his or her life writing does deal with many related aspects, such as the pertinent issues of sameness, difference, race, and gender.

Feminist literature has constantly endeavoured to bring to light the common experiences of oppression shared by women. It is significantly loaded with ideological gravity and nuances of politically laden discourses. Feminists down the centuries have dissected and thoroughly verified the category called the feminine. Gender equation is a major area of feminist concern, since it is a cultural construct. Being a woman is a biological categorisation, but being feminine is a cultural construct. The category called the feminine is constructed in relation to the male, the masculine, the norm, the centre: "Just as for the ancients there was an absolute vertical with reference to which the oblique is defined, so there is an absolute human type, the masculine" (Beauvoir

5). Simone de Beauvoir further elaborates the process of cultural "Othering": She is defined and differentiated in relation to man, while he is not in relation to her; she is the inessential in front of the essential. He is the Subject; he is the Absolute. She is the Other. (6)

This process of taking the masculine as the yardstick against which the deviant called feminine is measured and analysed creates a negating effect on feminine identity, as she starts denigrating herself. This process is accentuated by the hegemonic pursuits of different societal institutions. The ideology of patriarchy tends to reinforce an already entrenched system of exploitation, and gender equations attain threatening dimensions within the framework of patriarchal dominance. Juliet Mitchell sees patriarchy as a dominant feature with cultural rooting, maintained by operational ideology. It is perpetuated through a process by which subjectivity is culturally constructed. Gendered subjectivity can be seen as constituted ideologically, ensuring the continuous reproduction of dominant masculinity and dominated femininity. Patriarchy is not merely an ideology; it is a set of organised power structures with the key position occupied by man or his supporting mechanism. The position of hierarchy, the authority to dominate and subjugate, is nonetheless enjoyed by man, who creates the norms that establish his superiority.

Literature is a representation of the pulses and vibrations of society, and it is against this configuration that literature should be analysed. The literature produced by male authors, indoctrinated by patriarchy, provides a prejudiced, mutilated graph of women. Women are misrepresented either as angels – the true emblem of purity and innocence, of service and sacrifice – or as the evil temptress – the demon ready to tempt and lead man to havoc. Male-constructed literary texts stereotype women either as the paragon of virtues or the demon of vices. The realistic portrayal of women, who stand between these extremes, is conspicuous by its absence in literature produced by male writers. These stereotypical images are intended as prescriptions for women, dictating to them what they should be and what they should not be. The discourse of patriarchy reads woman's desire for choices or liberation as forms of aberration.

Women writers face numerous challenges in their attempt to model an act of utterance and experience. The available model of literary history is essentially male-centred, and women are aliens here. Being caught in a world structured by male-centred concepts, it is a challenge for women to have a way of knowing or representing themselves. Subjectivity, historically constructed and expressed through the phenomenological equation of self/other, necessarily rests on masculine "selfhood" and feminine "otherness." The 'self' and the 'other' make a pair in which the 'other' is subordinated. Man is identified as the 'self' and woman as the 'other'; the 'self' treats the 'other' as supplement, thus womanhood is negatively constructed in patriarchy. The subject centre of dominant discourses in terms of power, agency and autonomy has been a universal subject which has established its identity through the invisible marginalisation or exclusion of femininity.

Femininity can be regarded as a powerful ideology: a code of do's and don'ts often masquerading as free choices. The apparent choices offered are male-constructed and patriarchally conditioned. The biological differences are irreducible, but the meanings built around these differences are constructed. Radical feminist theory perceives that one group, defined by biological sexual difference, is violently oppressed and controlled by the other. The category called woman, defined by biological sexual difference, is further disempowered through the socialisation process that both creates and reinforces her inferior status. Ideology is the principal means by which the interests of one group are maintained and guaranteed through the creation and simultaneous subordination of the other. The disturbing fact is that these sets of commonly held ideas, values and beliefs always serve the interests of the dominant group. The term dominant ideology suggests widespread acceptance of one set of ideas, values and beliefs over the others, and their relationship with power makes them signifiers of frailty and dependence.

Hélène Cixous focuses attention on the patriarchal value system, which, in dealing with sexual difference, validates a hierarchical construction of binary oppositions. The biological opposition of male/female is used to construct a series of negative female values, which are then imposed as definitions of the female. The male is equated with activity and power, and the female with passivity and powerlessness. For meaning to be acquired by one, it must destroy the other; supremacy is attached to the male, and the battle is one in which the female must always lose. The Greeks conceptualised the universe in terms of various binary oppositions, which included limit/infinity, light/darkness, reason/unreason, mind/body, good/evil, and masculine/feminine. In this sequence of binaries, the second term is subordinated to the first. The terms on the left of the opposition are identified as positive by the Greek thinkers, and the terms on the right represent the treacherous, the negative.

The binaries rarely represent different but equal relationships, as they are inherently unstable. "Tension may be temporarily relieved by subordinating one half of the binary to the other. Thus whites rule blacks, men dominate women, reason is thought superior to emotion in ascertaining truth, facts supersede opinion in evaluating knowledge, and subjects rule objects. The foundations of intersecting oppressions become grounded in interdependent concepts of binary thinking, oppositional difference, objectification, and social hierarchy. With domination based on difference forming an essential underpinning for this entire system of thought, these concepts invariably imply relationships of superiority and inferiority, hierarchical bonds that mesh with political economies of race, gender, and class oppression" (Collins 78). African American women occupy a position whereby the inferior half of a series of these binaries converges, and this placement has been central to their subordination. Black women have recognised the fundamental injustice of a system that relegates them to the bottom of the social hierarchy, and this continues from one generation to the next.

The oppositions are hierarchical, as the terms are structured on the principle of dominant versus subordinate. The metaphorical structures place women in the realm of negativity. The binary oppositions have been extended to the realms of gender and sexuality to circumscribe female identity and to restrict female sexuality. Articulating the specificity of her experience in itself becomes problematic. She is often ordained to be mute, silent and obedient, and it is this ideology-laden scenario that feminist writers seek to unveil and scrutinise. The task of the feminist writer is to uncover the forces of oppression that circumscribe the life and possibilities of a woman. Women have been the victims of an interior colonisation; being denied the resources of language, they have been led into silence or euphemism or even circumlocution. The feminist writers' attempt is to define and retrieve new horizons of dignified, fruitful existence so as to thwart the powerful play of gender equations that always pushes women to the margin, to the vacuum.

The word feminist is derived from the French word *femme*, meaning 'woman.' Feminism is concerned with the liberation of women in all realms of society, including literature. It is the belief in social, political and economic equality of the sexes, and a movement organised on the belief that gender should not be the pre-determinant factor for shaping a person's social identity or socio-eco-politico rights. The resurgence of feminism in the 1960s and 1970s was based on the shared recognition that women were oppressed, and that there is a need to develop theory that would further the process of women's liberation. Some feminists drew inspiration from Marxism and ascribed the economic exploitation of the have-nots as the basis for women's oppression.

The Marxist feminists and the Socialist feminists seek to incorporate feminism into Marxist critique, or to extend Marxism to encompass the politics of women's liberation. The Radical feminists, however, perceive the analysis of patriarchal ideology as a system of male dominance requiring theoretical priority. The Psychoanalytic feminism unravels the silent ways in which patriarchy controls the structured female psyche. Patriarchy operates subtly and moulds them into passive, diffident femininity. In this context, Juliet Mitchell points out, "Under patriarchal order women are oppressed in their very psychologies of femininity, once this order is retained only in a highly contradictory manner, this oppression manifests itself. Women have to organise as a group to effect a change in the basic ideology of human society" (qtd. in Jackson 11). Juliet Mitchell advocates specific struggle against patriarchy; that is, women should decolonise their minds and subsequently decolonise their bodies to rediscover autonomous female identity and unrestricted female sexuality.

The ideologically conditioned cultural parameters validate the activities of men and degrade women, and literature both shapes and responds to this culture. It perpetuates patriarchal ideals through representations of women which omit the reality of female experience.

It is this political scenario that feminist writers and critics seek to unveil. They try to bring forth the powers of oppression which work cunningly and viciously. The struggle to achieve self-definition and break free from the predominantly male power to attain ideal womanhood is explored in depth by many feminists. By articulating, women exhibit resistance to the oppression of patriarchal logic.

The theories of feminism—be it Marxist, social, radical, psychoanalytical, or poststructuralist—treat the position of women as a generalized category with a similarity of experiences and ethos. This generalization of women as a stable collectivity is challenged by many Black women writers. They find feminism as practised in the present to be an extension of the viewpoints of white heterosexual middle-class women. The issues projected herein affect the lives of white women, which necessarily are exempt from many of the oppressive forces that define the lives of Black women. The Black feminist Hazel Carby exemplifies this point: "When white feminists emphasise patriarchy alone, we want to redefine the term and make it a more complex concept. Racism ensures that black men do not have the same relations to patriarchal/capitalist hierarchies as white men" (Carby PDF). Carby stresses the need for both feminist theory and practice to recognise the fact that white women stand in a power relation as oppressors of Black women. Black women generally occupy an overlapping space of oppression constituted by racism, sexism, and classism. The way the gender of Black women is constructed differs from the constructions of white femininity because of racism. Sojourner Truth pictures the ways in which 'womanhood' is denied to the Black woman:

> *That man over there says women need to be helped into carriages, and lifted over ditches… Nobody ever helps me into carriages, or over mud-puddles! And ain't I a woman? Look at me! Look at my arm! I have ploughed and planted, and gathered into barns, and no man could head me! And ain't I a woman? I could work as much and eat as much as a man – when I could get it – and bear the lash as well! And ain't I a woman? I have borne thirteen children, and seen most all sold off to slavery, and when I cried with my mother's grief, none but Jesus heard me! And ain't I a woman? (qtd. in Loewenberg and Bogin 235)*

Sojourner Truth underlines the concept of woman as a culturally constructed one. Her life as a second-class citizen has been filled with hard physical labour, with no assistance from men. "Her question, 'and ain't I a woman?' points to the contradictions inherent in blanket use of the term woman" (Collins 18). The theory of feminism, as such, fails to encompass the life dimensions of those women whose lives are traversed by the forces of oppression. The experiences of women differ from race to race and culture to culture. Feminism needs to address the issues of women specifically in the context of their situation.

Black feminism is a revolt against the mainstream feminism dominated by white women, which largely ignores the plight of Black women. White women have been accused of focusing on oppression in terms of gender while ignoring the issues of racism and classism. Black feminists maintain that the white woman's voice is not their voice, since their experiences are ingrained in race and sex. Women of colour perceive the feminist movement as an upper-middle-class white women's movement which does not speak for the coloured women who have to bear the triple burden. Hence, Black women join hands to voice their fight against this triple oppression. Unlike white women, Black women suffered multiple oppressions, being Black and woman at the same time. In resistance to this marginalisation, the theory of Black feminism came into being. This theoretical concept is developed to focalise attention on the multiple oppressions experienced by Black women, reflecting and defining their everyday experiences. Black feminist thought is focused on the liberation of Black women in search of self-awareness and self-empowerment.

The nineteenth-century Black women intellectuals such as Anna J. Cooper, Frances Ellen Watkins Harper, Ida B. Wells-Barnett, and Mary Church Terrell exemplify the tradition of merging intellectual work with activism. These women analysed the intersecting oppressions that circumscribed Black women's lives and worked for social justice. Black feminists like bell hooks, Sojourner Truth, Angela Davis, Barbara Smith, Maria Stewart, Audre Lorde, and Alice Walker are prominent voices in the field. In a move to reject the vocabulary of the whites, Black women call their movement "womanism," a term given by Alice Walker.

The term *womanist* first appeared in Walker's *In Search of Our Mothers' Gardens: Womanist Prose* (1983), wherein she attributes the origin of the word to the Black folk expression of mothers to female children: "You acting womanish, i.e. like a woman … usually referring to outrageous, audacious, courageous, or wilful behaviour. Wanting to know more and in greater depth than is considered 'good' for one … [A womanist is also] a woman who loves other women sexually and/or non-sexually. Appreciates and prefers women's culture … and women's strength … committed to survival and wholeness of entire people, male and female. Not a separatist … Womanist is to feminist as purple is to lavender" (11–12). The introduction of womanism into the feminist lexicon in the early 1980s marks a historic moment in feminist engagement in the United States. The late 1970s and 1980s witnessed an internal insurgency in feminism led by women of colour who vigorously fought against the sexual politics of the previous decade, only to be confronted by the feminist politics of exclusion a decade later. Excluded and alienated by feminist theorising and thinking, Black women insist that feminism must account for different subjectivities and locations in its analysis of women, so as to bring into focus the issue of difference, particularly with regard to race and class. If feminism does not fully account for the experiences of Black women, it would be necessary to find other terminologies that could carry the weight of those experiences. It is in this regard that Walker's "womanism" intervenes and makes an important contribution.

In 1984, in *New York Times Magazine*, Walker states, "I don't choose womanism because it is 'better' than feminism … I choose it because I prefer the sound, the feel of it; because I cherish the spirit of the women (like Sojourner) the word calls to mind and because I share the old ethnic-American habit of offering society a new word when the old word it is using fails to describe behaviour and change that only a new word can help it more fully see" (94). In other words, feminism needs a new word that would capture its complexity and fullness. Despite Walker's claims to the contrary, she suggests in her definitions of womanism that the womanist, referring to a Black woman, is stronger and superior to the feminist, referring to a white woman. Walker's construction of womanism and the different meanings she invests in it is an attempt to situate the Black woman in history and culture and, at the same time, rescue her from the negative and inaccurate stereotypes that mask her in African American society. In 1993, the word *womanism*, with the meanings Alice Walker bestows on it, was added to the *American Heritage Dictionary*.

Black feminism affirms, articulates, and provides a vehicle for expressing the specific consciousness intending to empower African American women and to stimulate resistance as well. The importance of Black women in producing Black feminist thought exhibits that the primary responsibility for defining one's own reality lies with the one who lives that reality, who personally experiences it. Black women intellectuals from all walks of life must aggressively push the theme of self-definition because speaking for oneself and crafting one's own agenda is essential for empowerment.

The nineteenth-century African American women writers assumed literary power through their personal narratives and written records of the struggle for freedom, despite historical, political, and sociological constraints. In an attempt to recreate and represent the experiences of Black women, by shaking, twisting, and sometimes breaking the existing types of life writing, the Black women writers created a new literary form. The nineteenth-century African American women recorded their narratives for themselves and continued to speak for their needs as well as for their communities.

Life writing is the African American way of preserving cultural memory; at the same time, it challenges their marginalisation and oppression by the establishments. The method of life writing is necessarily more creative, subversive, original, and reflective of the cultural traditions. Despite its inherent conflict between the individual self and the collective self, it is a vehicle of literary expression for many mid-nineteenth-century African American women. Literate nineteenth-century African American women writers were in possession of knowledge with the acumen to use and manipulate the language of the oppressors. Power is inherent in such knowledge, and Black women writers used this power to outwit the white male literary hegemony. Through their resistance to oppression, these women weakened the hold of the oppressor. Their writings are more than just literary exercises; they have the potential of being social discourses too. The early struggle of Black women writers to achieve an authorial voice is clearly associated with the quest for freedom.

The nineteenth-century Black women's writing is much more than a personal narrative that merely records her personal growth; it is a social discourse that applies a unique Black woman's voice for the interpretation of life experiences within a historical context that perceived Black Americans' endeavour to establish their humanity and self-worth in the eyes of dominant white American society. The white man's representation of the African as a barbarian, or at most as the noble savage, and later the African American woman's representation in the mainstream American canon as a sexually provocative woman are notable instances of unrealistic, politically or culturally motivated representations. These contradictory representations are doubly imposed on Black women. During slavery, Black women were considered sexual objects for the masters' pleasure or a 'mammy' figure that devotes all her time to her master's family instead of her own. Unwanted sexual harassment forced Black women to take on the de-sexualised role of the 'mammy' in order to escape the horrible sexual acts committed against them.

In the last forty years or so, Western feminist scholarship has been seriously engaged in redefining culture and reinvestigating the cultural memory and gender interface. The feminist focus is more and more on the retrieval and inclusion of women's works in the form of memories, life histories, stories, songs, and artefacts. Memory is vitally significant from the feminist perspective, for the narrated memories of the African American women's agonising journey in slave ships to the United States, and later of their harrowing experiences in tea plantations, sparked off the Civil War. The vast body of Native, Aboriginal, African, and African American literature has been resurrected and reinvented from the memories of grandmothers and great-grandmothers. "The best instance of employing the apparatus of memory – cultural as well as collective – for various purposes, for instance in the reconstruction of past, in the nurturing of ethnic consciousness or as a therapeutic device one comes across in the Afro-American women's writing" (Dimri 260). There is substantial contested literature on Black women's experience of racial oppression that distinguishes it from the experiences of men.

Literature by African American women is important for its aesthetic qualities, and it also illuminates the social issues which these authors have confronted in life. This act of penning one's own stories is a way for African American women to create their own identities, rather than those formally created and promoted by the whites. The question of woman's identity is crucially important for any formulation of feminist discourse. Women need to search for a sense of self as a way out, an exit, from an exclusive identity and discover a positive feminine identity. "Power and domination are the two defining and sustaining imperatives of a woman's identity" (Dimri 91). Elaine Showalter, in her gynocritical project, refers to three major phases common to all literary subcultures: namely, a phase of initiation; secondly, a phase of protest; and the last phase as "a phase of self-discovery, a turning inward, freed from some of the dependency of opposition, a search for identity" (128).

The image of woman is gender, caste, class, and culture specific. The valorisation or polarisation of a female image is not an innocent act and "is polemically related to the dynamics of patriarchy and representation" (Dimri 71). Mary Ann Fergusson convincingly argues "how the female social stereotypes throughout history have been reinforced by archetypes. Consequently, in every age, woman has been perceived primarily as mother, wife, mistress, sex object in relationship to man" (4–5). The change in socio-political reality is bound to affect and gradually transform the image of woman in a specific community or society, and the socio-cultural images of woman are primarily responsible for the construction of the literary archetypes to be eventually translated or transcreated into stereotypes.

At the beginning of the twentieth century, Black women were still considered practically worthless. bell hooks emphasises the fact that little has changed since the times of slavery: "As far back as slavery, white people established a social hierarchy based on race and sex that ranked white men first, white women second, though sometimes equal to Black men, who are ranked third, and Black women last [...] Most Americans, and that includes Black people, acknowledge and accept this hierarchy; they have internalised it either consciously or unconsciously" (52–53). Black women were not only at the bottom of the social hierarchy, but also negative stereotypes were attributed to them, "[T]hese negative myths and stereotypes have effectively transcended class and race boundaries and affected the way Black women were perceived by members of their own race and the way they perceived themselves" (bell hooks, *Ain't I a Woman* 70).

In fact, it becomes necessary for Black women to dispose of the negative false images and to create their own true self-images. One major reason is that the previous sources of these images were unreliable and based their constructions on stereotypical, prejudiced, and distorted representations and ideologies. "Black woman, writing her life story, is probably writing in order to free herself from the stereotypical and derogatory images that have been inflicted on her historically" (Davies 20). The need to challenge and reinvent the images of Black people, and particularly women of colour, has led to the establishment of life writing as an important way of creating new images and encountering old images. The redefinition of the self through self-narrative places power in the hands of the writer to define herself. "Black women are beginning to experience the documentation of their lives as an important way to utilise their experiences and knowledge, for the expansion of their knowledge of self and others" (Davies 36). This is the initiation for change in the global societal views of Black women.

There is a need for Black women to write their lives—both to correct the history of their lives and for the personal benefit they gain from engaging in the process of life writing. Their exclusion from the mainstream literary tradition led them to develop and employ alternative means of communication, drawing upon their personal experiences of oppression and resistance to shape their texts. The creation of self and community are as much sociological explorations of the writer's environment as they are examinations of an individual's life. The Black woman thus becomes a historian of her community.

For life writing, the writer has to view herself beyond her identity as Black or as a woman, and even beyond her membership in a particular family, to see herself as an individual human being. The presentation of knowledge of her "self" through life writing is significant because it provides readers with personal perceptions that determine self-identity, which necessarily relies on culture, environment, upbringing, and general background, as well as on sex, sexual preference, and other factors that impinge upon her life. She thinks, writes, and speaks from a Black woman's perspective, living in a significantly racist society where the majority of people are prejudiced against Black women.

Black women are marginalised, considered dark and ugly, rather than dark and lovely. They write to express what life has been to them, as well as to release their anger and pain stemming from the mistreatment and marginalisation they experience in a hostile society. They examine their cultural experiences, what and how they were taught as children, and how their upbringing has made them who they are today. Thus, life writing is a channel to know the writers. Black women are recognising their responsibility for telling their stories so that others can gain firsthand information about them as individuals and about the communities they come from. Life writing permits the reader to enter the world and culture of the writer, who expresses deep feelings about subjects rarely spoken of to those outside the community. It has the capacity to unravel culture in the sense that it allows outsiders to know the people better and enhance the value of individual experiences. Life writing by a Black woman opens the door to greater understanding of her culture and how she is able to forge her self-identity despite travails. It captures how they coped with marginalisation both at home and in the geographical and cultural places they migrated to. These works offer a glimpse into the world of the writer and the great skill that one must master to survive.

Black Americans have endured numerous hardships since their involuntary migration and subsequent enslavement. The physical captivity of slavery has been transformed into mental captivity, in the way that mainstream American culture has systematically fostered racism and discrimination. The despicable imprisonment of African slaves—especially physical and mental—still affects Black American values, identities, and ideologies. These hardships and issues were, and still are, present in the lives of Black women. The representation of Black women throughout history has affected how Black people and American society perceive them in general.

Amidst the harsh repression of slavery, Americans of African descent—and particularly Black women—managed to preserve the culture of their ancestry by articulating their struggles and hopes in their own words. A growing number of Black female artists and writers emerged during the Civil War and Reconstruction eras, before finally bursting into mainstream American culture in the 1920s with the dawn of the Harlem Renaissance. After playing significant roles in both the Civil Rights Movement and the Women's Movement of the 1960s, the rich body of creative work produced by Black women has found wider audiences in the late twentieth and early twenty-first centuries.

"Being situated on the margins of American society gave African American women autobiographers an advantage in that they were able to observe much of what was happening within a society from which they were virtually excluded; they were not deemed worthy of the dominant society, but because they were not deemed worthy of much concern, members of the dominant society took little notice of them or of the discourses they were producing" (Stover 75). The first examples of literature written by African American women appeared around 1859, known as the Renaissance of Black literature. It includes Harriet E. Wilson's autobiographical novel *Our Nig; or, Sketches from the Life of a Free Black*. Harriet Jacobs' *Incidents in the Life of a Slave Girl* (1861) is the first autobiography by a former female slave that describes sexual exploitation resulting from the slavery of Black women. Jacobs critiques racism, the institution of slavery, and even patriarchy, descriptively characterising how it feels to be a slave girl. It also provides an early example of Black female strength in the face of adversity.

The Civil War era witnessed memorable autobiographical works by African American women, such as that of the former slave Elizabeth Keckley: *Behind the Scenes; or, Thirty Years a Slave and Four Years in the White House* (1868). There are not many women's slave narratives, but of the few, a deep understanding and recognition of the emotional anguish and suffering come forth.

Over the first two decades of the twentieth century, continuity of racial injustice and widespread reports of lynching and mindless violence inspired a literature of protest. "Hope was rising—though discrimination, prejudice, and closed doors on account of race and sex were by no means eliminated" ("Black History and Women: People and Events in African American and African Women's History," web. 23 Dec. 2016). In this environment, a flowering of music, fiction, poetry, and art in African American intellectual circles—known as the Harlem Renaissance—took place. Based in the African American community of Harlem in New York, it was part of a larger flowering of social thought and culture.

The Harlem Renaissance marked a turning point for African American literature. Prior to this, books by African Americans were primarily read by other Black people. With the Renaissance, African American literature and art began to be absorbed into mainstream American culture. Among the most eloquent voices of the Harlem Renaissance are Nella Larsen, Jessie Fauset, and Zora Neale Hurston. The women writing during the Harlem Renaissance asserted the validity and strength of Black women and provided means for other women to redefine themselves.

The socio-political changes in the Black community in the 1960s and 1970s sought to change the way African Americans were defined and treated. The Black Arts Movement sought to change how Blacks were represented and portrayed in literature and the arts. Anchored in political change, the Black Arts Movement furthered the concept that the artist is part of their community and that their work should speak for the needs and aspirations of that community. Its goals were the promotion of self-determination, solidarity, and nationhood among African Americans. "The 'tell it like it is' temper of the 1960s spurred an unprecedented candour about race and placed a premium on authentic self-expression in African American Autobiography" (Andrews, web. 12 Jan. 2017).

The hardships of the Depression and World War II redirected African American literature towards social criticism. *The Autobiography of Malcolm X*, written with Alex Haley and published in 1965, influenced similar memoirs by Black female activists like Anne Moody and Angela Davis. The growth of the Women's Movement and its impact on the consciousness of African American women, in particular, fuelled the 'Black Women's Literary Renaissance' of the 1970s. Writers like Toni Morrison, Maya Angelou, and Alice Walker are names to be reckoned with, and they inspired a generation of younger Black female writers. "As a sign of a new power, a new African-American slogan—'Black is Beautiful'—was heard across the country" ("Toni Morrison: African American Women's Writing," web. 13 Jan. 2017).

The 1970s and 1980s saw the flowering of African American women's writing as a result of the intersection of the women's rights movement and the Black Power movement. The women's rights movement inevitably led to an increased awareness of the inequality faced by Black women, who were known in folk wisdom to be "de mule uh de world" (Bloom 82). African American women writers started attracting increased attention because of the growing public interest in women's issues. Many of them, like Toni Cade Bambara, June Jordan, Audre Lorde and Alice Walker, had been activists in the Civil Rights Movement and the Women's Movement, and they began to explore racism in the women's movement and sexism in the Black Power movement.

African American women continue to tell their passionate tales, deeply rooted in African culture and focusing mostly on the triple marginalization of the Black woman. Written works by contemporary Black women primarily focus on being a woman—specifically, a Black one. Each woman expresses her rejection of racism, sexism and classism, as these constructs limit her voice. They embrace writing as an act of resistance and present an account of the obstacles that the white male American culture put in place to minimize and control her. Each shows the actions she took to overcome these obstacles in order to assume authority over her life. The authors selected for study are Zora Neale Hurston, Maya Angelou, Paule Marshall, Anne Moody and Charlayne Hunter-Gault.

Though she died penniless and forgotten, Zora Neale Hurston is now recognized as a major figure in African American literature. Several book-length biographies have been written on Zora Neale Hurston, which include *Zora Neale Hurston: A Literary Biography* (1980) by Robert E. Hemenway, *Zora Neale Hurston: A Storyteller's Life* (1992) by Janelle Yates, *Zora Neale Hurston* (1994) by Paul Witcover, *Zora Neale Hurston: Southern Storyteller* (1996) by Della A. Yannuzzi, *The Assertive Woman in Zora Neale Hurston's Fiction, Folklore, and Drama* (1998) by Pearlie Mae Fisher Peters, *A Zora Neale Hurston Companion* (2002) by Robert Wayne Croft, *Wrapped in Rainbows: The Life of Zora Neale Hurston* (2003) by Valerie Boyd, *Speak, So You Can Speak Again: The Life of Zora Neale Hurston* (2004) by Lucy Anne Hurston, *Zora Neale Hurston: A Life in Letters* (2007) by Carla Kaplan, *Zora Neale Hurston: A Biography of the*

Spirit (2007) by Deborah G. Plant, *Zora Neale Hurston* (2009) by Harold Bloom, *Critical Companion to Zora Neale Hurston: A Literary Reference to Her Life and Work* (2009) by Sharon Lynette Jones, and *Zora Neale Hurston: Harlem Renaissance Writer* (2010) by Katie Marsico.

The critical works written on Zora Neale Hurston are: *Zora Neale Hurston: Storyteller of the South* (1993) by Roz Calvert, *Social Rituals and the Verbal Art of Zora Neale Hurston* (1996) by Lynda Marion Hill, *Critical Essays on Zora Neale Hurston* (1998) by Gloria L. Cronin, and *Zora Neale Hurston and a History of Southern Life* (2005) by Tiffany Ruby Patterson. Other works are: *Zora Neale Hurston: An Annotated Bibliography and Reference Guide* (1997) by Rose Parkman Davis—a reference book, a comprehensive guide to the large body of work written about her in the last seventy-five years, which includes annotated entries for books, dissertations and theses written about Hurston's life and literary career. *Women, Violence and Testimony in the Works of Zora Neale Hurston* (2003) by Diana Miles examines numerous scenes of violence against women in her fictional works. *Zora Neale Hurston: "I've Been in Sorrow's Kitchen"* (2007) by Laura Baskes Litwin explores why Hurston is one of history's most influential African American writers. *Zora Neale Hurston: Collected Plays* (2008) by Jean Lee Cole and Charles Mitchell includes eleven of her forgotten dramatic writings published together for the first time. *Zora Neale Hurston on Florida Food: Recipes, Remedies and Simple Pleasures* (2015) by Fred Opie is a collection of food stories, folklore and remedies for those who love to cook and eat.

Book-length studies have also been done on Hurston's novels: *Zora Neale Hurston's Their Eyes Were Watching God: A Casebook* (2000) by Cheryl A. Wall, *Zora Neale Hurston's Their Eyes Were Watching God* (2009) by Harold Bloom, *Women's Issues in Zora Neale Hurston's Their Eyes Were Watching God* (2012) by Gary Wiener, and *Zora Neale Hurston, Haiti, and Their Eyes Were Watching God* (2013) by La Vinia Delois Jennings.

There are a number of biographies written on Maya Angelou in the twentieth century, namely: *Order Out of Chaos: The Autobiographical Works of Maya Angelou* (1990) by Dolly Aimee McPherson, *Maya Angelou: Woman of Words, Deeds, and Dreams* (1993) by Stuart A. Kallan, *Maya Angelou* (1994) by Miles Shapiro, *Maya Angelou: Greeting the Morning* (1994) by Sarah E. King, *Maya Angelou: Journey of the Heart* (1998) by Jayne Pettit, *Maya Angelou* (1999) by Judith E. Harper, *Maya Angelou:*

The Poetry of Living (1999) by Margaret Courtney-Clarke, *Maya Angelou* (1999) by Pamela Loos, and *Maya Angelou* (1999) by Terrasita A. Cuffie.

In the twenty-first century also, a number of biographies on Maya Angelou have been published: *Maya Angelou* (2006) by L. Patricia Kite, *Maya Angelou: A Glorious Celebration* (2008) by Marcia Ann Gillespie, Rosa Johnson Butler and Richard A. Long, *Maya Angelou: Poet, Performer, Activist* (2009) by Don Nardo, *Maya Angelou* (2009) by Gail Stewart, *Maya Angelou: A Creative and Courageous Voice* (2009) by Jill Egan, *Maya Angelou* (2009) by Vicki Cox and Miles Shapiro, *Maya Angelou: A Biography of an Award-Winning Poet and Civil Rights Activist* (2013) by Donna Brown Agins, *The Very Best of Maya Angelou: The Voice of Inspiration* (2014) by Frank Johnson, and *Maya Angelou: A Biography* (2017) by Alex Roberts.

The critical works on Maya Angelou are: *Heart of a Woman, Mind of a Writer, and Soul of a Poet: A Critical Analysis of the Writings of Maya Angelou* (1997) by Lyman B. Hagan, *Readings on Maya Angelou* (1997) by Mary E. Williams, *Maya Angelou: A Critical Companion* (2002) by Mary Jane Lupton, *Maya Angelou* (2014) by Harold Bloom, and *Maya Angelou: Adventurous Spirit* (2015) by Linda Wagner-Martin. The critiques on her life writing are: *Maya Angelou's I Know Why the Caged Bird Sings: A Casebook* (1999) by Joanne M. Braxton, *Maya Angelou's I Know Why the Caged Bird Sings* (2004) by Harold Bloom, and *I Know Why the Caged Bird Sings, by Maya Angelou* (2010) by Mildred R. Mickle.

Likewise, several book-length studies have been carried out on Paule Marshall's work. The prominent ones are: *The Fiction of Paule Marshall: Reconstructions of History, Culture, and Gender* (1995) by Dorothy Hamer Denniston, *Toward Wholeness in Paule Marshall's Fiction* (1995) by Joyce Owens Pettis, *Places of Silence, Journeys of Freedom: The Fiction of Paule Marshall* (1998) by Eugenia C. DeLamotte, *Voices of Black Feminism: The Novels of Paule Marshall* (1999) by Harihar Kulkarni, *Caribbean Waves: Relocating Claude McKay and Paule Marshall* (1999) by Heather Hathaway, and *A Human Necklace: The African Diaspora and Paule Marshall's Fiction* (2013) by Moira Ferguson.

Though Anne Moody and Charlayne Hunter-Gault played pivotal roles in the Civil Rights Movement, there are no critical works written on them. Except for Maya Angelou's *I Know Why the Caged Bird Sings*, no other life writing chosen for this study has been explored by anybody.

The research proposes to analyse the writings of the select writers to scrutinize their lives in different time spans. By writing their lives, the writers empower themselves, and the stories of the lives of these empowered women, resultantly, empower other women. The selection of these authors is for the reason of their serious engagement with the feminist issues of identity, race, subjectivity, sexuality and resistance. These writers have been chosen from different periods and time spans to make a comprehensive statement and bring forth their marginalization because of being poor, Black and female.

Zora Neale Hurston (1891–1960), a novelist, short story writer, folklorist, and anthropologist, is unparalleled in her fictional and factual accounts of Black heritage. Born in Notasulga, Alabama, to John Hurston and Lucy Ann (Potts) Hurston, her father was a Baptist preacher, tenant farmer, and carpenter, and her mother was a schoolteacher. When Hurston was three, the family moved to Eatonville, Florida, which was one of the first all-Black towns to be incorporated in the United States in 1887. Hurston later used Eatonville as a backdrop for her stories, for it was a place where African Americans lived independently. In her 1928 essay, *How It Feels to Be Coloured Me*, Hurston describes her experiences of growing up in Eatonville. Later, her father was elected the mayor of the town in 1897, and in 1902, he became a preacher of the largest church, Macedonia Missionary Baptist Church.

After her mother's death in 1904 and her father's subsequent remarriage, Hurston was sent to a Baptist boarding school in Jacksonville, Florida. After some time, they stopped paying her tuition fees, and she was expelled from school. She lived with different family members for the next few years. To support herself and manage her education, Hurston tried different jobs and even worked as a maid to a lead singer in the Gilbert and Sullivan Touring Theatrical Company. In 1917, she attended Morgan College, the high school division of Morgan State University, a historically Black college in Baltimore, Maryland, from where she graduated in 1918. She studied at various universities and collected folklore from the South, the Caribbean, and Latin America. Being an outstanding folklorist and anthropologist, she recorded the stories and tales of many cultures, including her own African American heritage.

In 1918, Hurston joined Howard University and earned an associate degree in 1920. She co-founded *The Hilltop*, the university's student newspaper, and published one of her earliest works in it. In 1921, she wrote a short story, *John Redding Goes to Sea.* A few years later, she moved to New York City's Harlem neighbourhood, where she befriended Langston Hughes and Countee Cullen. The Harlem Renaissance was at its peak, and she soon became one of its seminal writers. Her academic interest led her to Barnard College on a scholarship, where she pursued anthropology under Franz Boas. Her short story *Spunk* was selected for a landmark anthology of fiction, poetry, and essays, *The New Negro*, which focussed on African American art and literature.

Hurston returned to Florida to collect African American folk tales in 1927 and later published a collection of these stories entitled *Mules and Men* (1935). She also contributed articles to magazines like *Opportunity* and *The Journal of American Folklore.* She worked with Langston Hughes on a play, *Mule-Bone: A Comedy of Negro Life*, and wrote several other plays like *The Great Day* and *From Sun to Sun.* In 1934, Hurston released her first novel, *Jonah's Gourd Vine.* She received a Guggenheim Fellowship two years later to conduct ethnographic research in Jamaica and Haiti, which helped her work on *Their Eyes Were Watching God* (1937). She also penned *Tell My Horse* (1938) and *Moses, Man of the Mountain* (1939).

Her life writing *Dust Tracks on a Road* (1942) was received well by critics; it is a remarkable account of her early life, her love, and energy for life. This is a joyous song, offering a judgement on society and an insight into Black America at that time. It is Hurston's unrestrained account of her rise from childhood poverty in the rural South to prominence among the leading artists and intellectuals of the Harlem Renaissance. Her writing offers a rare, poignant glimpse of the public and private life of a premier African American writer. *Dust Tracks on a Road* narrates what it is to make tracks by following the path of life. Even when the dust threatens to build up and overwhelm, there's still the steady pace; this provides a rich and inclusive look at this woman of genius.

In 1948, she published *Seraph on the Suwanee*, known for its focus on white characters, which was her last published work. Hurston struggled financially and personally during her final decade. She kept writing but faced difficulty in getting her work published in spite of her accomplishments. She experienced adverse reactions for her criticism of the 1955 U.S. Supreme Court decision of *Brown vs. Board of Education*, which called for the end of school segregation. A few years later, living in the St. Lucie County Welfare Home, she suffered several strokes. On 28th January 1960, Hurston died poor and alone and was buried in an unmarked grave in Fort Pierce, Florida.

Alice Walker sought Hurston's grave in 1973 and planted a grave marker calling her "A Genius of the South." She wrote about Hurston in the essay "In Search of Zora Neale Hurston" (1975) in *Ms.* magazine. This helped to revive interest in Hurston, and her work introduced Hurston to a new generation of readers and encouraged publishers to print new editions of Hurston's writings. Like Alice Walker, contemporary Black women scholars believe that "people do not throw their geniuses away," and that "if they are thrown away, it is our duty as artists, scholars, and witnesses for the future to collect them again for the sake of our children … if necessary, bone by bone" (Walker, *Living by the Word* 92). Among other writers, Maya Angelou, Toni Morrison, and Ralph Ellison were highly influenced by Hurston. Her manuscript *Every Tongue Got to Confess*, a collection of folk tales gathered in the 1920s, was published posthumously in 2001 after being discovered in the Smithsonian archives. Zora Neale Hurston's hometown of Eatonville, Florida, celebrates her life in an annual festival and is home to the Zora Neale Hurston Museum of Fine Arts, named in her honour. Every year, her legacy is celebrated at the Zora Neale Hurston Festival of the Arts and Humanities. On 7th January 2014, the 123rd anniversary of Hurston's birthday was commemorated by Google Doodle.

Maya Angelou (1928–2014), a multi-talented and celebrated American author, poet, educator, dramatist, producer, actress, historian, filmmaker, civil rights activist, and autobiographer, has been hailed as "America's most visible Black female autobiographer" by Joanne M. Braxton. She is one of the most renowned and influential voices of the times. She published seven life writings, three books of essays, several books of poetry, and was credited with a list of plays, movies, and television shows spanning over fifty years. Born Marguerite Ann

Johnson on 4th April 1928 in St. Louis, Missouri, Angelou had a difficult childhood, as her parents separated when she was very young, and she and her brother Bailey were sent to their father's mother, Anne Henderson, in Stamps, Arkansas. As an African American, Angelou experienced firsthand racial prejudices and discrimination in Arkansas. During a visit to her mother, Angelou was raped by her mother's boyfriend at the age of eight. Traumatised by the experience, she stopped talking to anyone and spent years as a virtual mute.

During World War II, Angelou moved to San Francisco, California, where she won a scholarship to study dance and acting at the California Labour School. During this time, she became the first Black female cable car conductor, a job she held briefly in San Francisco. In 1944, she gave birth to a son, Guy, at the age of sixteen; thereafter, she did a number of jobs to support herself and her child. In 1952, she married Tosh Angelos, a Greek sailor, the future literary icon from whom she took her professional name – a blend of her childhood nickname, Maya, and a version of his surname.

In the mid-1950s, Angelou's career as a performer started with a role in **a** touring production of *Porgy and Bess*. Later, she appeared in the off-Broadway production *Calypso Heat Wave* in 1957 and released her first album, *Miss Calypso*, in 1957. In 1958, she moved to New York, where she joined the Harlem Writers Guild. She organized and starred in the musical revue *Cabaret for Freedom* to benefit the SCLC (Southern Christian Leadership Conference), serving as the SCLC's northern coordinator. Being a civil rights activist, Angelou appeared in an off-Broadway production of Jean Genet's *The Blacks* with James Earl Jones, Louis Gossett Jr., and Cicely Tyson in 1961. The play earned good reviews, and Angelou moved on to other pursuits, spending much of the 1960s abroad in Egypt and then in Ghana, working as feature editor for *The African Review* and freelance writer for *The Ghanaian Times*. Angelou also taught at the University of Ghana's School of Music and Drama for some time.

After returning to the United States, Angelou was urged by a friend and fellow writer, James Baldwin, to write about her life experiences. Her efforts resulted in the enormously successful *I Know Why the Caged Bird Sings* (1969), about her childhood and young adult years, which made literary history as the first nonfiction bestseller by an African

American, and made Angelou an international star. James Baldwin called the book "a beginning of a new era in the minds and hearts of all black men and women" (qtd. in Cox 7). *I Know Why the Caged Bird Sings* is written at a time when life writings by black women had begun to proclaim women's significance in the mainstream as thinkers and activists. It conveys the difficulties associated with the mixture of racial and gender discrimination endured by a southern black girl, and how she confronted racism, sexism, violence, and loneliness, dismantling the prevalent stereotypes of women. At the same time, she speaks of many other issues, such as the relationship between parents and children, child abuse, and the search for one's own path in life. "According to scholar Hilton Als, up to that point, black female writers were marginalized to the point that they were unable to present themselves as central characters in literature they wrote" ("Maya Angelou Poems: Reception and Legacy," web. 21 Jan. 2017). Angelou's depictions of her experiences of racism have forced white readers to explore their own privileged status and their feelings about race.

I Know Why the Caged Bird Sings, the first volume of the seven-volume series, is a coming-of-age story that illustrates how strength of character and love of literature can help overcome racism and trauma. "The Caged Bird," a symbol for the chained slave, is an image Angelou uses in her writings. It narrates the story of the first seventeen years of her life, and in the course of the text, she is transformed from a victim of racism, with an inferiority complex, into a self-possessed, dignified young woman capable of responding to prejudiced treatment. It is a testament of the power of art, protest, and memory.

Angelou is best known for her series of seven life writings, namely, *I Know Why the Caged Bird Sings* (1969), *Gather Together in My Name* (1974), *Singin' and Swingin' and Gettin' Merry Like Christmas* (1976), *The Heart of a Woman* (1981), *All God's Children Need Travelling Shoes* (1986), *A Song Flung Up to Heaven* (2002), and *Mom & Me & Mom* (2013). *I Know Why the Caged Bird Sings* continues to be regarded as her acclaimed life writing. After publishing *Caged Bird*, Angelou continued to break new ground—not just artistically, but educationally and socially too. She published several collections of poetry, including *Just Give Me a Cool Drink of Water 'Fore I Die* (1971), which was nominated for the Pulitzer Prize. She wrote a play, *Georgia, Georgia*, in 1972 and became the first African American woman to have a screenplay produced. Among other honours, she earned a Tony Award nomination for her role in the play *Look Away* (1973) and an Emmy Award nomination for her work on the television mini-series, an adaptation of Alex Haley's *Roots* (1977). In 1982, she earned the first lifetime Reynolds Professorship of American Studies at Wake Forest University in Winston-Salem, North Carolina.

Maya Angelou was active in the Civil Rights Movement and worked with Martin Luther King Jr. and Malcolm X. She is widely recognised as an international ambassador for goodwill across race and culture. She is called "the black women's poet laureate" and her poems have been called the anthems of African Americans. One of her poems, "On the Pulse of Morning," was recited by her at President Bill Clinton's inaugural ceremony in January 1993. She went on to win a Grammy Award, Best Spoken Word Album, for the audio version of the poem. In 1995, she was lauded for remaining on *The New York Times'* paperback nonfiction bestseller list for two years—the longest-running record in the chart's history. Seeking new creative challenges, she made her directorial debut in 1998 with *Down in the Delta*, starring Alfre Woodard, thus becoming the first African American woman to direct a major motion picture. She also wrote a number of inspirational works, from the essay collection *Wouldn't Take Nothing for My Journey Now* (1994) to her advice for young women in *Letter to My Daughter* (2008).

Angelou also published cookbooks, including *Hallelujah! The Welcome Table: A Lifetime of Memories With Recipes* (2004) and *Great Food, All Day Long* (2010). She was given numerous honours: The Chicago International Film Festival's 1998 Audience Choice Award, a nod from the Acapulco Black Film Festival in 1999 for *Down in the Delta*, and two NAACP Image Awards for outstanding literary work in the category of nonfiction—for the 2004 cookbook *Hallelujah! The Welcome Table: A Lifetime of Memories with Recipes* and the 2008 *Letter to My Daughter.* Martin Luther King Jr., Angelou's close friend, was assassinated on 4th April 1968—her birth date. She stopped celebrating her birthday for years afterward, and sent flowers to the widow of King, Coretta Scott King, for more than thirty years, until Coretta's death in 2006.

Angelou's friend, TV personality Oprah Winfrey, organized several birthday celebrations for the award-winning author, including a week-long cruise for her 70th birthday in 1998. She was awarded the Presidential Medal of Arts in 2000 and received the National Medal of Arts in the same year. She penned the poem, "Amazing Peace: A Christmas Poem," for President George W. Bush and delivered the poem at the White House Christmas tree lighting ceremony in 2005. The Presidential Medal of Freedom, the country's highest civilian honour, was presented to her by President Barack Obama in 2010.

She received dozens of awards and more than fifty honorary degrees. After experiencing health issues for a number of years, Maya Angelou died on 28th May 2014 at her home in Winston-Salem, North Carolina. The news of her passing spread quickly, with many people taking to social media to mourn and remember Angelou. President Barack Obama also issued a statement about Angelou, calling her "a brilliant writer, a fierce friend, and a truly phenomenal woman." He wrote Angelou "had the ability to remind us that we are all God's children; that we all have something to offer" ("Maya Angelou – Poet, Civil Rights Activist, Author, Activist – Biography," web. 20 July 2017). The New York Public Library writes, "Her words and actions continue to stir our souls, energize our bodies, liberate our minds, and heal our hearts" ("A Celebration of the Life of Maya Angelou," web. 12 Sept. 2014). Angelou is and will be highly respected as a spokesperson for black people, especially black women, as she has set all barriers apart, reached for the stars, and turned seemingly impossible fantasy into reality.

Paule Marshall (1929–2019), winner of the prestigious MacArthur Fellowship, is a journalist, short fiction writer, essayist, and an educator. She was born Valenza Pauline Burke on 9th April 1929 in Brooklyn, New York, to Barbadian parents who had migrated to New York in 1919. She visited her parents' homeland, Barbados, for the first time at the age of nine. The influence of her West Indian ancestry has been profound in her writing, with an emphasis on history and the legacy of slavery, the search for identity, and the need for Black Americans to reclaim their cultural heritage. She is known for her works on Caribbean and African American identity. She graduated from Hunter College, New York, in 1955. She worked as a librarian for some time and then joined an African American magazine, *Our World*, where she worked as a food and fashion editor from 1953 to 1956. She married Kenneth Marshall in 1957, whom she divorced six years later in 1963. She remarried Nourry Menard, a Haitian businessman, and her second marriage also ended in divorce.

In 1959, her first novel *Brown Girl, Brownstones* was published, which was considered a seminal work in twentieth-century Black American women's literary history and was republished by the Feminist Press in 1981. She received the Guggenheim Fellowship in 1960 and, in 1961, published *Soul Clap Hands and Sing*, a collection of four novellas, for which she won the National Institute of Arts Award in 1962. In 1965, she was chosen by Langston Hughes to accompany him on a State Department-sponsored world tour, and in 1966 she wrote her most acclaimed short story *To Da-duh, in Memoriam*, which conveys her experiences on her first trip to Barbados. In 1969, she published a novel *The Chosen Place, The Timeless People*, and her novel *Praisesong for the Widow* (1983) won the Before Columbus Foundation American Book Award (1984). Her 1991 novel *Daughters* is centred on a father-daughter relationship that resembles the relationship she had with her father. Her works focus on the complexities of race, nationality, gender relationships, Black culture, and Black women's search for self-identity. Barbara Christian observes in the *Dictionary of Literary Biography*, her novels "present a black woman's search for personhood within the context of a specific black community rather than in reaction to a hostile white society. As such, they acknowledge the existence of a rich black culture" (qtd. in Gale, "Marshall, Paule 1929 – Contemporary Black Biography," web. 14 Jan. 2017).

Marshall taught at several universities and has been a Distinguished Professor of English and Creative Writing at New York University. She taught at Virginia Commonwealth University, the University of California, Berkeley, Iowa Writers' Workshop, and Yale University before holding the Helen Gould Sheppard Chair of Literature and Culture at New York University. In 1993, she received an honorary L.H.D. (Doctor of Humane Letters) from Bates College, and has been a MacArthur Fellow and a winner of the Dos Passos Prize for Literature. She was designated as a Literary Lion by the New York Public Library in 1994 and was inducted into the Celebrity Path at the

Brooklyn Botanic Garden in 2001. Her life writing, *Triangular Road: A Memoir*, published in 2009, won a Lifetime Achievement Award from the Anisfield-Wolf Book Awards in 2010, and presently she lives in Richmond, Virginia.

Paule Marshall's *Triangular Road: A Memoir*, written at the age of eighty, is an account told from the vantage point of nearly eight decades that narrates how a writer discovered and learned her vocation, and of the influences of place, family, race, and history that shaped it. It is adapted in part from lectures delivered at Harvard University in 2005, and it documents her early years as a writer and meditates on the slave trade. The title alludes to the "Triangular Trade," beginning in the seventeenth century: raw materials sent from the New World back to Europe, which produced manufactured goods that were shipped to Africa, where they were exchanged for human beings transported to America and sold into slavery. The title reflects three phases of her life: the Brooklyn birthplace; the Caribbean, from where her parents had emigrated and where she lived on and off for several years as an adult; and the ancestral Africa that she is yet to discover.

Triangular Road portrays a young Black woman's coming of age as a novelist in a literary world dominated by white men. It is a recollection of her personal quest as a young Black female writer trying to find footing in the white patriarchal field of literature. She tells the story of her years as a young writer in the 1960s. *Triangular Road* is a self-discovery, a tribute to Langston Hughes, and to other influences on her work. In the course of her journeys to Europe, Barbados, and eventually Africa, Marshall is able to comprehend the historical enormity of the African diaspora, an understanding that strengthens her sense of purpose as a writer.

Anne Moody (1940–2015) was born Essie Mae Moody on 15th September 1940, near the town of Centreville in Mississippi's Wilkinson County. She was a daughter of poor African American sharecroppers. Being the eldest of several children in the family, she started working for the white families in the area as early as fourth grade because her father had left the family, and her mother was unable to make both ends meet by herself. She endured a turbulent childhood, experiencing racial hatred and prejudice with rising racial tensions in the community. She earned perfect grades in school and also helped at

Mount Pleasant Church. She graduated with honours from a segregated, all-Black high school. She was a devoted and popular student, played for the basketball team, and eventually was able to earn an athletic scholarship for two years to all-Black Natchez Junior College. She also earned an academic scholarship to Tougaloo College, from where she graduated in 1964.

As a student, Moody was involved in the growing Civil Rights Movement, joined CORE (Congress of Racial Equality), SNCC (Student Nonviolent Coordinating Committee), and the NAACP (National Association for the Advancement of Coloured People), and led the voter registration drives. After graduation, Moody became a full-time worker in the Civil Rights Movement, participated in protests and sit-ins to desegregate the Woolworth's lunch counter, along with other demonstrations in Jackson. She also took part in the historic 1963 March on Washington. After her graduation, Moody worked at Cornell University as its Civil Rights Project Coordinator until 1965. Eventually, she became disenchanted with certain aspects of the Civil Rights Movement and distanced herself from it, and she moved to New York. There she wrote *Coming of Age in Mississippi* (1968), detailing her rural childhood, difficult times with her family, and subsequent activism. She fought racism and segregation since childhood in Centreville, Mississippi, and continued doing so throughout her adult life around the South.

Anne Moody's *Coming of Age in Mississippi* is an unforgettable personal story, laced with truth. To read her book is to know what it is to have grown up poor and Black in Mississippi in the 1940s and 50s, and to have survived with pride and courage. Her life writing exhibits a young Black girl's struggle to overcome racism in the South. It mirrors Anne Moody's dissatisfaction with the slow pace of the Civil Rights Movement and shows that there is no conclusive end to the struggle against racism. The text is an account of her struggle both against racism among white people and sexism among her fellow Civil Rights activists. In telling the story of her life, she shows why this movement was such a necessity, and the depth of injustice that it intended to correct. Her powerful story brings the reader into the world of Negroes, where on a daily basis they faced bigotry, discrimination, and prejudice. It is a story of a fighter for equality that just won't quit, manifesting that when times are tough, you don't run and hide. The long-lasting appeal of the text lies in its basic humanity. Herein, Anne Moody underlines the sights, smells, and sufferings of growing up in a racist society and candidly reveals the soul of a Black girl who had the courage to challenge it. The result is a touchstone work, an accurate, authoritative portrait of Black family life in the rural South.

The text is divided into four sections that reflect different phases of her life. In the first section, entitled "Childhood," Moody remembers her childhood years spent in the poverty of rural Mississippi. She exhibits her acts of resistance and rebellion against the racist society. "High School," the second section, reveals her political awakening during her teenage years with the death of Emmett Till. She realises the extent of white supremacy and the powerlessness of the blacks. The third section, "College," documents her increasing commitment to political activism to fight against segregation and racial inequality. "Movement," the last section, chronicles her involvement in the Civil Rights Movement in the form of sit-ins, rallies, demonstrations, freedom votes and so on and so forth. It ends with her discontent with the movement to bring about any change, and she wonders if they will ever succeed in overcoming racism.

Coming of Age in Mississippi received high praise on its publication, including honours from *The Nation*, *The Chicago Tribune*, and *The New York Times Book Review*. It also won the Best Book of the Year Award from the National Library Association and the Brotherhood Award from the National Council of Christians and Jews. It is acclaimed for its realistic portrayal of life during the Civil Rights Movement of the 1960s by a young African American. It is a moving account of Moody's impoverished childhood, her struggle against the pervasive racism of the Deep South, and her work as a Civil Rights Activist; it is praised as a historical personal document.

In 1967, Anne Moody married a white man, Austin Strauss, who was a New York University graduate, and in 1971 she gave birth to her son, Sasha Strauss. In 1972, her family moved to Berlin after she received a full-time scholarship, and they remained there until 1974. Afterwards, they returned to America. Moody published her fiction collection *Mr. Death: Four Stories* in 1975. She earned another award from *Mademoiselle* magazine for the story "New Hopes for the

Seventies." She wrote a sequel to *Coming of Age in Mississippi* entitled *Farewell to Too Sweet*, paying homage to her mother, which was never published. She was also involved in the anti-nuclear movement and worked with anti-poverty initiatives in New York. Prior to her death, she had been working on her novel *The Clay Gully*. She died on 5th February 2015 at the age of 74 at her home in Gloster, Mississippi, under the care of her younger sister, Adline Moody.

Charlayne Hunter-Gault (b. 1942) from Due West, South Carolina, is an African American journalist and former foreign correspondent for National Public Radio and the Public Broadcasting Service. She has staked her claim as one of the leading journalists in the United States, having won many honours for excellence in investigative reporting. She and her two younger brothers mainly grew up in Georgia, though her family was often moving from one place to another due to her father's work as an army chaplain. Her father was often on duty for long tours away from home, leaving the children in the care of their mother and grandmother. Her grandmother was a role model for her. Though not educated beyond the third grade, she read three newspapers a day and sparked a healthy curiosity about the world in the future reporter. As a child, Hunter-Gault admired a comic strip, *Brenda Starr*, about a reporter whose life was full of adventures. In the hope of having an exciting career of her own, she decided to study journalism in college.

Being an African American student, her college options in the South were limited. After standing third in her class at Atlanta High School, she wanted to go to the University of Georgia at Athens, for it offered a good journalism program, but they did not admit African Americans. She was approached by a group of Atlanta's black civil leaders who were looking for talented students to challenge segregation in the colleges and universities of Georgia. They decided to apply to the University of Georgia, but her request for admission was denied by the university in 1959, so she studied at Wayne State University, Detroit, Michigan. In January 1961, a court ruling came that allowed Hunter-Gault and her school classmate, Hamilton Holmes, to enrol at the University of Georgia. Thus, Hunter-Gault and Holmes became the first two African American students to integrate the university, and Hunter-Gault became the first African American woman to enrol there.

Amid shouts of protest, taunts, and racial epithets, they got registered for classes. They encountered a lot of hostility, were suspended for their safety, and then readmitted on another court order. The entire experience helped Hunter-Gault mould her future career in journalism, as she learned by observing the style and techniques of reporters who chronicled the event. Before graduating with a journalism degree in 1963, she married Walter Stovall, a fellow white journalism student, had a daughter, and got divorced due to diverging career paths, but remained close friends.

Hunter-Gault went to work at *The New Yorker* after graduation, where she handled administrative tasks and also wrote for the magazine. She received a Russell Sage Fellowship to study Social Science at Washington University in St. Louis, and in 1967 she joined as a reporter and anchor for WRC–TV in Washington, D.C. In 1968, she became a reporter for *The New York Times*, eventually becoming the newspaper's Harlem bureau chief. She brought about a significant change in the editorial policy of the newspaper, convincing the editors to drop their use of the word "Negro" with reference to African Americans. In 1971, she got married to Ronald Gault, an investment banker, thus becoming Charlayne Hunter-Gault and a mother of a son.

Charlayne Hunter-Gault joined PBS's *MacNeil/Lehrer Report* in 1978 as a correspondent and became its national correspondent in 1983 when it became the *MacNeil/Lehrer NewsHour.* While at PBS (Public Broadcasting Service), Hunter-Gault covered both national and international stories as a correspondent and reported on topics including Vietnam veterans, racism, life under apartheid, drug abuse, and human rights issues. However, she became frustrated with the network and left *NewsHour* in 1997. In addition to her work on *MacNeil/Lehrer*, Hunter-Gault hosted her own show, a human rights-focused series called *Rights & Wrongs*, but the programme did not receive national distribution on PBS. She worked as the chief correspondent for National Public Radio in Johannesburg, South Africa from 1997 to 1999. After working as the Johannesburg Bureau Chief for CNN (Cable News Network) from 1999 to 2005, she returned to National Public Radio. Her skills as an interviewer resulted in her meeting with some of the most famous people in the world, including British Prime Minister Margaret Thatcher, Archbishop of

Cape Town Desmond Tutu, U.S. President George Bush, German statesman and Chancellor Helmut Schmidt, and many more.

In 1988, Hunter-Gault became the first African American to give the commencement address at the University of Georgia. She was asked to deliver the address in recognition of her personal success and the social, economic, and political advancements of the people of colour in the United States over the past few decades. She wrote two life writings about her experience with integration and civil rights, *In My Place* (1992) and *To the Mountaintop: My Journey Through the Civil Rights Movement* (2012). She authored *New News Out of Africa* (2006), a book documenting positive developments in Africa. She also wrote *Corrective Rape* (2015), a book about violence against gay women in South Africa.

In My Place by Hunter-Gault gives a moment-by-moment account of her walk into history, when, as a nineteen-year-old girl, she challenged southern law and southern violence to become the first Black woman to attend the University of Georgia. Her book is a witness to the brutal realities of segregation. In this warm-hearted, well-observed writing, Hunter-Gault reflects on her childhood and adulthood, including her historic role as one of the two Black students who desegregated the University of Georgia in 1961, a high point in the Civil Rights Movement. She describes how she grew up in a segregated society and what enabled her to successfully challenge the old Southern laws that were created to keep her and all Black people 'in their place.' Her writing is a story of growing up in Alaska on a military base and in small towns in Georgia during the stable 1950s and coming of age during the turbulent 1960s.

In My Place addresses the universal adolescent search for one's place in the family, among one's peers in the community, and eventually in the world. It is an inspiring historical journey and compelling documentation of the turmoil of the times. She recalls her early years growing up Black and female in the Deep South, as well as the turmoil of entering the University of Georgia. *In My Place* downplays her courage in living through the adversity of her college years, giving credit instead to the Black community and her family for supporting her and paving the way for her giant step ahead. She shows how she was emotionally equipped to face loneliness, ostracism, and even violence for the cause of the Civil Rights Movement. Her first encounter with prejudice over race occurred when she, as a child, was mocked by other Black children for being a mulatto, a person of racially mixed ancestry. Hunter-Gault's text conveys the omnipresent textures of racism and the strength and vitality of Black culture that defied and transcended racism's seemingly unalterable codes.

Hunter-Gault received the George Foster Peabody Broadcasting Award for her documentary *Apartheid's People* and National News and Documentary Emmy Awards for excellence in broadcast journalism. Hunter-Gault was one of the first correspondents allowed into the West Indian nation of Grenada after the American-led invasion in 1983, and she won an Emmy Award for her Grenada coverage. She also received the Journalist of the Year Award from the National Association of Black Journalists in 1986, the Sidney Hillman Award in 1990, the Good Housekeeping Broadcast Personality of the Year Award, the American Women in Radio and Television Award, and two awards from the Corporation for Public Broadcasting for excellence in local programming. In 2005, she was inducted into the National Association of Black Journalists Hall of Fame and was honoured with a Lifetime Achievement Award by the Washington Press Club Foundation in 2015. She held her ground against racism to become a voice of consciousness in the field of American broadcast journalism.

The book aims at exploring the expressions of marginality in the context of race, identity, and gender in the life writings of five selected African American women writers. It honours the women who have recorded their lives in the face of enormous disadvantages. Writing their lives helps them share their rich experiences as self-defining women who can speak for themselves. Their life writings encourage coming generations to strive for self-identity, empowerment, self-knowledge, and posterity.

Chapter 2

Growing Up Poor, Black and Female: Triple Marginalization

Honey, de white man is the de ruler of everything as fur as Ah been able tuh find out. Maybe it's some place way off in de ocean where de black man is in power, but we don't know nothin' but what we see. So de white man throw down de load and tell de nigger man tuh pick it up. He pick it up because he have to, but he don't tote it. He hands it to his womenfolks. De nigger woman is de mule uh de world so fur as Ah can see.

– Zora Neale Hurston,
Their Eyes Were Watching God

The birth of African American literature is a witness to the irresistible human urge for freedom. It provides fertile ground for the creation of new literature that is produced by the oppressed ones. Generally, Africans were considered an inferior race, incapable of producing literature. The Scottish philosopher David Hume asserts, "I am apt to suspect the negroes, and in general all the other species of men to be naturally inferior to the whites. There never was a civilized nation of any other complexion other than white," ("Go There To Know There: Phillis Wheatley: African American Foremother of Poetry," web. 13 Sept. 2016). Yet African Americans produced literature that has both richness and variety. It is the literature of pain and survival, of triumphs and defeats, of fears and dreams, and of struggle for freedom, equality, and identity.

"Black women have repeatedly asked themselves: how does a black woman handle the claims of being both a black and a woman? There has been no simple answer because the solution varies with each individual. Some women see themselves as being black first and female second; others reverse that order. Still others see the condition more fluidly and believe that the claims don't conflict. They see black women as people and their race and sex as aspects which contribute to their total being" (Scott PDF). In an attempt to answer this question, black women have used life writing to discover or assert their identity. Writing is an assertion of self as well as an expression of the search for a dignified ethnic identity.

Life writing "is a form of therapy, self-healing, and emotional release… a source of pleasure, creativity, and self-affirmation… an act of remembering, self-defense, or survival" (Bell-Scott 19–20). In a unique and personal tone, black women speak emphatically of their concerns and ring out their voices profoundly, sharing their experiences that cross class, cultural, and geographical boundaries. As they record their experiences, they see the critical paths established by the oppressive forces of racism, classism, and sexism. The life experiences of these women are running commentaries of their personal journeys from childhood into womanhood. In exploring what it means to be poor, black, and female, they present mirror images of "self" and the "other" to the world. The presentation of the knowledge of their "self" to others through life writing is significant because it provides the readers or listeners with personal perceptions that determine their self-identity, which is necessarily reliant on their culture, environment, upbringing, general background, and other factors that substantially impact their lives. "Moving from silence into speech is for the oppressed, the colonized, the exploited, and those who stand and struggle side by side a gesture of defiance that heals, that makes new life and new growth possible. It is that act of speech, of 'talking back,' that is no mere gesture of empty words, that is the expression of our movement from object to subject – the liberated voice" (bell hooks, *Talking Back* 9).

Within the marginalized blacks in America, women are at a triple disadvantage. Gloria Wade-Gayles aptly describes the precarious position of African American women: "America is an oppressive system that divides people into groups on the basis of their race, sex, and class, creating a society in which a few have capital and therefore are able to influence the lives of many. There are three major circles of reality in American society, which reflect degrees of power and powerlessness. There is a large circle in which white people, most of them men, experience influence and power. Far away from it, there is a smaller circle, a narrow space in which black people, regardless of sex, experience uncertainty, exploitation, and powerlessness. Hidden in this second circle is a third, a small, dark enclosure in which black women experience pain, isolation, and vulnerability" (3–4). Being poor, black, and female makes them the most vulnerable and easy target for the male-dominated community. African American women writers "give voice to women who had long been silenced and devalued – women who, according to Zora Neale Hurston, have the status of a mule" (Ampadu PDF).

Zora Neale Hurston is a significant black woman writer and anthropologist of the first half of the twentieth century. *Dust Tracks on a Road* (1942) is her story written in her own words, wherein she recalls what it is to grow up poor, black, and female. Hurston's fame reached its zenith in 1943 with a *Saturday Review* cover story honouring the success of *Dust Tracks on a Road.* Here she recounts her life vividly from childhood to adulthood. Despite the fact that she was born in Notasulga, Alabama, Hurston cites Eatonville, Florida, as her place of birth, where she spent much of her childhood. "It could be said that Hurston rewrites her own personal history in order to create a particular persona and be able to claim as a birthright the status of being from an all-black town. Given her rise to prominence during the New Negro movement, this may not be surprising, since that movement placed a premium on cultural and ethnic origins. Originating from an all-black town would fit into the movement's ideas of black pride, consciousness, and heritage" (Jones, Sharon 28).

Coming *of Age in Mississippi* (1968) by Anne Moody stands out as one of the classic life writings of American literature. Her writing is about growing up in rural Mississippi in the mid-twentieth century as an African American woman. It "represents the flowing together of the personal and historical and the action between them" (Wynn, web. 20 Jan. 2017). It is a story of growing up or coming of age in Mississippi during the turbulent times of struggle. Anne Moody is a unique, compelling voice of the oppressed rural blacks. Being an African American female, she experiences discrimination and racism herself. Her writing portrays the timelessness of black oppression in America. She grows up in Wilkinson County, a rural county marked by extreme poverty and racism.

Maya Angelou is one of the most accomplished and powerful voices of African American literature. Her work has a deep feministic strain which strongly connects her with the black feminist literary tradition. She is best known for her strong portrayal of African American women. *I Know Why the Caged Bird Sings* (1969) tells the story of a black female's hard life growing up in the American South during the 1930s and 40s, the segregated era characterized by discrimination. The title of the book is taken from the poem "Sympathy" by the black poet Paul Laurence Dunbar. The title means that African Americans must have a voice in order to earn freedom. Angelou writes:

The caged bird sings with a fearful trill of things unknown
but longed for still and his tune is heard on the distant hill
for the caged bird sings of freedom.
(*The Complete Collected Poems of Maya Angelou* 194)

Maya Angelou was herself a caged bird, but she broke those bars and soared high in the sky beyond the reach of any human cage. "Cages" are things that restrict people, and Angelou's cage manifests the black, poor and triply marginalised female. She has been looked down upon for being black, has lived in those segregated black tenements, and as such, witnessed the poverty and displacement of the black community in America. Hilton Als states that *I Know Why the Caged Bird Sings* marked one of the first times that a black life writer could, as he puts it, "write about blackness from the inside, without apology or defense" ("Maya Angelou Poems: Reception and Legacy," web. 21 Jan. 2017).

Charlayne Hunter-Gault's *In My Place* (1992) is the story of her life from her birth in the Deep South to her historic role in desegregating the University of Georgia, a high point in the Civil Rights Movement.

It is about the growing up of an African American woman in the Jim Crow South and a coming-of-age story during the turbulent 1960s. Derrick Bell reviews the book in the following words, "*In My Place* is Charlayne Hunter-Gault's richly readable reminiscence of growing up black and middle class in the segregated South, and acquiring in that warm and caring environment the cold courage required to desegregate the University of Georgia" (3-4).

Paule Marshall's *Triangular Road* (2009), at the age of eighty, portrays a young black woman's coming of age as a novelist in a literary world dominated by white men. Her writing is a map of her development as a writer, and she writes with sensitivity, compassion and effectiveness, maintaining tight control over the personal details she chooses to share. It reveals pieces of her family history and her path to become an established author. *Triangular Road* consists of four chapters, an account of how a writer discovers and learns her vocation, and of the influences—notably of place, family, race and history—told from the vantage point of nearly eight decades. In *The New York Times*, Marshall explains the title of *Triangular Road* as "Africa, Barbados, Brooklyn – that's the triangle that defines me and my work" (Lee C1).

The first of the many places that Charlayne Hunter-Gault calls "my place" (*In My Place* 5) is Due West, a small village in an isolated little corner of South Carolina, where she is born on 27th February, 1942. Being born black in Due West in 1942 gives her a distinct sense of place, as "Negroes or colored people in those days – had their place" (9). Due West has the distinction of having Erskine College since 1839 for white male students, established by the members of the Associate Reformed Presbyterian Church. There were around one hundred and five white families and fifty Negro families in Due West in 1938. Like her grandmother, most of the blacks worked for the white people of Due West, either for the college as maids, janitors and in similar jobs, or in the homes of people associated with the college in one way or another. "African-American women's confinement to domestic work revealed how race and gender influenced Black women's social class experiences" (Collins 245).

Hunter-Gault's mother's people were from Georgia, and after her grandfather Rochell Brown's death, her grandmother Frances Wilson Layson Brown goes to Due West to take care of the mother of the

Todds, a white family for whom she had worked in Covington, Georgia, who had suffered a stroke and was confined to a wheelchair. The Todds are good employers, and she has no complaint about them unlike the other white families she had worked for. "When Black folks stayed in their place, they got along just fine with the white folks of Due West" (10). After Lady Todd's death, she marries a part-time bricklayer, Ollie Jones, her third husband and last marriage.

There was no hospital in Due West, only an infirmary associated with the college. "Anybody seriously ill either suffered through it, died, or went twenty miles to the town of Anderson" (11). It was wartime and money was scarce, so the black folks were thankful to Hitler, because the war brought desperately needed work to the poor folks of Due West. Hunter-Gault's mother adds income and fills some of her lonely hours by teaching in a school. She does not have a college degree, but she had graduated from one of the most prestigious high schools in Chicago, Hyde Park. Her mother had sent her to live with her father's sister, as her parents were deeply committed to her education and she could not get it in the coloured school in Covington. Moreover, they wanted to protect their daughter from the advances of white men who had their eyes on this very beautiful girl. She gets the job without a college degree because white folks did not care what black folks have; they only cared about the fact that someone is ready to do the job.

Covington, Georgia, is the place of her mother's family; her ancestors lived there—some white and some Native American—and therefore, Hunter-Gault and her mother are light-skinned, choosing to appropriate their African American identity. Hunter-Gault's mother, Althea, hears of the University of Georgia from Renee, granddaughter of Mrs. Cooper, for whom her mother works. Renee talks of going there, and Althea knows that she will never be able to go there and never dreams that her child will ever go there as a student. So, when Renee goes to the University of Georgia, Althea's mother sends her to high school in Chicago. Althea does not go to college; she comes back home from Chicago and starts working as a secretary in the Covington branch of the black-owned Atlanta Life Insurance Company. She lives at home and helps her mother with washing and ironing for the white families. Her father has a barbershop, but he does not earn much, and they all work hard to make both ends meet. Her mother earns two dollars a week as a cook, and she adds to her income by selling toilet articles—face creams, lotions, deodorants, etc. Black folks do not have cars, so they walk everywhere to sell their articles. Both mother and daughter are active members of the black church in the county; her mother is usually the president of the Missionary Society, and Althea is elected secretary as she could take notes because of her expertise in Gregg shorthand.

Although Althea's mother is not educated, she is intelligent and smart. If she had a little education, she would have been a powerful woman; she organizes clubs and delivers speeches. It is through church speaking that Althea meets Charles, Hunter-Gault's father, a young preacher. After listening to her speech in church, Charles introduces himself and compliments her on the speech. Four months later, they get married, for Althea's father has no objection to dark-skinned Charles: "As light as they all were, they always identified themselves proudly as Black, even when they could have easily passed as white in some other location" (29).

"I've Known Seas: The Caribbean Sea, Barbados, Part I," the third chapter of *Triangular Road*, is about the island of Barbados, which is the parental birthplace of Paule Marshall. Her mother, Adriana Viola Clement, grew up in a hilly district called Scotland on the Atlantic or windward coast. Her father, Sam Burke, neither mentioned his family nor the name of his birthplace ever. Adriana Viola Clement and Sam Burke immigrated from the north to Big America after World War I, separately, as they did not know each other by then. Physically, Adriana Viola Clement was like her father, Prince Albert Clement, who died of rum drinking when she was a child. Adriana was eighteen years old when she reached New York and presented her papers to the authorities along with "show money" (65) required of those emigrating from the Caribbean.

She explains the term to her American-born children: "If you was from the West Indies, you had to have fifty big U.S. dollars to show to the authorities when you landed, to prove you wasn't a pauper or coming to country to be a pauper. Back then, if you was black, you cun [couldn't] set foot in big America without fifty dollars cold cash in you' hand" (65–66). She was able to pay her passage to the north with the

Panama Money—money named after the canal which began in 1905—from an elder brother, Joseph Fitzroy Clement. Her brother, hearing of the money to be made on the canal, had eagerly left to work there, sent home the better part of his pay dutifully, and died there like most of the other islanders. The Panama Money was largely responsible for "the West Indian wing of black America's Great Migration North, the momentous exodus that, figuratively speaking, saw 'a black million-man march' from the South to the northern cities of America in the early twentieth century" (67). This migration could not have taken place without Panama Money.

"The Great Migration, or the relocation of more than 6 million African Americans from the rural South to the cities of the North, Midwest and West from 1916 to 1970, had huge impact on urban life in the United States. Driven from their homes due to unsatisfactory economic opportunities and harsh segregationist laws, many blacks headed north, where they took advantage of the need of industrial workers that first arose during the First World War. As Chicago, New York and other cities saw their black populations expand exponentially, migrants were forced to deal with poor working conditions and competition for living space, as well as widespread racism and prejudice" ("Great Migration," web. 5 June 2017).

In the Clement family, the remittances from the elder brother were used to purchase small plots of sugarcane or "canepieces" (68), as they called it. They rented them out until one of the Clement children or grandchildren was of an age to travel. A "canepiece" was sold to pay his or her passage to America, England, or Canada. Alberta Jane Clement, Adriana's mother—called "M' Da-duh" by her children, a pet name that on their lips became an honorific title (68)—was in charge of the entire operation. "She was both the 'Chancellor of the Exchequer' in charge of the Panama Money as well as the architect and administrator of the 'canepiece' plan" (68). She had married Prince Albert Clement, had borne him fourteen children (of whom nine survived), struggled with her husband over his rum drinking (of which he died), and she outlived him for decades.

Marshall remembers meeting "M' Da-duh," her grandmother, only once when she was seven and her sister eleven. In her eighties, she had written a letter to Adriana saying that her last wish in the world was to see her "American-born grands" (69). She had already sold a good-sized canepiece to pay for their passage and the money required on the way. Marshall's father opposes the trip and thinks of doing "something big" in America rather than wasting so much money in going to meet their grandmother, but Adriana, as a dutiful daughter, ignores him and they set sail to meet M' Da-duh. Marshall just remembers the sight of the small, black old woman, and her grandmother appears in one guise or another in every book she has written. She describes her grandmother in an introduction to the story published in 1983: "She's an ancestor figure, symbolic for me of the long line of black women and men ... who made my being possible, and whose spirit I believe continues to animate my life and work" (Gale, "To Da-duh, in Memoriam," web. 5 June 2017).

Adriana, at the age of eighteen, lands in New York, and with the help of an elder brother, Winston Carlyle Clement, is able to find a job in less than a month. The work is to clean the ten-room house of a white lady whom she is to call "Madam" (71). She serves as nursemaid for three small children and attends to her sick old mother too. The Madam teaches her how to cook like white people; they make her work hard throughout the day, and the nights are even harder. In the evenings, she could go to her basement room, where flies give her company; she misses her family and home and cries for them. "No matter how loved they were by their White 'families,' Black women domestic workers remained poor because they were economically exploited workers in a capitalist political economy" (Collins 81).

After two years in this job, on one Sunday (an off day), she meets Sam Burke at her brother's place in Brooklyn—a fellow from home—and develops a liking for him. Sam Burke was an "illegal alien" (72), with no visa, passport, documents, birth certificate, or official papers of any kind. He paid no "show money," for he came to New York by way of Cuba, and no Panama money was given to legally finance his passage north. Desperate for a chance, he turns to a contract-labour scheme that occasionally sent young men like him from the smaller islands to work for a limited time on the larger islands. He signs the papers and is chosen for Cuba in Oriente Province, where, to his surprise, most of the people are Black. The work is to cut canes from morning till evening on a plantation—work that he was doing in Barbados too—

only it was twice the size of Barbados. He finds the work harder here because of the comparatively hotter weather. He loves to help in transporting raw sugar from the plantation mill to the seaport of Nuevitas. He soon finds a job in a Brooklyn mattress factory where Adriana's brother is a supervisor. He likes Adriana, a sweet-faced Bajan or Barbadian girl, and she too likes him, and soon they get married. Sam rescues her from cleaning a ten-room house, and she becomes a wife, a mother, and "a Madam in her own right" (76) in her own home. Like all Bajans, they were determined to progress.

Hurston is born in Eatonville, Florida, "a pure Negro town" (Dust Tracks on a Road 1). Eatonville is the first attempt at organized self-government on the part of Negroes in America. "She argues that this town carries a special status, noting that it 'made history by becoming the first of its kind in America, and perhaps in the world'" (Jones, Sharon 29). John Hurston, Zora Neale Hurston's father, is born near Notasulga, Alabama, "in an outlying district of landless Negroes, and Whites not too much better off" (7). He is a tall, heavy-muscled mulatto, who, in his late twenties, leaves Macon County, Alabama, because he cannot do anything better there, and the trials and tribulations of sharecropping on the southern Alabama cotton plantation are humiliating for his ambition. In sharecropping, ignorant Negroes in the power of unscrupulous landowners and merchants sank to a condition hardly better than slavery. Even the most diligent, persistent, frugal, and industrious Blacks were often unable to overcome the ironlike grip of the Whites on the land, or the low wages. "Most observers of the Blacks in the rural Deep South during these decades were struck by the continuity with the prewar era: Negroes laboring in the fields on white-owned plantations in much the same manner as they had during slavery. They were also struck by the deplorable living conditions" (Schweninger 162).

Between cotton-chopping and cotton-picking, John Hurston somehow learns to read and write and is, in a way, satisfied with it. He goes to Macedonia Baptist Church on the right side of the creek, where once he meets dark-brown Lucy Ann Potts and falls in love with her. Knowing that he is an "Over-the-creek nigger" (8), who lives on one or the other white man's plantation and lets himself be hired by poor white trash, Lucy Ann Potts does not think about him, but as he is handsome, she cannot help noticing him. He keeps impressing her by slipping love notes between the leaves of hymn books and other things of the sort, and a few months later, she agrees to marry him.

In spite of violent opposition from her family, she wears a little silk dress which she had made herself and sets out on her wedding night alone, as none from the family except her brother Jim could bear the sight of her great come-down in the world. "She who was considered the prettiest and the smartest black girl was throwing herself away and disgracing the Pottses by marrying an over-the-creek nigger, and a bastard at that. Folks said he was a certain white man's son" (8). She walks two miles at night by herself to keep her pledge to him at the church. Her father had decided that his daughter would neither go alone nor walk to her wedding, so he pulls the buggy and goes with her. Lucy Ann Potts keeps her word and takes her stand for life and goes off to a cabin on a white man's plantation with him, and that is all they have right now.

Her father softens soon, but not her mother, and her daughter's husband is never John Hurston to her till death—he is always "dat yaller bastard" (9). After his marriage, Hurston's father begins to want things; his plantation life begins to bother and restrain him, so he leaves his wife and three children and goes out in search of better opportunities. "Accordingly, one of the hallmarks of the black historical experience has been limited employment opportunities, which restricted them to low-wage menial jobs. Thus, opportunities open to Blacks for economic betterment through advancement on the job were practically nonexistent: hence the paucity of skills, high unemployment rates, relatively low incomes, and abject poverty among a disproportionate number of these citizens" (Henry 11).

Anne Moody, in *Coming of Age in Mississippi*, "provides a telling glimpse into that period in southern culture between 1940 and 1965 when African Americans still labored in fields as sharecroppers for white landowners" ("Coming of Age in Mississippi: Researchomatic," web. 19 Jan. 2017). Anne, born in Mississippi, named Essie Mae by her parents, lives on Mr. Carter's plantation, and in the very first line she admits, "I'm still haunted by dreams of the time we lived on Mr. Carter's plantation. Lots of Negroes lived on his place" (3). They all are farmers like her parents. They all live in "rotten wood two-room shacks" with no electricity or indoor plumbing, while Mr. Carter lives in luxury in his "big white house" (3). In the evening, when light is lit in the white house, her mother tells her that Mr. Carter stays up at night counting money he has made from the Black plantation workers. "The close correlation between race and poverty clearly has its roots in historic racism – and, for Black people, the legacy of slavery, which was a very direct system of building white wealth at the expense of black people" (Nolan, web. 25 Jan. 2016). Anne is four years old, and Adline, her sister, is a six- or seven-month-old crying baby. Their parents go to the fields early in the morning and return by six in the evening. In between, her mother's eight-year-old brother, George Lee, looks after them. Resentful of babysitting, one day he accidentally sets the wallpaper on fire while trying to scare them with matches in a fit of anger and blames it on Essie Mae. Her father punishes Essie Mae for the crime she has not committed, which foreshadows the injustice and tyranny that is in store for her. Septima Clark, civil rights activist, describes her experiences: "I found all over the South that whatever the man said had to be right. They had the whole say. The woman couldn't say a thing" (Collins 10).

Amid anxiety over fire, money, and the death of his best friend, her father, Diddly, leaves her pregnant mother for his best friend's beautiful widow, Florence, who was a "mulatto, high yellow with straight black hair" (11). Every woman on the plantation is jealous of her. Her mother gives birth to a boy and calls him Junior. After the birth of Junior, they leave their father's house for good and move to Aunt Cindy's place. In Toni Morrison's *Sula* (1974), Eva Peace's husband runs off, leaving her with three children and no money. Despite her feelings, "the demands of feeding her three children were so acute she had to postpone her anger for two years until she had both the time and energy for it" (Morrison 32). The demands of providing for children in intersecting oppressions are sometimes so intense for many Black mothers that they have neither the time nor the patience for affection.

Essie Mae's mother cries a lot, but she is a strong woman and a survivor. Soon, she is able to get a job at the Cook's house, where she works for only two weeks. After that, she gets a better job in the town at a Negro café and earns twelve dollars a week, with which she supports her children. Her mother's resourcefulness and ability to survive in the face of poverty and crisis influence Essie Mae and give her strength to face the hardships of life. African American mothers place a strong emphasis on protection to shield their daughters as long as possible from the penalties attached to their derogated status and to teach them skills of independence and self-reliance so that they will be able to protect themselves. This is presented in the following verse from a traditional blues song:

I ain't good lookin' and ain't got waist-long hair
I say I ain't good lookin' and ain't got waist-long hair
But my mama gave me something that'll take me anywhere.
(Perry and Brownley 144)

Black mothers teach their daughters necessary skills that will take them anywhere in life, making them self-reliant and independent.

Maya Angelou was born in St. Louis, Missouri, on 4th April, 1928, and was named Marguerite Johnson. She was a daughter of Vivian Baxter Johnson and had a brother, Bailey. Marguerite Johnson relates her experience of displacement as she moves from one place to another with her brother Bailey to be raised by different family members. After their parents' divorce, three-year-old Marguerite and four-year-old Bailey are shipped all alone from California to Stamps, Arkansas, to their grandmother, Mrs. Annie Henderson, with tags on their wrists – "To Whom It May Concern" (*I Know Why the Caged Bird Sings* 5). She does not remember much about the trip, but after they reach the segregated South, Negro passengers give them food to eat, feeling sorry for the poor little motherless darlings, left alone by their parents to cover such a long journey unlike any white child. As young children, Marguerite and Bailey struggle with the pain of being rejected and abandoned by their parents. Marguerite is disheartened to be sent alone by their parents at such a tender age; however, years later, she discovers that the United States had been crossed thousands of times by frightened Black children travelling alone to their newly affluent parents in northern cities or back to grandmothers in Southern towns when the urban North reneged on its economic promises. Thus, Black children have had to suffer for being born to Black parents, who neither could afford them a better life like white children, nor could accompany them on such journeys.

The segregated southern town of Stamps reacts to the newcomers as they had reacted to all new things. They regard kids with caution, and when they are considered harmless, the people of the town "closed in around us, as a real mother embraces a stranger's child" (6). In Stamps, they live with their grandmother, who runs Wm. Johnson General Merchandise Store, "the only Negro store in Stamps" (12), with crippled Uncle Willie, the son of Mrs. Annie Henderson. The grandmother, usually called 'Momma' by the kids, is a successful businesswoman in Stamps. Along with a mobile lunch counter, she also helps the workers by giving them money on interest. In the heart of the Black section of town, the Store provides food and all sorts of articles for the cotton pickers who work in the surrounding fields.

Most of the population of Stamps comprises poor Black peasants who work as cotton pickers on "the remains of Slavery's plantations" (7). The white, ruthless masters are tyrannical and oppressive, with no humane feelings for the poor Black peasants who are made to work as slaves picking cotton in the fields for meagre wages. In the morning, the Store is filled with "laughing, joking, boasting and bragging" workers; the tired field workers would "fold down, dirt-disappointed, to the ground" (8) at the end of the day. They toil hard the whole day with no reward, and Angelou describes their predicament: "No matter how much they had picked, it wasn't enough. Their wages wouldn't even get them out of debt to my grandmother, not to mention the staggering bill that waited on them at the white commissary downtown" (8). Against the discrimination towards the Blacks of Stamps, they had to unite together in order to overcome the misfortune. A feeling of fellowship and brotherhood exists in the Black community, for they suffer at the hands of the whites in one way or another.

Physical hardships like "the fingers cut by the mean little cotton balls" (8) are minutely observed by her at Momma's store. Black people are in a cave, chained to cotton, held by poverty and ignorance. They are treated like slaves by the white masters, even after the abolition of slavery. They work hard every day to earn enough for the whole year, knowing pretty well that they would end the season as they had started. Angelou describes the hopelessness of the cotton pickers who are victims of the system: "In cotton-picking time the late afternoons revealed the harshness of Black Southern life, which in the early morning had been softened by nature's blessing of grogginess, forgetfulness and the soft lamplight" (9). The rigid caste system of the South during the Great Depression is realistically portrayed by Angelou through the tragic plight of the poor Black peasants. The white cotton balls are symbolic of the tyranny and oppression of the white man, whose humane feelings are never aroused by the innumerable sufferings of the poor Black peasants.

The revival meetings ignite anger in Marguerite. She questions the lifestyles of peasants and their quiet acceptance of hard work. When the cotton pickers return from the fields, "Their minds sagged. In the Store the men's faces were the most painful to watch, but I seemed to have no choice. When they tried to smile to carry off their tiredness as if it was nothing, the body did nothing to help the mind's attempt at disguise" (120), they are back to the Store from where they had started in the morning. "The women's feet had swollen to fill the discarded men's shoes they wore" (121). Marguerite is disheartened to see her people working like oxen who struggle to survive a pitiful existence. She considers it shameful that they try "to pretend that things were not as bad as they were," and she yearns to make them stand up and "assume the posture of a man" (121), rather than being treated like an animal all through their lives.

In spite of facing innumerable hardships, they lean on God's mercy, having full faith in the merciful master. "People whose history and future were threatened each day by extinction considered that it was only by divine intervention that they were able to live at all" (120). Marguerite is indignant because, instead of resting at home after a whole day of hard physical labour, the peasants waste their time going to the church for the revival meeting. She says, "Go to church in that cloud of weariness? Not go home and lay those tortured bones in a feather bed? The idea came to me that my people may be a race of masochists and that not only was it our fate to live the poorest, roughest life but that we liked it like that" (121). She is not able to comprehend the relation between the poor Black people and a white God. The minister at the revival meeting preaches charity. He says, "Charity is simple.... Charity is poor.... Charity is plain." Through this, he reassures the Black people that "although they might be the lowest of the low they were at least not uncharitable, and 'in that great Getting' Up Morning, Jesus was going to separate the sheep (them) from the goats (the whitefolks)'" (128). The church appears silly to her because the religion it preaches offers no comfort to her anguished mind. "Angelou's account suggests that she considers the preacher's message that African Americans should endure and resign themselves to their lot in life to be an inadequate response to their plight" (Megna-Wallace 90).

According to the minister of the revival meeting, God loves the poor and hates the rich, and adds that the Black man can assure his place in the land of milk and honey by suffering on this earth and being charitable. The collection comes last in the service, and the revival members give from their small means in the name of charity. "They basked in the righteousness of the poor and the exclusiveness of the downtrodden. Let the whitefolks have their money and power and segregation and sarcasm and big houses and schools and lawns like carpets, and books, and mostly – mostly – let them have their whiteness. It was better to be meek and lowly, spat upon and abused for this little time than to spend eternity frying in the fires of hell" (131). Thus, the Blacks are trapped in a life of drudgery and exploitation. Though the church preaches big words like charity and forgiveness to the Blacks, the whites are kept out of the responsibility of being charitable to their fellow humans. The Blacks are exploited even in the name of religion, yet they exult in the righteousness and promise of heavenly bliss after death. They are victims of discrimination in the South and ask God how long they have to suffer on this earth.

Momma Henderson has a religious orientation and she rears her grandchildren on strictly religious principles. She not only educates her grandchildren about religion but also about discipline and good manners. She makes her grandchildren participate in the activities of the community church, the Episcopal Methodist Church, of which she is an active member. She is genuinely protective and loving towards her grandchildren, from whom Marguerite learns to resist by enduring the sorrows of life. Black mothers are often described as strong disciplinarians and overly protective, yet they manage to raise daughters who are self-reliant and assertive. Gloria Wade-Gayles, in *Sage: A*

Scholarly Journal on Black Women, explains this apparent contradiction and suggests that "Black mothers do not socialize their daughters to be 'passive' or 'irrational.' Quite the contrary, they socialize their daughters to be independent, strong and self-confident. Black mothers are suffocatingly protective and domineering precisely because they are determined to mold their daughters into whole and self-actualizing persons in a society that devalues Black women" (12).

Hurston's mother is very optimistic and inspires her children "to 'jump at de sun.' We might not land on the sun, but at least we would get off the ground" (*Dust Tracks on a Road* 13). Her father is not that hopeful and believes that Negroes should not have this spirit. He always threatens to break Hurston's spirit, and her mother always comes to her rescue. She knows that she is impudent and given to talking back, but she believes that she is just like her and does not want her to grow up like a doll who cannot fight for herself. Alice Walker attributes the trust she has in herself to her mother. Mary Helen Washington describes this relationship, pointing out that Walker "never doubted her powers of judgement because her mother assumed that they were sound; she never questioned her right to follow her intellectual bent, because her mother implicitly entitled her to it" (Perry and Brownley 145). Walker's mother exhibits the value of a free mind by giving her daughter a library card.

A. P. Porter, in *Jump at de Sun: The Story of Zora Neale Hurston*, states, "Her ability to keep running after she'd lost her shoes, to strut when others expected her to crawl, was a blessing and a curse. It was a blessing because it kept her going when times were bad, and times were often bad. It was a curse because it separated her from those who had less faith. Jumping at the sun ain't easy" (90). Hurston did jump at the sun by overcoming adversities and accomplishing her goals. In the foreword to this book, Lucy Ann Hurston, daughter of Zora Neale Hurston's youngest brother, writes, "The road for an African American has always been uphill. Aunt Zora didn't care. In some ways, a woman has always had a tougher time than a man. She didn't care about that either. Aunt Zora would just not quit. Her courage and persistence inspired me to go back to school, to write, to lecture, to jump at the sun" (7).

At the time of Hurston's birth, her father, a successful carpenter, is away on building business for months. On the news of her birth, he threatens to cut his throat, as he believes that he could stand only one daughter, Sarah, his favourite child, and that one girl is enough. "Plenty more sons, but no more girl babies to wear out shoes and bring in nothing" (19). Literature, as far as it mirrors the world, reflects the predominant attitude which frequently values men and masculine pursuits more highly than women and feminine pursuits. "Black women had to suffer from triple oppression as poor, black and female, while their counterparts suffered double oppression as poor and black" (Karthikeyani PDF).

No grown folks are around when Hurston's mother delivers her, as the people were busy digging sweet potatoes and killing hogs. She sends one of the smaller children to fetch the midwife, Aunt Judy, who had gone to eat a hog-killing. Her mother has to do it all alone, and after the baby comes out, she is too weak to do anything for herself or the baby. A white man who knows the family well, listening to the loud cry of the newborn baby, reaches their house just a few minutes after Hurston's birth, cuts the navel cord with his knife, offers them fresh meat and sweet potatoes, and by the time the midwife arrives, he does all that is there to be done. The next day, Mrs. Neale, her mother's friend, comes in and reminds her that she had promised to let her name the baby in case a girl is born. She had read a name somewhere, picked it up, for she thought it was very pretty, and thus she names the baby Zora Neale Hurston.

Marshall is born four years after her sister's birth, and she believes that her parents wanted a boy and, to their disappointment, she was born. "It was a grievous and permanent disappointment for Adriana. This I knew before I even fought my way out of her womb. Because hadn't I, during my nine months there, heard her praying nonstop for a boy-child, Adriana believing that a little Sam Burke, Jr., would miraculously transform his father into a provider on the order of her brother, Winston Carlyle, and the other Bajan men who were all steadily progressing in spite of 'the discrimination n' thing in this man country'" (*Triangular Road* 82–83). Adriana pins her hopes on the birth that she hopes will bring the required change in her husband. Shirley Chisholm once noted, "The emotional, sexual, and psychological stereotyping of females begins when the doctor says, 'It's a girl'" (qtd. in Jule 45). Over half of the world's population is female, yet they unjustly receive an unfair balance in life from conception.

Another girl-child in the family is a matter of disappointment for the parents, moreover one who is not even as pretty as their first child. Marshall's father loves her no less for being a girl, and her mother recites the list of her physical flaws almost daily. There are her personality flaws as well: "Hard-ears!" "Willful!" "Own-ways!" (*Italics original* 83–84). Almost from the beginning, Marshall follows her own way. In 1905, Fannie Barrier Williams lamented, "The colored girl … is not known and hence not believed in; she belongs to a race that is best designated by the term 'problem,' and she lives beneath the shadow of that problem which envelops and obscures her" (qtd. in Washington, *Invented Lives* 150). Marshall's father falls in love with all things Spanish and names his daughters accordingly: Valenza, after Valencia, for Marshall, and Anita for her elder sister. Marshall is called by her middle name, Pauline, which she changes to Paule, with a silent "e" (80), at the age of thirteen.

Hunter-Gault, as a young girl, questions her mother about her unusual name. Her mother tells her that she thought she would have a boy, whom she would name Charles after her husband. She chooses her middle name, Alberta, in honour of her husband's mother. She calls her Charlayne, as she "wanted it to be as close to Charles as possible and yet make it feminine" (*In My Place* 6). Hunter-Gault loves her name, and to her, it always meant feminine strength. She always thinks of being beautiful, feminine, soft and smart like her mother. Her mother suffers extreme pain for four days during her birth, yet she feels herself to be the luckiest woman in the world, though she had been expecting a boy.

"The position of the girl child in India is still more deplorable, primarily because the discrimination against girls is rooted in our social and cultural prejudices which value a son as an asset but look upon a girl as a liability and a drain on the resources of the family.… As such, the birth of a female child is often viewed with disappointment and at best, indifference" (Luthra 63). The novel *Nectar in a Sieve* by Kamala Markandaya exposes the traditional attitude of Indians towards a female child right from her birth: "Rukmani's disappointment at the birth of a girl child is typical in India, especially for Indian farmers who need manpower for reaping and harvesting. Her reaction at the sight of the first-born is, 'what woman wants a girl for her first-born?'" (19). She sheds tears of weakness and disappointment; she supports her husband's view that "a male child is an asset and a girl child is a liability to the family" (Varghese 16). Preference for a son over a daughter is common throughout the world, be it India or America. In *I Know Why the Caged Bird Sings*, Angelou's brother, Bailey, is loved more than her, and he enjoys a freer life compared to her because he happens to be a boy.

In Marguerite's world, Bailey is the "greatest person" (21), and she feels it her good fortune that he is her brother only and she need not share him with anyone else. She compares herself to her brother and tells how handsome he is in contrast to her: "Where I was big, elbowy and grating, he was small, graceful and smooth. When I was described by our playmates as being shit color, he was lauded for his velvet-black skin. His hair fell down in black curls, and my head was covered with black steel wool. And yet he loved me" (22). It is very painful for her that she was the only ugly child in a handsome family. "Pecola Breedlove, an unloved, 'ugly' 11-year-old Black girl in Toni Morrison's novel *The Bluest Eye* (1970), internalizes the negative images of African-American women and believes that the absence of blue eyes is central to her 'ugliness.' Pecola cannot value her Blackness – she longs to be White so that she can escape the pain of being Black, female, poor, and a child" (Collins 102).

Angelou relates the dissatisfaction with her looks with lack of love and abandonment and believes that her quest for love can only be actualized through beauty. She associates being beautiful with the set standards of the "blond-blue-eyed-angel-like" girl and connects this standard to social acceptance. Family members, friends and neighbours remind her about her ugliness time and again. bell hooks, in *Outlaw Culture: Resisting Representations*, describes the colour-caste system mentioned above as a practice that values lighter shades of blackness as better and more beautiful: "the lighter one's skin, the greater one's social value" (203). Bailey is her protector and comes to her defence when adults say unkind things pertaining to her physical appearance. He is also an all-time partner and companion to her. For Marguerite, her "pretty Black brother was my Kingdom Come" (23), and "he was the pride of the Henderson/Johnson family" (22), and she loves her brother immensely.

I Know Why the Caged Bird Sings begins with a prologue wherein Marguerite painfully remembers a terrible day when she had to recite a poem at the church on the occasion of Easter in a new dress which she had imagined to be very beautiful, which actually is "a plain ugly cut-down from a white woman's once-was-purple throwaway" (2). She thinks, "I was going to look like one of the sweet girls who were everybody's dream" (2). Marguerite is a Black, poor female with "skinny legs," "small and squinty" eyes, and a "kinky mass" of hair (2). She fails to fulfil even the Black standards of beauty: "Her sense of impotence and worthlessness is underscored in the opening pages when she dreams of waking up transformed into a beautiful white girl with blond hair and blue eyes" (Megna-Wallace 4). She believes that she is actually white but a wicked, jealous fairy had turned her "into a too-big Negro girl, with nappy black hair, broad feet and a space between her teeth that would hold a number-two pencil" (3). She feels herself to be an ugly Black child who would never measure up to the standards of pretty white girls. Dealing with prevailing standards of beauty – particularly skin colour, facial features, and hair texture – is one specific example of how controlling images derogate African American women. A children's rhyme often sung in Black communities proclaims:

Now, if you're white you're all right,
If you're brown, stick around,
But if you're black,
Git back! Git back! Git back!

Prevailing standards of beauty claim that no matter how intelligent, educated, or "beautiful" a Black woman may be, those Black whose features and skin colour are most African must "git back." "Within the binary thinking that underpins intersecting oppressions, blue-eyed, blonde, thin White women could not be considered beautiful without the Other – Black women with African features of dark skin, broad noses, full lips, and kinky hair" (Collins 97–98).

The cultural idea of 'Black Is Beautiful' – the reclamation of African American beauty – rises up from these pages as Angelou writes about growing up in a world that equates beauty with whiteness. The prologue conveys Marguerite's displacement in the already marginalised Black community. The preface states, "If growing up is painful for the Southern Black girl, being aware of her displacement is the rust on the razor that threatens the throat" (4). She is fully aware of the hardships a young Southern Black girl will have to face in a racially discriminated and segregated society. The racist society convinces her that she can be nothing more than a poor Black girl in a white man's world. In the *Southern Humanities Review* titled "The Song of a Caged Bird: Maya Angelou's Quest after Self Acceptance," Sidonie Smith says that this "primal childhood scene brings into focus the nature of the imprisoning environment from which the self will seek escape. The Black girl child is trapped within the cage of her own diminished self-image around which interlock the bars of natural and social forces" (368).

One Christmas, Marguerite and Bailey receive gifts from their parents who lived separately in California. They feel sad on receiving the gifts and go out and cry. Marguerite had thought her parents to be dead till she receives gifts from them on Christmas. Her father sends his photograph, and her mother sends her a tea set and a doll "with blue eyes and rosy cheeks and yellow hair painted on her head" (52). The gifts brought up so many questions to their mind as to what wrong they had done that their parents sent them alone from California to Stamps at the age of three and four, with tags put on their arms. The parents fail to understand the feelings of their little kids and gift a blue-eyed doll which ironically pictures the white standard of beauty. Both of them tear the stuffing out of the doll as a revolt against the unattainable standards of beauty and save the tea set in case their parents return. In *The Bluest Eye* (1970), Toni Morrison presents the character of Claudia, a 10-year-old Black girl who, "to the chagrin of grown-ups, destroys White dolls by tearing off their heads and who refuses to share her classmates' admiration of light-skinned, long-haired Maureen Peal. Claudia's growing awareness of the 'Thing that made her [Maureen Peal] beautiful and us ugly' and her rejection of that Thing – racist images of Black women – represents yet another reaction to negative images of Black womanhood" (Collins 104).

One day, her father, Bailey Henderson Sr., comes to Stamps. He is very handsome, and Marguerite thinks that Bailey is his son, for he was as handsome as their father, and that she "was an orphan that they picked up to provide Bailey with company" (55). For three weeks, people who had gone to school with her father or heard about him came to meet him. To Marguerite, her father "sounded more like a white man than a Negro. Maybe he was the only brown-skinned white man in the world" (58). She gets very upset to know that their father has come to take them with him to St. Louis to their mother, as she does not want to leave Momma. She does not even care about anything during the journey; all she knows is that, "we were being driven to hell and our father was the delivering devil" (59). When they reach St. Louis and meet their mother, Bailey falls in love with her at first sight. Marguerite realises that her mother is too beautiful to have children, so she had sent them away as "unwanted children" (60). Both children are amazed at the beauty of their mother. She is modern, open, strong-minded, and supports her children "efficiently with humour and imagination" (207). She is a very positive person and refuses to be subservient to men or white people.

For Marguerite, her parents are like strangers, and it does not bother her when, after a few days, her father leaves for California. She has no feelings for them, but Bailey likes them both, and they share the same physical beauty and personality as their parents. She struggles to accept herself and her body, even though she feels inferior to others. Uncle Tommy, her mother's brother, used to tell her often, "Ritie, don't worry 'cause you ain't pretty. Plenty pretty women I seen digging ditches or worse. You smart" (67). Though her brain is appreciated, her belief in her ugliness is affirmed further. Angelou writes in a letter to her friend Rosa Guy, "My belief [as a child] that I was ugly was absolute, and nobody tried to disabuse me – not even Momma. Momma's love enfolded me like an umbrella, but at no time did she try to dissuade me of my belief that I was an ugly child" (qtd. in Braxton, *Maya Angelou's I Know Why the Caged Bird Sings: A Casebook* 24).

In St. Louis, Marguerite notices how the marginalised Negro community is plunged into the world of crime, paying no heed to law and order. She becomes a victim of male oppression and exploitation when Mr. Freeman, her mother's boyfriend, molests and rapes her at the tender age of eight. She confuses his embrace with paternal love and affection when he first molests her: "From the way he was holding me, I knew he would never let me go or let anything bad ever happen to me. This was probably my real father, and we had found each other at last" (73). Mr. Freeman threatens to kill Bailey if she tells anything to anybody. Subsequently, Mr. Freeman rapes her, which is physically and mentally painful. She considers herself guilty of some forbidden crime and keeps the incident a secret out of fear and guilt, though she is sick with terrible pain. She thinks, "What he did to me, and what I allowed, must have been very bad if already God let me hurt so much" (81). Mr. Freeman chooses the weakest target, a black female child, to exert his cruel male power, symbolising the tyranny of a sexist society.

Later, the family hospitalises her; she feels like spending the rest of her life in the hospital as she relishes the attention, love, care and protection given to her by the Baxter family. "Mother brought flowers and candy. Grandmother came with fruit, and my uncles clumped around and around my bed, snorting like wild horses. When they were able to sneak Bailey in, he read to me for hours." (83) Literature has a therapeutic effect on her mind and body, and she looks forward to such reading sessions. In the court, Freeman's lawyer symbolises male oppression as he verbally brings up the whole incident of rape. He belittles her in the name of justice and asks her, to her dismay, "Do you know if you were raped?" (84). She denies any prior physical contact with Mr. Freeman because she fears that her uncle will kill her, her grandmother will get angry and stop talking to her, her mother will be disappointed and Bailey will know that she had kept a secret from him, "And all those people in the court would stone me as they had stoned the harlot in the Bible" (85). She prefers retreating into silence rather than answering the lawyer's intimidating questions after experiencing extreme physical and mental turmoil. The rape of a child is the cruelest action as Angelou shares why she writes about her rape, "You write so that perhaps people who hadn't raped anybody yet might be discouraged, people who had might be informed, people who have not been raped might understand something, and people who have been raped might forgive themselves" (Braxton, *Maya Angelou's I Know Why the Caged Bird Sings: A Casebook* 12).

The court of law punishes Mr. Freeman for one year and one day, but someone gets him released that very afternoon. Marguerite comes to know that he had been found kicked to death, probably by her uncle. She feels that Mr. Freeman is dead because she told a lie in court. She decides to stop talking, or someone else might die. "I could feel the evilness flowing through my body and waiting, pent up, to rush off my tongue if I tried to open my mouth. I clamped my teeth shut; I'd hold it in" (86-87). Except for her brother, she communicates with no one and remains mute for several years. Her family accepts her behaviour as a "post-rape, post-hospital affliction" (87), but even after the doctor tells her that she is healed, she refuses to be the child she once was. Even after necessary punishments and thrashings, she does not retain her usual self and is called "impudent" (88). She copes with the rape by refusing to talk. "The context of silence is varied and multi-dimensional. Most obvious are the ways racism, sexism, and class exploitation act to suppress and silence" (bell hooks, *Talking Back* 8). Her innocence is stolen from her, and she is not a carefree child again. After some time, the loving and caring Baxter family grows tired of her silence and grim presence and sends Marguerite and Bailey back to Stamps, where they are placed in the care of their loving grandmother, Mrs. Henderson. The people of Stamps accept Marguerite's muteness; she feels at ease in the Southern community and believes that the barrenness of the small town is precisely what she wants.

The oppression of women stems largely from men's desire for power and control. The same need which, throughout history, has driven men to try to conquer and subjugate other groups or nations, and to oppress other classes or groups in their own society, drives them to dominate and oppress women. "Since men feel the need to gain as much power and control as they can, they steal away power and control from women. They deny women the right to make decisions so that they can make them for them, leave women unable to direct their own lives so that they can direct their lives for them" (Taylor, web. 30 Aug. 2012). Society is constructed on the historical notion that men are stronger, more dominant, more capable, superior, and more knowledgeable than women.

John Hurston hears about folks building a town of coloured people in Florida and regards it as a good place to live in. Later on, he is elected Mayor of Eatonville for three terms, and he even writes the local laws; the village of Eatonville is still governed by the laws formulated by Hurston's father. Her mother joins her father a year after he settles in Eatonville, and they both begin their life anew. They buy land, build a roomy house, plant, reap, and the children keep coming, "more mouths to feed and more feet for shoes" (10). Neither of them minds that, and her father boasts of his house full of young ones and also of the fact that he never allowed his wife to go out and work for anybody, even for a single day in her life. He has his weaknesses, and her mother is unhappy at times, but they never think of ending their relationship, so she believed that her father and mother were really in love.

Hurston and her family live on a big piece of ground with two big Chinaberry trees shading the front gate. There are plenty of fruits growing in their yard and a five-acre garden with eatables growing in it. They have all that they wanted – chicken, meat, eggs, and fish – and the guests are also served with hospitality. There are eight rooms in their house, eight children in the family, and their house is noisy from morning till bedtime. They have a big barn and a ground well covered with grass, and the village children come to play in their yard. They are not allowed to go and play at the houses of others, as their mother believes that they have plenty of space to play, plenty of things to play with, and plenty of them to give each other company. She tells them that there is no need for them to live like poor Negroes and poor white trash – who are so poor as to sit and play in their house and to go to someone else's house. Any of her children who have such a tendency might have got it from the Hurston side and not from the Pottses, "Things like that gave me my first glimmering of the universal female gospel that all good traits and leanings come from the mother's side" (13). Her mother identifies the characteristics that make her children her own: "Lucy Potts Hurston intends to provide a stable environment for her children. In a move that criticizes John Hurston's background and anticipates his argument for breaking Zora's spirit, the author's mother identifies any tendency to devalue the family home with the Hurston side; the maternal inheritance would encourage the child's creativity and ambition and would also ultimately yield her success, Lucy Potts Hurston implies" (Rodriguez 35).

The white man who had helped her mother in the delivery of Hurston comes the next day to enquire about the baby, and with the passing of time, he keeps track of Hurston's welfare. Hurston is a curious child like other children and has the know-how of all things; she asks many questions but gets few answers. While playing outdoors in the moonlight, she is happy to think that the moon follows her whichever way she goes. She confides her secret to her friend Carrie Roberts; she is hurt by the fact that the moon follows her also, and they both quarrel over the moon. Soon others get to know the reason for their quarrel, they laugh at them and tell them that the moon follows everyone. Hurston is hurt to know that the moon is not her exclusive friend, but still she is among those who showed the way to the moon. This way, she keeps on probing to know more, no matter whether her probings make her happier or sadder.

Hurston used to climb to the top of one of the huge Chinaberry trees, which guarded their front gate, to look out over the world. The most interesting thing that she sees is the horizon; she turns in all directions, and it is there at the same distance. She feels like walking out to the horizon to see the end of the world. She shares it with her friend Carrie Roberts and asks her to accompany her the next morning. Hurston is not able to sleep at night due to the excitement of finding out the end of things, which she had desired for months. The next morning, after breakfast, she waits for her friend, and when she does not turn up, she goes to her house and meets her on the way. Carrie is coming to tell her that she cannot go with her, as they may be late to come back, for it looks so far, and they both will be punished for that. Hurston persuades her friend to join her, and when she does not agree, she hits her and then feels sorry too. She believes if she has something to ride on, she can go alone to the end of the world.

A few days before Christmas, her father asks them what they want from Santa Claus. Her siblings ask for toys of their choice; Hurston asks for a fine black riding horse. On hearing this, her father gets angry, "It's a sin and a shame! Lemme tell you something right now, my young lady; you ain't white. Riding horse!! Always trying to wear de big hat! I don't know how you got in this family nohow. You ain't like none of de rest of my young'uns" (29). He warns her that, being a Negro, she should not be too ambitious, for they are not whites. Hurston replies that if he cannot give her a riding horse, then she wants nothing. Still, on Christmas, she gets a doll, not a horse to ride off to the end of the world. John Hurston, being a practical man, "knew no other way to protect his boisterous child from the harsh and unforgiving racism of the South than by teaching her to act as a black girl was expected to act – by blacks as well as whites" (Witcover 31).

Hurston watches the world go by, taking a seat on top of the gate post; the carriages and cars pass before her on the way to Orlando. Often the white travellers hail her, but more often she hails them and asks if she could join the ride with them. She is always invited to come along; she rides up the road half a mile with them and comes back walking on her own, and when her family finds out about it, she is badly beaten. Her grandmother had known slavery, so she worries a great deal about her erratic ways, "Git down offa dat gate post! You li'l sow, you! Git down! Setting up dere looking dem white folks right in de face! They's gowine to lynch you, yet. And don't stand in dat doorway gazing out at 'em neither. Youse too brazen to live long," (34), but Hurston keeps gazing at them and also goes for a ride whenever offered. Harihar Kulkarni writes in the context of slavery, "The brutal treatment that the black women received during slavery invariably left profound scars on their psyche. Their physical bondage ultimately turned into a psychological bondage causing mutation and mutilations of their world. The external forces operating at the socio-economic levels came to bear an unmistakable relationship to the internal fears, worries, anxieties and feelings of inadequacy and frustration. The poisonous fangs of slavery manifested themselves in innumerable ways and finally determined the behavioural pattern of black women" (59). Harriet Jacobs, an enslaved light-skinned woman, was sexually harassed because of her looks. Her straight hair, fair skin, her appearance as a dusky white woman, made her physically attractive to white men. The fact that she was black made her available to white men as no group of white women had been. In describing this situation, Jacobs notes, "if God has bestowed beauty upon her, it will prove her greatest curse. That which commands admiration in the white woman only hastens the degradation of the female slave" (qtd. in Washington, *Invented Lives* 17).

Marshall's father goes about life, insisting by his manner that his is a higher calling than the series of factory jobs he has held over the years. In his eyes, he possesses the talent and ability to be much more, and so he joins many courses like radio repair, accounting, and trumpet lessons but never completes any of them. He also works as a salesman, part-time or on weekends. He pursues such selling ventures until they either fail to give profit or he simply grows tired of repeating the same sales pitch. Finally, he decides that selling door-to-door is beneath his talents. Still, he remains optimistic and thinks that a job is only a matter of time. He always remains playful with his daughters, and every morning he wakes them up with, "Ladyfolks, ladyfolks, rise and shine and give God the glory!" (Triangular Road 80). Whenever Adriana complains about his frequent job changes, abandoned mail-order courses, and selling ventures, Sam Burke sings the same "Satan go 'way" hymn for her, and she stops complaining.

Marshall is born in the cold-water flats in Red Hook on Fulton Street. They live in a series of walkups that at least have steam heat, hot water, a gas stove, and a bathtub in the bathroom. They, the Burke family, manage to move to "the heights" (85). Their circumstances do not really improve, but with Adriana supplementing Sam Burke's weekly salary by doing day's work at the Madams again, they are able to lease an old Victorian brownstone on Hancock Street No. 501 uptown. It is a reddish-brown four-storey building with trees in the front and backyard, a sun parlour on the second floor, and two upper-floor apartments that can be rented out to pay the greater part of the lease. It is best for Marshall as it is at a short distance from a local branch of the Brooklyn Public Library, "A necessary home away from home" (85). She is so fond of books that her mother considers her a bookworm. She considers the library a necessary home, and at the age of twelve, she summons up the courage one day to ask the white librarian for a list of books by coloured writers.

Sam Burke spends his weekends in the sun parlour at 501, recovering from the factory job he is doing at the moment and dreaming up other pursuits that may free him from such jobs. Adriana is ashamed to lease a house when every Bajan is buying one. She does not feel like going to her brother's house, whose wife shows her nice things to make her feel bad. She is ashamed to have married a man who always tries one foolish scheme after another that does not produce money. Sam Burke abandons silencing her with his playful hymn. He attacks her for having wasted the Panama money years ago on the visit home to her mother, which could have been a down payment for the house. Nine years after Marshall's disappointing birth, a boy-child is born—the long-hoped-for son—named Franklin Edsel, who arrives too late to bring about any miracles, as by then Sam Burke, in his endless seeking, finds God. "God in the person of a short, brown, bald and rotund fellow named George Baker from Georgia, who, having migrated north, had somehow metamorphosed into a god called Father Divine, with his heavenly kingdom an old, outsized brownstone mansion in Harlem" (91). He declares himself to be the one and only father to his followers. All his followers are his deemed children, and no matter what their familial roles are, they are brothers or sisters now to their spouses and to their children as well.

Sam Burke, Marshall's father, becomes Brother Burke, and everyone in his family has to address him as such. The short little self-proclaimed god from Georgia relieves him of the burden of being both a husband and a father. Adriana verbally attacks them both, for her husband quits his latest factory job and proudly announces that Father Divine has chosen him to administer a branch of the kingdom being established in Philadelphia. His so-called god delivers him at last from the long, futile search for a vocation worthy of his still undefined talents. With this, Sam Burke, now Brother Burke, vanishes from their lives, and with him is gone everything, beginning with 501 Hancock.

Adriana cannot manage the lease, not even with the rent from the two upper floors. She cannot ask her brother, having broken off all contact with him due to his boasting wife, and other family members are of no help. In consequence, they return to the series of cheaper walkups this time. They are usually evicted for back rent, with their belongings piled up on the sidewalk; they become nomads, wandering from one brief resting place to another in central Brooklyn until they finally end up in the cramped third-floor apartment of a brownstone owned by a fellow Bajan. This is the ultimate humiliation for Adriana. With Sam Burke gone, plunging them into poverty, she spends hours putting her adolescent daughters on guard against his kind, threatening them in an effort to save them from a fate similar to her own. In *The New York Times* review of the book, Felicia R. Lee says, "Marshall's parents presided over an ambitious household of failed dreams" (C1).

Rosalie Troester, in *Sage: A Scholarly Journal on Black Women*, discusses the mother-daughter relationship in Paule Marshall's *Brown*

Girl, Brownstones. She catalogues the ways mothers have aimed to protect their daughters and the impact this may have on relationships themselves: "Black mothers, particularly those with strong ties to their community, sometimes build high banks around their young daughters, isolating them from the dangers of the larger world until they are old and strong enough to function as autonomous women. Often these dikes are religious, but sometimes they are built with education, family, or the restrictions of a close-knit and homogeneous community.... This isolation causes the currents between Black mothers and daughters to run deep and the relationship to be fraught with an emotional intensity often missing from the lives of women with more freedom" (13).

Anne Moody's mother gives birth to James, a baby by Raymond, who is a soldier. His mother, Miss Pearl, does not like Essie Mae's mother and takes James along with her, saying that she will not be able to feed so many children. Her mother is disheartened by Miss Pearl's behaviour. At the end of the summer, they move into town, in Centreville, where she starts work. Before school is out, they move again. "It seemed as though we were always moving. Every time it was to a house on some white man's place and every time it was a room and a kitchen" (*Coming of Age in Mississippi* 28). One day after Christmas, Junior sets the house on fire by chance; the whole house is burnt to ashes along with the new clothes bought for Christmas. "These were the first she had ever bought us. All our other clothes had been given to us" (29). They eat the leftover food of the white family where her mother works, which is the best food they had ever eaten. This makes them realise that white folks have all kinds of food with meat, and they just have beans and bread. This reflects the poverty and helplessness of the poor blacks, and food represents the difference between the blacks and the whites. "Black feminism has always encompassed basic bread-and-butter issues which affect women of all economic groups" (Jones, Sharon 86).

Essie Mae's mother gets another domestic job and they shift house again: "We were the only Negroes in that section, which seemed like some sort of honor. All the whites living around there were well-to-do" (32). Essie Mae and her siblings sit and watch the white children play with their toys and wish to buy such toys one day. The white children play with expensive toys like bikes and skates; they have two apple crates and a tin can to play with. Soon they become friends and start playing together; the playhouse of the whites is far better than any house the blacks can even dream of. Essie Mae does not understand what makes her white playmates different from her and why they have better toys than them. She tries playing "doctor-doctor" and examines them to find an answer, but to no avail. This shows her early concern with the question of race, which she keeps pondering over and fighting for life.

Adline and Junior also start school when Essie Mae is nine and in fourth grade. It becomes really hard for their mother to feed them, buy clothes for the three of them, and keep them in school, as she earns five dollars a week. She cannot afford to buy bread for their lunch, so she makes biscuits and gives two to each of them with peanut butter. The children, being hungry, go to the water fountain to fill up on water; at times they eat the dinner leftovers given to their mother by her employer, Mrs. Johnson. Essie Mae starts working part-time, cleaning the houses of white families in order to put food on the family's table. She earns seventy-five cents and two gallons of milk a week in her first job, and afterwards she works for many employers. Like Anne Moody, black daughters learn to expect to work, to strive for an education so they can support themselves, and to anticipate carrying heavy responsibilities in their families and communities, because these skills are essential to their own survival and those for whom they will eventually be responsible. New Yorker Michele Wallace recounts, "I can't remember when I first learned that my family expected me to work, to be able to take care of myself when I grew up ... It had been drilled into me that the best and only sure support was self-support" (qtd. in Collins 198).

The employer that influences Moody the most is Mrs. Claiborne, who treats her like a daughter, allows her to eat at the table with the white family, and teaches her the ways of the white world. She always gives her things, encourages her to study hard and learn as much as she can. She pays her three dollars a week, which keeps them from being hungry at school and at home, and despite her impoverished condition, Moody turns out to be a bright student. "Poor black children are the recipients of the poverty and helplessness that are features of the reality of many poor black women. They have a need to resist and subvert such hopelessness, thus undermining the shame, humiliation, and despair that accompany intergenerational poverty" (Day 45). Essie Mae's mother gets pregnant again with Raymond's child, and seeing her mother's big belly, she feels sad thinking that she will have to quit school to take care of another baby.

Moody is always struggling, from a simple beginning in Mississippi, including an unfaithful father, an emotionally tortured and fragile mother, and too many children to feed on the family's budget. "Youth in Africa leave school too early and enter the labor market unprepared, limiting their contribution to economic growth and increasing their vulnerability to poverty and economic hardship" (Garcia and Fares 22). One day her mother tells her that Raymond has built a house for them and they are going to move there very soon. She is very happy for her mother, for after working so hard for seven years, someone is going to build a house for her, a place of her own. Since their parents separated, they have shifted six times, and now they are going to move off white people's places, probably for good. Raymond has built the house at the bottom of the Ash Quarters, right off Highway 24. They will now live next door to Raymond's mother, Miss Pearl, who does not like Toosweet, Essie Mae's mother, as she is black and they are better because they were "yellow" (49). For the first time, they go to buy furniture for their house; earlier, they had always been given old, discarded furniture. Essie Mae wants to buy a bed and a refrigerator like the Johnsons and the Clairbornes. Her mother tells her not to buy everything that the white folks have.

Everybody in Raymond's family speaks to the children, but no one speaks to Toosweet. That hurts her very much. She thinks she can make the adults accept her through the children. She makes them study their lessons twice so that they have the highest grades in the class—especially Essie Mae, who is set in competition with Raymond's sister Darlene, who is her age and in the same grade. Toosweet tries really hard to get Miss Pearl's approval, but she never succeeds and feels sad about it. Raymond is a coward who never has the courage to stand up for Toosweet against his mother. Toosweet delivers Raymond's second baby. Miss Pearl comes to meet the baby but does not talk to Toosweet at all. She feels very bad and cries, but Raymond does nothing, for he will never break with his family for Toosweet, and they will never accept her, even after her continuous efforts to make them like her. They hate Toosweet "for no reason at all than the fact that she was a couple of shades darker than the other members of their family. Yet they were Negroes and we were also Negroes. I just didn't see Negroes hating each other so much" (59). As lighter-skinned African Americans, they look down on her family with darker skin. They will prefer Raymond's marriage with a lighter-skinned woman than with dark Toosweet.

In one scene of Dorothy West's *The Living Is Easy* (1948), a key figure, light-skinned, middle-class Cleo, hustles her daughter past a playground filled with the children of newly arrived Southern blacks, observing that "she wouldn't want her child to go to school with those niggers." Cleo clings to her social class position, one that she sees as separating her from other African Americans, and tries to muffle the negative status attached to her blackness by emphasizing her superior class position: "Even though Cleo is more acceptable to the White world, the price she pays for her acceptance is the negation of her racial identity and separation from the sustenance that such an identity might offer" (Collins 103).

Essie Mae feels that her white employers are nicer to them than Miss Pearl and her family. She does not understand the reason for Miss Pearl's hatred towards Toosweet. Moody tells about "the destructive power of prejudice. There is the prejudice of whites against blacks, and also the prejudice of lighter-skinned blacks towards darker-skinned blacks, and of people with money against poorer people" ("Coming of Age in Mississippi: Themes, Motifs, and Symbols," web. 6 Feb. 2017). Moody experiences each kind of prejudice that causes great mental pain. Raymond buys cheap land and tries to cultivate it, which turns out to be a difficult process as he finds that the land is loaded with hand grenades and mines from the war. He tills the land and plants cotton; Essie Mae works on the farm, hates the sun, and is dreadfully afraid of getting sunstroke. Everyone puts a lot of hard work into the field, but they do not make enough money from it. Essie Mae realizes that farming is the hardest way of making a living and decides that she will never be a farmer. Mrs. Claiborne, one of her white employers, tells her that she is smart and can do a lot if she just had a chance: "I knew if I got involved in farming, I'd be just like Mama and the rest of them, and that I would never have that chance" (90). She does not want to live life like her mother and Raymond, as she wants to get out of this Black system of poverty.

At the new session of school, they go in their same old school clothes and broken shoes. One day they go to Mr. Wheeler's house to pick up pecans and the money that they earn to buy new school clothes and shoes. The next week, they pick up pecans for Miss Minnie, who asks Essie Mae to work for her and pays her three dollars a week. Essie Mae, in her eighth grade, is elected the homecoming queen as she is a beautiful young girl now. In the process, she raises a lot of funds for her school with the help of her classmates and teacher Mrs. Willis. Her father, Diddly, brings her a beautiful blue dress for her homecoming parade, making it one of the few joyful moments of her young life. As the parade passes through the street, everyone stands to watch it, Black as well as white. Essie Mae wants to tell the whites, "Negroes can be beautiful too" (112). Black theologian Howard Thurman, in *The Search for a Common Ground*, comments, "'Black is Beautiful' became not merely a phrase – it was a stance, a total attitude, a metaphysics. In very positive and exciting terms it began undermining the idea that had developed over so many years into a central aspect of white mythology, 'that black is ugly, black is evil, black is demonic.' In so doing, it fundamentally attacked the front line of the defense of the myth of white supremacy and superiority" (98).

From this experience, she learns a lot about organizing people from Mrs. Willis, and this skill she uses later in the Black Empowerment Movement. "The slogan 'black is beautiful' was an important popular expression of resistance to white supremacy (of course that expression loses meaning and power if it is not linked to a process of politicization where black people learn to see ourselves as subjects rather than as objects, where as an expression of being subjects we act to transform the world we live in so that our skin no longer signifies that we will be degraded, exploited).... We prepare ourselves to act most effectively for radical social change" (bell hooks, *Talking Back* 109). After she is crowned the queen, she changes her name. Mrs. Willis asks them to bring their birth certificates for school records as graduation is approaching. Essie Mae's birth certificate is lost when

Junior set the house on fire. New copies of it are made, in which instead of Essie Mae her name is Annie Mae, as Essie did not like her name and is happy to have Annie instead.

After two years of bad luck with the farm, Raymond gives up trying to be a farmer in Mississippi. Toosweet succeeds in sending Raymond to California to find a job: "In Centreville there weren't any factories or sawmills that employed unskilled Negro men. The nearest mills were fifteen to fifty miles away in Woodville, Crosby, and Natchez. White businesses in town employed Negroes as janitors only, and there was never more than one janitor in any single business. The Negro man had a hard road to travel when looking for employment. A Negro woman, however, could always go out and earn a dollar a day because whites always needed a cook, a baby-sitter, or someone to do housecleaning" (117). Raymond stays in Los Angeles for about a month. Unable to find a job, he goes back to Centreville. As Raymond is out of work and Toosweet is about to have another baby, a mother of seven children, it seemed to Annie "as though we were doomed to poverty and more unhappiness than we had faced before" (118). Poverty is a real curse for the Blacks: "Blaming the victim is typically tied to arguments rooted in the idea that a culture of poverty exists that accounts for racial differences in the United States, including racial economic differences. The culture of poverty argument suggests that the poor – particularly blacks – suffer from a learned helplessness and powerlessness that explains their lack of success in a so-called merit-based society" (Martin 84–85).

In vacation, Moody goes to New Orleans to earn money, and when school reopens, she returns home. Everyone appreciates the change in her appearance, but looking good becomes a problem for her. Whenever she goes to town, white men stare at her and follow her; her basketball coach Hicks and her stepfather Raymond are attracted to her. One day, she gets so disgusted and dismayed with Raymond that she threatens to kill him with a piece of glass. She runs away from home and goes to the sheriff, Ed Cassidy, to help her pick up her clothes from Raymond and her mother's house. She tells him, "I was old enough to go to New Orleans and Baton Rouge and work and buy them. I'm old enough to send myself to school too. I don't owe Raymond nothin' and I want my clothes from there" (208). She hates

Raymond for treating them like dirt, for fussing with her mother, and hates him more than all the whites in Centreville. She decides to move away to her Daddy Diddly's house in Woodville.

Diddly's new wife, Emma, is a strong woman whom Moody loves, for she is full of energy and warmth. Unlike Raymond, Emma stands up to her "yellow" family and makes her family love Diddly. They refuse Moody to work for white men around, as they passionately dislike most of the whites in Woodville. One day, Emma's brother-in-law, Wilbert, gets in a huge fight with his wife over financial issues and threatens to kill his wife. Emma gets in the way, injures her foot by Wilbert's shot, not meant for her. Moody realizes how much her Daddy loves Emma when he carries her to the truck all by himself, though she weighs a lot. She is taken to the hospital. Moody goes to Wilbert's house to see the children and finds the eldest of them, Leon, crying. He tells her how he will have to stop going to school and work to help his mother, Janie, take care of the children if his parents separate: "These white people here don't pay nothin' to grown men. You know they ain't gonna pay a twelve-year-old boy nothin'. I use to work for that old white lady who live up the road and she paid me four dollars a week to work like a slave" (225). Listening to Leon, Moody thinks about her own life after her parents separated and of all the white women she worked for who paid her too little to survive.

Moody spends a week with Emma in the hospital, and during this time, she learns to admire her strength even more. She is livelier than anyone who comes to visit her and refuses to let anyone feel sorry for her. She even cracks jokes with the doctor whenever he comes to examine her wound. Moody admires her more for the fact that she does not blame Wilbert for shooting her: "She placed the blame where it rightfully belonged, that is, upon the whites in Woodville and how they had set things up making it almost impossible for the Negro men to earn a living" (226). She believes that Wilbert and Janie will not fight if Wilbert gets a good job and makes enough money to take care of the family. The whites are starving the blacks to death, and she adds that blaming Wilbert will neither bring her foot back nor set things right. This shows how the white people and the American society made survival extremely difficult for the blacks. After discharge from the hospital and sitting alone at home, Emma starts feeling sorry for herself. The Emma Moody admired disappears gradually. She makes her work a lot and complains about everything. Moody begins to count the weeks to graduation, when she will leave them for good. A story of frustration and anger at the inequities found in everyday living, *Coming of Age in Mississippi* sums up the daily indignities which were a part of growing up black in the rural South in the mid-twentieth century.

Merriam-Webster Dictionary defines vision as something seen in a dream, trance, or ecstasy; especially a supernatural appearance that conveys a revelation. Hurston starts having visions at the age of seven—disconnected scenes after scenes—which she believes to be true: "a preview of things to come, and my soul writhed in agony and shrunk away" (*Dust Tracks on a Road* 41). She knows her fate, has knowledge before time, and knows that she will be an orphan and will be homeless one day; the comforting circle of her family will be broken and she will have to wander alone until she serves her time. Finally, she will come to a big house where two women will be waiting for her with strange white flowers, and this will be the end of her pilgrimage—not the end of her life—and then she will know peace and love. She does not disclose these strange things to anyone, as she thinks they will laugh at her as a fake storyteller. "… the visions call into question Hurston's own position as subject of her text. Serving as metaphors for a fragmented self and for the self as sign and interpreter, the visions effectively literalize the fragmentation of the self that they both foretell and document. The author's mute reaction to the experience – she tells no one about the visions even as they come true – illustrates this fragmentation. Having been betrayed by her own eyes, the young girl also does not speak about what she has seen; the body, represented here by the senses, and self, represented by the power to understand and to speak, become fragmented and to some degree lost from one another with the event" (Rodriguez 37).

Meanwhile, her mother falls sick and keeps getting worse day by day. Her chest cold never gets better, and finally, she takes to bed. She goes back to her old home to be with her sister during her sister's last illness. She stays there for two months till her death. It seems that there are other things that worry her; her mother never forgives her for the move she had made twenty-one years before in marrying John Hurston and refuses to give her any share in the parental property. Hurston recounts, "I do not think that the money part worried Mama as much as the injustice and spitefulness of the thing" (63). Then Cousin Jimmie dies during her visit; he goes for a party and the next morning, his headless body is found beside the railroad track with no blood. It was said that he was shot dead by a white man unintentionally, as he mistook him for a certain white man whom he was expecting to pass that way; his death remained an unsolved mystery.

Back home, her mother is weak and less active. One day, she calls Hurston and gives her instructions: "I was not to let them take the pillow from under her head until she was dead. The clock was not to be covered, nor the looking-glass" (64). She assures her mother that she will see to it and promises to follow her instructions. "Lucy Hurston wished to symbolically reject the folklore of her village. Eatonville, like many rural communities, believed that a person's dying hard was a bad sign, since the spirit might haunt the survivors; everything must be done to alleviate suffering. It was understood that a pillow under one's head prolonged dying, and that the looking glass should be covered because a reflection of the corpse might attach itself permanently to the glass. One covered the clock because it would be forever ruined if it was functioning when time ran out and the spirit looked upon the clock's face" (Hemenway 16). Though the reasons for these beliefs were unimportant, the community possessed a ceremony of dying, and Hurston was unable to prevent the adults from carrying out their rites.

Hurston had no idea that her mother would die the same day. In the evening, she dies, and Hurston fails to carry out her last wish, as the elders do not listen to her. "Hurston finds herself powerless and silenced; the event pits her loyalty to her mother against the power of communal ritual" (Rodriguez 41). She remains in agony for years over her failure to execute her promise to her dying mother, and this moment signals the end of a phase in her life. "I was old before my time with grief of loss, of failure, of remorse, of failure. No matter what the others did, my mother had put her trust in me. She had felt that I could and would carry out her wishes, and I had not" (66–67). With this begins Hurston's wanderings — not so much in geography and time, but in spirit.

Bob, her eldest brother, was in school in Jacksonville. He comes home after their mother has passed away, and he is in terrible grief. Her sister Sarah tries to handle two-year-old Everett, their youngest brother. Hurston loves her father, but she is her mother's child and knows that her mother has not been happy, so she wishes to know how sad her father is over her mother's death. The next day, her mother is carried to the church for the last time. After that, Bob and Sarah return to Jacksonville to attend school. Two weeks later, Hurston too is on her way to Jacksonville, as her father is mostly away from home for long. She is underage, but the school agrees to take her, keeping the circumstances in mind. On her way with her brother Dick to catch the midnight train to Jacksonville, at the curve on the road that skirts Lake Catherine, she witnesses her first vision. She sees herself upon that curve at night, leaving the village home, bowed down with grief, and she fears that her other visions too will come true. "Hurston's text takes up this immersion into the imaginary world and also witnesses the transformation of the familiar into the uncanny; the home created by her mother is replaced with the world of the visions" (Rodriguez 38).

The life at Jacksonville is that of a little coloured girl, as she becomes aware of her identification as a Black person. The white people neither welcome her nor give her a piece of candy or a bag of crackers, as in Eatonville. In school, the girls do not like her getting into the conversation. In an essay, *"How It Feels to Be Colored Me,"* she writes, "Sometimes I feel discriminated against, but it does not make me angry. It merely astonishes me. How can any [people] deny themselves the pleasure of my company?" (qtd. in Porter 9). She does well in her class, and her teachers are happy with her. Now she is deprived of the loving pines, lakes, violets in the woods, and the animals she used to know in Eatonville. At times, the schoolgirls are taken for a walk, lined up two and two. On one such occasion, she sees a woman sitting on a porch who, from a distance, looks like her mother, sitting in a rocking chair just like her mother. She thinks that maybe they are mistaken, that their mother is not dead, but before she reaches the porch in line, the woman gets up and goes inside. She makes up her mind to run to the house someday to meet her mother, but the hope is gone soon, and she accepts her mother's death. For a daughter, "a mother's death also means the loss of the consistent, supportive family system that once supplied her with a secure home base. She then has to develop her self-confidence and self-esteem through alternate means. Without a mother or mother-figure to guide her, a daughter also has to piece together a female self-image of her own" (Edelman xxvii).

Sarah is her father's favourite child, and she loves him more than anything on the earth. After two months, Sarah is sick and wants to go home, and her father arranges the same. Within two weeks, Sarah informs Hurston about the second marriage of their father, and consequently, he has little time or money for his children. All the children are hurt, but it is worse for Sarah, for her stepmother resents her father's tender indulgence toward her. Leaving school and coming back home has tragic results for Sarah, as the stepmother asks their father to throw Sarah out of the house and town. Sarah marries and goes down on the Manatee River to live with Everett.

John Hurston loves his first-born daughter, Sarah, from the day of her birth. "If she was not fore-told, she was certainly fore-wished" (74). He had three sons, but after the first son, he wanted a little girl child around the house, and when finally she arrives after years, his joy has no limit. He takes care of the baby girl and never allows her to cry as an infant, and her wishes are always fulfilled. He brings her the best dresses, shoes, ribbons, dolls — everything that she asks for. All the family members are to take proper care of her and do things as per her wishes. She is given music lessons on the piano even when she is not interested, and Hurston begs for music lessons but is not allowed. Whenever the children want to eat something, they get Sarah to ask for it, as their father will never refuse her. Neither does he allow anybody to beat her, nor does he ever hit her. At the provocation of his new wife, he hits Sarah, and this is too much for her.

Six years after Sarah's heartbreak, Hurston takes her sister's revenge on her stepmother. One morning, Hurston's stepmother threatens to beat her for her rude behaviour after a useless effort to instigate her father to hit her. Hurston is determined to kill her, irrespective of the consequences, so she fights with her, and when her stepmother realises that she is bent on killing her, she escapes. Her father is disturbed, seeing them fighting. He weeps and asks Hurston to stop while she is holding her stepmother's head between her fists and the wall. She is mad with anger and keeps on fighting until her father rescues her. Her stepmother demands that Hurston be arrested, but her father refuses point-blank to let her sleep in jail even for a night. She goes to the church, and the people laugh at her, for most of them are old friends of her mother, and they want something like this to happen. Her stepmother leaves her father with the understanding that he can get her back when he makes "them good-for-nothing nigger wimmens know dat she was Mrs. Reverend" (78).

In Jacksonville school, one day, the Second in Command informs her that her boarding fee is not paid and asks her how she is going to make the payment. For this, she has no answer. She stays for a year in school, and in lieu of that, she is put to scrubbing the stair steps every Saturday and is sent to help in the pantry and do what she can in the kitchen after school. Her brother hurries off to take a job during vacation, and she is to stay back. Every day, she keeps looking out of the window to see her father coming to take her home. Weeks pass, and nobody comes. Then a letter comes from her father saying that the school can adopt her. The Second in Command tells her about the letter and says that she has no place for a young girl and that she is too busy to bring up anybody. She offers her money to pay for the way back home by boat and asks her to tell her father to send the money back.

The boat trip is exciting for her; she feels like a wild thing back in the jungle. She enjoys everything in and around the boat docks at Sanford, from where she goes to the railway station to take the train for fifteen miles to Maitland. The conductor and the whole crew know her, and she is safely back to her father's gloomy house. Four elder children are gone for good, and the four younger ones are shifted to the homes of her mother's friends, one by one. She finds her stepmother sleeping on her mother's feather bed that she had brought from her father's house, and this is too much for her to bear. With the help of her brother Joel, she takes the mattress off the bed, and this leads to a fight. Her father asks the children to leave, and they are forced to make their way prematurely in the world. With this, the second picture of her vision transforms into reality, as she had seen herself homeless and uncared for. She knows that, in reality, she has become a vagrant. Her way is full of pain, but there is a promise of a happy ending to her journey.

Hurston's first five years of poverty are the worst; the untoward circumstances make her life depressing. In the five years after leaving school at Jacksonville at the age of ten, she is shifted from one house to another, but she does not find comfort anywhere. She feels miserable as she is without books to read, getting some only by chance. Off and on, she goes to school, but there is no peace, as she has no guarantee for how long the school intervals will last. At the age of fourteen, she thinks of supporting herself by finding a job, though she is too young for that. Housewives do not appoint her, as they want someone strong enough to do the work, and Hurston looks younger than her age because of her slow growth. Finally, when she does get a job, she does not find it interesting enough. "Shuttled from relative to relative, she began supporting herself at the age of fourteen. The following years, filled with hard work and uncertainty, had been difficult for a young woman who had learned to rely on her neighbors. In a world of strangers, Hurston discovered that she herself was the only person she could truly depend on" (Witcover 15).

Dust Tracks on a Road also documents her work experiences and how race relations come into play in her employment. Hurston is hired as an upstairs maid by a white family; Mrs Alice, the lady of the house, likes her for making friends with her two little girls. The cook, Miz Cally—the President in full in the house—is a fat, black old woman who had nursed the master of the house and is a fixture, a permanent worker. "No matter who hires you, the fixture can fire you" (89). From the very first day, she views Hurston as a threat to her job, so through her cunning strategy, she makes the master of the house fire her after a few days. "Hurston's experience thus reveals intraracial, as well as interracial, conflicts" (Jones, Sharon 37). Hurston is again out of a job and money, but is lucky to get a job easily, as somebody tells the woman she is staying with about another job. When she goes there, the sick lady, who has a little three-year-old girl, gives her the job. She does not like the house with gloomy faces—the sick lady, Mrs Moncrief, her two elder unmarried sisters, and the cook who never smiles.

Mr Moncrief does laugh, but not around the house. He walks with Hurston down the street, makes her feel uncomfortable, and tells her that he is tired of that house full of "sour-looking women" (94). He is sick of the town and everything in it, so he is selling out his business and going away to Canada, and wants to take her along. She refuses to go with him and tells him not to bother her. Finally, she tells his wife, who starts crying and says that, for the last three years, her husband has hoped to find her dead. She adds, "You don't know what it means to give birth to a child for your husband and find that your health is gone the day the baby is born, and for him not to care what becomes of the baby or you either" (95). Hearing this, Hurston cries and leaves the house, never to return. The next day, Mr Moncrief comes to the house where Hurston is and tells her that his wife has nothing to do with their going to Canada. He calls his wife an old maid whom he had married by mistake and asks Hurston to be ready tomorrow—he will come to pick her up at night, and she should not fool him. All he needs is a young coloured girl to sleep with and enjoy life, and Hurston is his preference. This reveals another power conflict—one based not only on race but also on gender. Hurston packs her bag and leaves the place. The next night, he comes to take her, searches the house for her, and cannot believe that she has escaped. Two weeks later, it is in the papers that he has gone with a coloured office girl of a well-known doctor, taking all his money and some other people's money as well. Hurston's situation highlights the "vulnerable position of black female in relation to white men. This episode can be traced back to white male–black female relationships in the antebellum South, when African-American female slaves found themselves viewed as sexual property by the white male slave owners, who had positions of power and authority over them" (Jones, Sharon 41).

Hurston leaves many other jobs. Sometimes she does not suit the people, and sometimes the people do not suit her. She is restless and unstable. She is not doing anything she wanted to, and this is breaking her from within. She wants family love, peace, books, school, and a resting place. Her third vision of aimless wandering is taking its toll. Her brother Dick marries and asks her to come to Sanford and stay with him. He sends her a ticket, and she goes, hoping to go to school again. As soon as she gets back to Sanford, her father orders her to stay at his house. In less than a month of staying there, Hurston has another fight with her stepmother. She finds her father a changed person, with no energy, his home in ruin, and is sorry for him. This further adds bitterness towards his wife. The misery of the situation continues for years. He drags himself around "like a stepped-on-worm" (98), his foundations rot, and within seven years everything is in wreck. Hurston cannot bear the air around, which is too personal and pressing with old memories, so she decides to go to another town.

Be it home or outside, her life is the same—dull, gloomy, depressing, and without hope. One day, in a pile of rubbish, she finds a copy of Milton's complete works that lifts her spirit up. She reads it without ever having heard that Milton was the greatest poet of the world. She keeps it in her things; she enjoys reading it in her leisure time. A young woman who works in a doctor's office asks her to be her substitute as she is going on a trip. Hurston and the doctor get along well, and he tells her that if the girl does not come back, he will train her as a nurse. At the same time, she receives a letter from her eldest brother Bob, who had just graduated in Medicine, telling her that he wants to help her with school. His wife sends love, and he assures her that she will love his three children and asks her to come at the earliest. She is mad with joy to have a home again, to go to school, and to be with her brother at last. She thinks, "My five haunted years were over" (99). She packs her things hurriedly and gets on the train, saying goodbye "to the town, to loneliness, to defeat and frustration, to shabby living, to sterile houses and numbed pangs, to the kind of people I had no wish to know; to an era. I waved it goodbye and sank back into the cushions of the seat" (99). Frustration awaits her, for there is no school and she is needed to work in the house.

Her brother takes her for a walk and explains that it will cause trouble if he puts her in school at once, as his wife will feel that he is pampering her. He asks her to work along and be useful around the house, and says he will soon work things out. Hurston is not happy, as she wants to get through high school: "I had a way of life inside me and I wanted it with a want that was twisting me. And now, it seemed I was just as far off as before" (100). This time, she is not getting paid for work and has no time off. Still, she is happy to be with her brother; the children are adorable, and she gets busy with them. She has to get up early in the morning and work without making any noise so as not to disturb her sister-in-law, who needs rest as she has borne her brother's children and deserves the best. After several months, she realises that it is not right, as she is not responsible for the children or her sister-in-law. They are her brother's responsibility.

Hurston befriends a poor white woman who has children of Hurston's age. She begins to take an interest in her and puts ideas in her head, like she ought to have gloves when she goes anywhere. Hurston is unhappy, for she cannot have them, as she is not in a position to buy even a handkerchief. Her friend finds her a job as a lady's maid to a singer at the theatre, where her husband is an electrician. Her maid is about to get married, so she is in search of a new one. Her friend's daughter, Valena, buys a neat, cheap and stylish dress for her, as she is to look nice for the job interview; she gives her a hat and car fare and sends her off to get the job.

The lady, Miss M—, hires her after a funny conversation about her age. Hurston says she is twenty, and the lady laughs to hear a little girl claim to be twenty years old. Eventually, she tells her she will be sixteen on her next birthday. The lady tells her that there is no need to bring up this age business again, as she thinks she is going to like her. She asks her name, does not ask anything about her family, and tells her that she will pay her ten dollars a week along with other expenses. Hurston is happy at the prospect of earning so much money and thinks that at this rate, she can soon own a bank. She does not go back to her brother's house, as she is afraid he will try to make her stay, and she sleeps on a cot in the room with Valena. At the end of the week, the company—Gilbert and Sullivan Repertoire—is to move on, so the lady gives her an advance to buy a suitcase for her clothes and the few things she has.

The company has its own coach, and Hurston is the only Negro on it, but that does not bother her at all, as the company welcomes her "like, or as, a new play-pretty" (104) and does not let her feel lonesome. They tease her all the time just to hear her talk, play all sorts of gags on her—with no wickedness in it—and stuff her mouth with ice creams, sodas and Coca-Cola, making her feel important. They share their love affairs and troubles with her. When Miss M— is in bed, Hurston is to stay with her and listen to her affairs. She pays for a course in manicuring for Hurston, and she practises it on everybody until she becomes an authority.

This comes to an end when Miss M— gets a part in another show whose rehearsals are to start after two weeks, and she takes Hurston to her home in Boston. Four months later, Miss M— meets a wealthy businessman from Newark and decides to marry him and leave the stage. She does not want Hurston to work for anyone else and thinks that she should not work at all but ought to be in school. She believes Hurston has a mind and it would be a shame for her not to receive further training. She inquires about schools in Baltimore, gives her some money that she can spare, tells her to keep in touch, and promises to do whatever she can to help her out.

The eighteen months that Hurston spends with Miss M— seem to her as if she has been in school. She does some reading, as the tenor—a Harvard man—has books with him and allows her to read them. She learns music, the classics, and becomes familiar with the best parts of the light opera field. She sees more than thirty people of all classes and races living a communal life. She learns life lessons through her day-to-day experiences, such as, "The passers-by don't hurt you, but if you go around like that, they make you hurt yourself" (118). The personal experiences that others share with her make her reflect on things.

The whole experience on the job gives her an approach to racial understanding. It discourages any sensitiveness on her part, for she is still not conscious of her race, no matter where she is. She is happy that she is going back to school, as the wish to return has never left her. Before this job, she had been lonely and devoid of comfort and love. Working with these people has brought her peace. Now, she feels scared to go alone by herself again. Seven of her unhappy visions have passed, and she hopes that from now on, everything will be just fine.

Money is what Hurston needs to get back to school. She has not saved much, as theatrical salaries were uncertain. She does not get her salary half the time, and she never worried when she was not paid. Now, she needs it. Miss M— informs her by mail that she is having troubles at home and is trying to help her folks. Hurston never directly asks her for anything more and does not even harbour any bitterness towards her, as the whole experience has been a pleasant one.

She tries being a good waitress, and along with other difficulties, she comes down with appendicitis—"Not a sensible sickness for poor folks to have" (122)—and is to be operated on right away, so she goes to the free ward of the Maryland General Hospital. She does not fear death, as nobody will miss her much and she has no treasures to leave behind. The operation is successful, and she finds another job as a waitress. She tries several other things and gets tired of making money for school, just to satisfy her soul. Finally, she joins the night high school in Baltimore.

Hurston studies there only for a few days, and the next week she shifts to Morgan College to register in the high school department. She has neither money nor family to refer to, still she goes there to talk to the Dean, William Pickens, a Black. He gives her a brief examination and credit for two years' work in high school and assigns a class to her. A few days later, Mrs. Pickens tells her that she has a job for her that will enable her to stay in school. A white clergyman, Dr. Baldwin, one of the trustees of Morgan, wants a girl to look after his wife with a broken hip, and he will give her a home and pay her two dollars a week. Hurston accepts the job and goes to live with the Baldwins. They have a great library, and she reads all the books with such eagerness as if the books will run away.

She studies hard because she realises that she is three years behind schedule, and study has never been difficult for her. Soon she gives competition to the well-dressed students of the school. There are eighteen people in class—six boys and twelve good-looking, well-dressed girls from Baltimore's best Black families—and her class is the best-looking class on the campus, college or prep. Sitting with these pretty girls, Hurston feels out of place, and to make things worse, she has only one dress. Soon they become her friends and lend her something to wear whenever there is a programme or a get-together. In the absence of an English or History teacher, Hurston is put in charge of the class, and her classmates love her teaching. Thus, Zora Neale Hurston struggles through hardships one after the other during her childhood but never gives up and perseveres to achieve coveted goals. "Her experiences being employed as a maid and a servant illustrate the limited opportunities for black women during this time period. More broadly, in her attempts to support herself, she finds many different but all short-lived jobs; her writing was the one sustaining force throughout her life" (Jones, Sharon 37). Her life writing shows an energetic woman who overcomes odds to achieve a liberated, rewarding life.

At the age of seventeen, Marshall secretly gets enrolled in Hunter College, which was free to all New York residents with qualifying grades. Her mother wants her to join the telephone company: "College?! Book writing?! Look, get from out my eyesight! You ain' hear that the telephone company is starting to hire colored? You best march yourself down there and beg for a job!" (Triangular Road 95). But Marshall, being hard-ears, wilful and doing things her own way, finds two part-time jobs at branches of the New York Public Library to support her family and chooses to be a writer. In the *Dallas Morning News*, the book review of *Triangular Road*, Karen M. Thomas writes, "This isn't just a memoir. It's a book that provides a rare, honest look at the deep, personal well where one writer draws her strength, a gift that anyone interested in understanding literature should cherish" (5).

In *I Know Why the Caged Bird Sings*, Maya Angelou recounts the events of her life in chronological order amidst the racist and sexist American society. Her life is full of ups and downs, but in spite of her trials and tribulations, she finds a way to accomplish her goals. "Angelou shows how to be black and female is to be oppressed twice, and that for black women to survive, they must be strong" (Sickles PDF). She portrays most of her difficult life events from the age of three to sixteen in her life writing, showing her hard upbringing, poverty, racism and sexual abuse. She undergoes painful experiences in life but eventually succeeds in overcoming them. She suffers tremendous hardships in her life, and her life writing visualises all the hardships she faced. For women across the globe, Angelou's life is a source of inspiration and immense strength. She says, "All my work, my life, everything I do is about survival, not just bare, awful, plodding survival, but survival with grace and faith. While one may encounter many defeats, one must not be defeated" (qtd. by Haas 300).

These African American women writers encounter many defeats but do not give up fighting against the racist, sexist society. These life writings show in a unique way that "Black women can validly be seen as microcosmic figures, encapsulating and representing the lives and struggles of all women, and also the struggles of all suffering humanity – male and female" (Bell-Scott 413). The remarkable thing is that African American women, long regarded as 'de mule uh de world', have at last found their own voice and have produced a steady stream of literature that commands an audience which is both Black and white. Writing about their life brings them face to face with the question of power; it forces them to resolve the question, to act, to find their voice, to become that subject who could place themselves and those like her at the centre of feminist discourse, transforming their consciousness and being. bell hooks avers in *Talking Back*, "It has been a political struggle for me to hold to the belief that there is much which we – black people – must speak about, much that is private that must be openly shared, if we are to heal our wounds (hurts caused by domination and exploitation and oppression), if we are to recover and realize ourselves" (3).

The longing to tell one's story and the process of telling is symbolically a gesture of longing to recover the past in such a way that one experiences both a sense of reunion and a sense of release. Writing their lives is a way to evoke the particular experience of growing up southern and Black in segregated communities, and a way to recapture the richness of Southern Black culture. Bringing one's past and memories together in a complete narrative allows one to view them from a different perspective, "not as singular isolated events but as part of a continuum" (bell hooks, *Talking Back* 159). Life writing enables them to look at their past from a different perspective and to use this knowledge as a means of self-growth to usher change in an emphatic way.

Chapter 3

Coming of Age: Experiences, Influences and Accomplishments

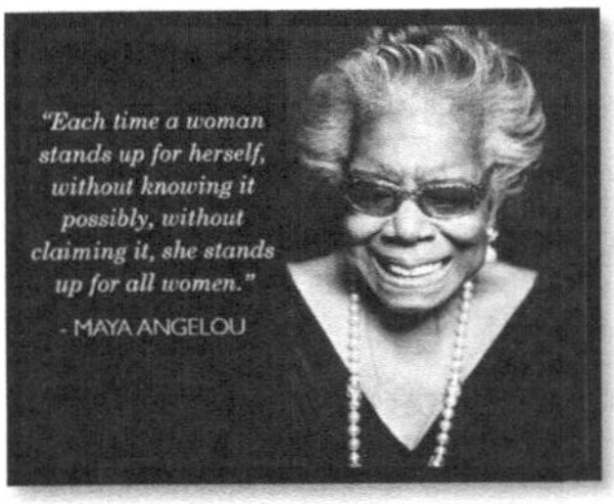

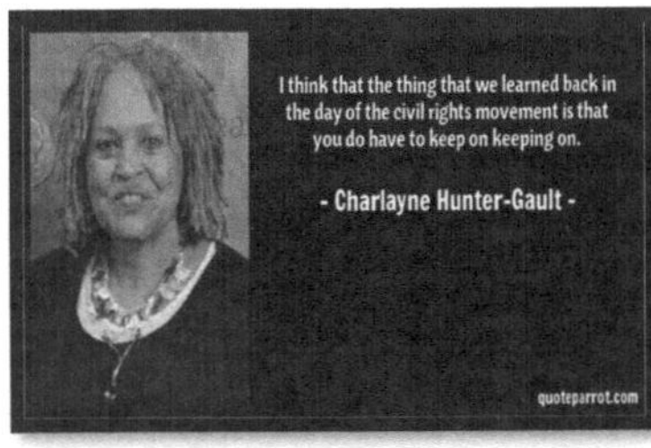

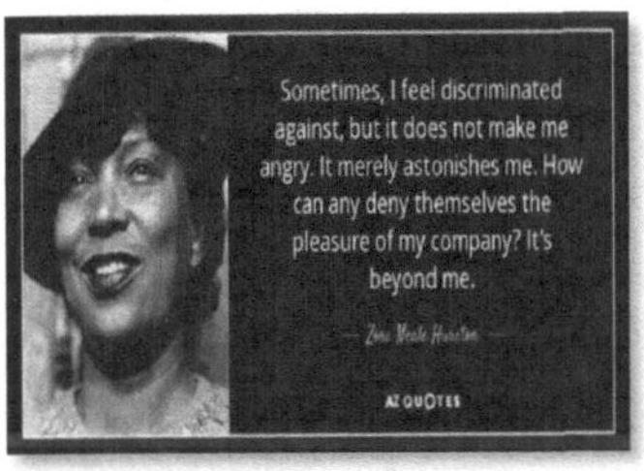

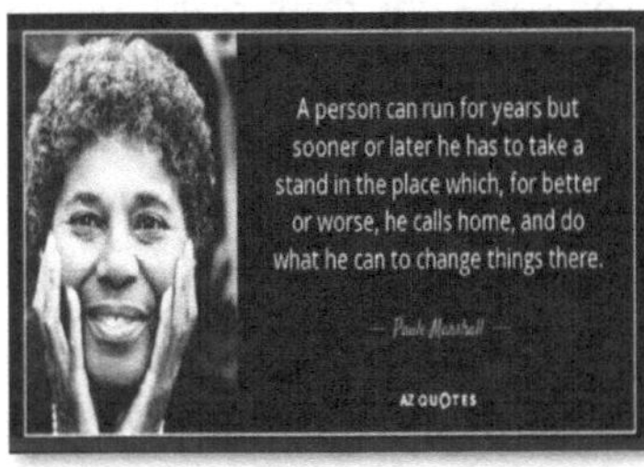

A person comes into being and knows herself by her achievements, and through her efforts to become and know herself, she achieves.

– Dickerson (qtd. in Tomm 203)

Feminism is a sociopolitical and cultural movement that aims at administering rights and legal protection to women. It involves political and sociological theories and philosophies concerned with issues of gender difference, as well as "a movement that advocated more gender-specific rights for women and [campaigned] for women's rights and interests" (Grisso, web. 16 Jan. 2016). The feminist movements and theories had leaders who were predominantly middle-class white women from Western Europe and North America. However, since Sojourner Truth's 1851 speech "Ain't I a Woman" to American feminists, women of other races have appropriated alternative feminisms. This trend accelerated in the 1960s with the Civil Rights Movement in the United States and the collapse of European colonialism in Africa.

"The phrase 'Women's Liberation' was first used in the United States in 1964 and first appeared in print in 1966" (Bottaro 124). One of the most vocal critics of the Women's Liberation Movement has been the African American feminist and intellectual Gloria Jean Watkins, with the pseudonym bell hooks. She highlights the lack of minority voices in the women's movement in *Feminist Theory: From Margin to Center* (1984). Feminist leaders like bell hooks, Audre Lorde, and many other Black feminists negotiate space for race-related subjectivities. bell hooks asserts, "The feminist scholarship is informed by the longing for a subject-to-subject encounter, by the longing for a meeting place, a place for solidarity where women can speak to and/or about men in a feminist voice, where our words can be heard, where we can speak the truth that heals, that transforms – that makes feminist revolution" (133).

A Black woman working with hooks at the phone company wanted her to write a book that would make their lives better by making other people understand the hardships of being Black and female. *Ain't I a Woman* expresses hooks' deep, passionate longing for change in the social status of Black women.

Maria W. Stewart, a women's rights activist, challenges African American women to counter the negative images of Black womanhood prominent in her time, and points out that race, gender, and class oppression are fundamental causes of poverty. Maria Stewart is not content to point out the source of Black women's oppression; she urges Black women to forge self-definitions: "It is useless for us any longer to sit with our hands folded, reproaching the whites; for that will never elevate us," she exhorts. "Possess the spirit of independence … Possess the spirit of men, bold and enterprising, fearless and undaunted. To Stewart, the power of self-definition was essential, for the survival of Black women was at stake" (Collins 3–4).

Contemporary Black feminist thought reflects Black women's increasing willingness to oppose gender inequality within Black civil society. Contemporary Black women intellectuals draw on the tradition of using everyday actions and experiences for their theoretical works.

In the African American literary tradition, the twentieth century has been an epochal era owing to the significant contributions made by African American women writers. It has been a period of intense literary activity because, for the first time, the writers expressed themselves freely. Their works undoubtedly portray their struggle, growth, and accomplishments. They have given powerful insights into grim issues such as race, gender, and class. According to Jayne Cortez, poet and president of the Organization of Women Writers of Africa, "Black women writers from around the globe have been struggling against racism, exploitation, gender oppression, and other human rights violations" (qtd. in Ampadu PDF). Right from the days of slavery to the present, African American women have been facing the triple oppression of racism, sexism, and classism—being at the receiving end, at the margins of society.

"Women are half the human race, and they are half of Black history, as well" ("Harlem Renaissance Women: African American Women Dreaming in Color," web. 27 Dec. 2016). With a new self-awakening, African American women writers, after being liberated from their past inhibitions, are breaking the boundaries set by the white patriarchal society and are finally writing and defining themselves, rather than being defined by others. Women come to power through the act of speaking, telling their stories, sharing history, and engaging in feminist discussion. Breaking through long silences, many women have given voice for the first time to personal sorrow, anguish, rage, bitterness, and hatred. This speech is a part of women's struggle to resist the silence imposed by male domination.

The coming of age of African American women writers in the twentieth century has not been an easy process; the journey has been arduous and tortuous. "In spite of isolation, multiple disadvantages, and attempts by others to stop them, they write defiantly of lives lived and dreamed in all their complexities" (Bell-Scott 25). Emerging out of enslavement, struggling against the odds, and facing discrimination and prejudice, the route has never been an easy one. The influence of different individuals in their lives helped them achieve what they aspired to and attained by their own choice.

The quest for Black female identity amidst a racist and sexist society pulsates through the entire oeuvre of Maya Angelou. *I Know*

Why the Caged Bird Sings traces Angelou's journey from a helpless victim, Marguerite Johnson, to her evolution into a young, confident Black mother who not only resists racial-sexual discrimination but converts it into a triumph story. "It is first and foremost about the coming-of-age of a young Black girl in the South" (Sickels PDF). Through her experiences, she learns the true meaning of courage, independence, and trust. She realises that hardships and experiences in life make one stronger: "Maya Angelou employs two voices to tell her story: that of a young girl, searching for an identity and trying to survive, and the now-accomplished adult, narrating the tale of a young Black girl growing up in the South in the early twentieth century" (Braxton, *Maya Angelou's I Know Why the Caged Bird Sings: A Casebook* 25). She conveys the difficulties of racial and gender discrimination faced by young Southern Black girls by touching on subjects from child abuse to the purpose of life with an intense sense of displacement and marginalisation.

Her life writing is a "coming-of-age as a Southern Black girl, confronting racism, sexism, violence and loneliness" ("I Know Why the Caged Bird Sings by Maya Angelou: Key Facts," web. 20 Jan. 2017). Angelou is raped by her mother's boyfriend, Mr. Freeman; she retreats into silence, and everyone gives up on her. Mrs. Bertha Flowers, an aristocratic lady of Black Stamps, throws Marguerite her "first life line" (93). According to Angelou, "She was our side's answer to the richest white woman in town" (93), for she was a beautiful, educated Black woman. She appeals to Marguerite, for she had never personally seen people like her, and she made her proud to be Black just by being herself. She feels fortunate that she never saw Mrs. Flowers in the company of the powhitefolks. During long afternoons of talking and reading aloud, she restores Marguerite's desire to communicate. "Mrs. Flowers is credited as being the person who showed Angelou the power of written and spoken word" (Agins 16). She teaches Marguerite a lesson that the human voice is necessary to infuse words with meaning, that one should be intolerant of ignorance but understand illiteracy, for some people who are unable to go to school are actually more educated and intelligent than the so-called educated ones. She encourages her to come up, assists her in finding her strongest defence, and kindles her love for literature so as to open the barriers and end her silence: "It is Mrs. Flowers who opens the door to the caged bird's silence with the key of loving acceptance" (Smith, *Where I'm Bound* 130). This enhances her courage and willingness to conquer other barriers. She inspires her to traverse the beautiful, mysterious land of literature and helps her get rid of her silence, overcome the trauma of rape, and find her own identity. According to Marcia Ann Gillespie et al., "it was during this period of silence when Angelou developed her extraordinary memory, her love for books and literature, and her ability to listen and observe the world around her" (22). Books are her best companions, and they offer adventure and beauty to her which is otherwise denied to her in real life.

Alice Walker, in *The Color Purple*, creates the character of Celia, a Black adolescent girl who is sexually abused by her stepfather. "Even I found it almost impossible to let her say what had happened to her as she perceived it… And why? Because once you strip away the lie that rape is pleasant, that children are not permanently damaged by sexual pain, that violence done to them is washed away by fear, silence, and time, you are left with the positive horror of the lives of thousands of children… who have been sexually abused and who have never been permitted their own language to tell about it" (Walker, *Living by the Word* 57). Celia finds her voice by writing letters to God and forming supportive relationships with other Black women. "By creating Celia and giving her the language to tell of her sexual abuse, Walker adds Celia's voice to muted yet growing discussions of the sexual politics of Black womanhood" (Collins 133). Her voice enables her to transcend the fear and silence of her childhood.

On getting into George Washington High School, California, Angelou finds that she is one of the "three Black students in the school, and in that rarefied atmosphere I came to love my people more" (214). She develops new allegiance with Miss Kirwin, her teacher, who makes an imprint on her mind for the rest of her life: "Miss Kirwin never seemed to notice that I was Black and therefore different" (216). In the evening classes, she takes up drama and dance along with grown-up whites and Blacks. She develops a sense of belonging with the city and sets goals for herself: "The city became for me the ideal of what I wanted to be as a grownup. Friendly but never gushing, cool but not frigid or distant, distinguished without the awful stiffness" (211). The city exemplifies beauty and freedom for

Marguerite, who is now "a thirteen-year-old Black girl, stalled by the South and Southern Black life style" (212).

Marguerite perceives the adjustments her grandmother has to make in California: "an old Southern Negro woman who had lived her life under the left breast of her community learned to deal with white landlords, Mexican neighbors and Negro strangers" (202). Her mother marries Daddy Clidell, a successful businessman, and the family moves to San Francisco. Marguerite shares a wonderful relationship with Daddy Clidell, a simple man with no inferiority or superiority complex; the two even resemble each other. According to her, he is "the first father I would know" (208). He earns his living by deceiving white people, who, in turn, believe they can always win over blacks by deception. He and his partners use their intelligence to pry upon the door of rejection and not only become wealthy but get some revenge in the bargain, for they choose their victims from wealthy whites and use the victims' prejudice against them. Marguerite trusts and respects him as she learns valuable lessons from him. He considers himself her father, takes care of her, and tells her stories about the blacks who were able to overcome their condition. From him, she learns the "Principle of Reverse" (221), with which he resists oppression and triumphs over white people.

Once her father and Dolores, her father's live-in girlfriend, invite her to spend the summer with them in Southern California, she is genuinely excited and accepts their invitation. One day, Dolores gets into an argument with Marguerite and ends up calling her mother a whore; she reacts by slapping Dolores in anger, proving herself a young, courageous woman who dares to stand against wrongs. Dolores assaults her, which makes her run away from home; she spends a month as a resident of a junkyard among other homeless run-away children. "Homelessness is a complex phenomenon that is not simply about the lack of shelter. This is now accepted by most specialists in the field. Along with the loss of accommodation, homelessness is linked with the loss of a home, social exclusion, and relegation to the margins of mainstream society. This in turn can lead to a homeless person becoming detached from the system of societal values and norms and to a fundamental change in their lifestyle" (Vagnerova et al., 9).

Homelessness has a profound effect on Marguerite's way of looking at the world. She makes friends with "a collage of Negro, Mexican and white races" (252). After a month, her way of thinking changes so much that she hardly recognises herself: "The unquestioning acceptance by my peers had dislodged the familiar insecurity.... After hunting down unbroken bottles and selling them with a white girl from Missouri, a Mexican girl from Los Angeles and a Black girl from Oklahoma, I was never again to sense myself so solidly outside the pale of the human race. The lack of criticism evidenced by our ad hoc community influenced me, and set a tone of tolerance for my life" (254). She openly accepts her peers and wipes away the feeling of insecurity that has been haunting her for a long time. They accept her as a human being, completely disregarding the colour of her skin, and initiate her into the brotherhood domain. Never again would she encounter such harmony of different races coming together to fend for life: "Working collectively to confront difference, to expand our awareness of sex, race and class as interlocking systems of domination, of the ways we reinforce and perpetuate these structures, is the context in which we learn the true meaning of solidarity" (bell hooks, *Talking Back* 25). She learns to be strong and self-assured after she survives living on her own. She proves that everything is possible if one puts one's mind to it. Her confidence develops, and she gets an opportunity to think about herself; from here on, she constructs her self-image in a positive way, is able to see her talents and her gifts, and disregards her worries about her physical appearance: "The uncaged bird of Maya Angelou, no doubt leaps on the back of the wind, it is only the caged bird who knows the real meaning of freedom" (Dimri 95).

At the age of fifteen, she decides to be independent and do something on her own. Her mother, Vivian Baxter, believes in self-sufficiency; therefore, she easily consents to let her work. However, when she first tells her mother that she plans to get a job on the streetcars, Vivian Baxter rejects the proposal, as they do not accept coloured people on the streetcars. But she is determined "to break the restricting tradition" (265). Realising that Angelou has made up her mind, she gives her unconditional encouragement and support. Her mother has always been a positive influence on her and strengthens her convictions with: "That's what you want to do? Then nothing beats a trial but a failure. Give it everything you've got. I've told you many times, 'Can't Do is like Don't Care'" (265), which manifests that nothing is impossible. The positive encouragement and support of her mother pave the way for her mission to become the first black female streetcar conductor in San Francisco. Her mother encourages her to give her best: "Life is going to give you just what you put in it. Put your whole heart in everything you do, and pray, then you can wait … God helps those who help themselves" (269). This helps her get through the difficulties created by her superiors.

With the positive support of her mother, she confidently challenges the racist order and fights with an invincible spirit till she achieves success. Her mother teaches her resistance by refusing to be subservient to men or to white people; she also teaches her children to be free and responsible for their choices. Her sense of displacement disappears, as her mother is her support system, and she blossoms into a confident young woman. Offering them a sense of their own unique self-worth, African American mothers often try to protect their daughters from the dangers that lie hidden. Many black women writers report the experience of being given at an early age a sense of specialness that encouraged them to develop their talents. Patricia Hill Collins shares, "My own mother marched me to the public library at age five, helped me get my first library card, and told me that I could do anything if I learned how to read" (202).

Katz, in the 1975 edition of *Webster's New Collegiate Dictionary*, defines racism as "a belief that race is a primary determinant of human traits and capacities and that racial differences produce an inherent superiority of a particular race…. The same dictionary defined sexism as prejudice or discrimination against women" (204). Racism subordinates a person or a group owing to the colour of their skin, and sexism undermines a person or a group on the basis of sex. There is dual oppression of both race and gender on Black women, and they fight for Black civil rights as well as for women's equity to overcome this oppression. One of the best examples in this context is Maya Angelou, who, being a determined girl, does not let discrimination get in the way of her goals. The white receptionist in the office of the Market Street Railway Company is surprised to see Angelou—a Negro female—in the office. Angelou categorically tells her that she is applying for the job listed in *The Chronicle* and would like to meet the manager. The receptionist tries to dissuade her and tells her that the manager is out for the day: "The receptionist was not innocent and neither was I. The whole charade we had played out in that crummy waiting room had directly to do with me, Black, and her, white" (267). Even after a rebuke from the receptionist, she does not give up; she continues to apply and calls on Negro organisations for help. She goes to the Streetcar Office daily, does not give up, and finally one day she is given the application form: "Maya assumes control over her own social destiny and engages in the struggle with life's forces. She has broken out of the rusted bars of her social cage" (Smith, *Where I'm Bound* 373). Thus, through her perseverance and diligence, she succeeds independently and becomes the first Black female conductorette on the San Francisco streetcars at the age of fifteen, at a time when it was virtually impossible for a Black female.

In "Learning to Live: When the Bird Breaks from the Cage," Opal Moore rightly states, "The story of this one black girl declaring 'I can' to a colour-coded society that in innumerable ways had told her 'you can't, you won't' transcends its author" (49). Angelou is strong in mind and principles and overcomes all the limits that restricted her. She displays that a young girl can be an independent woman regardless of her skin colour. Although the white bigots surround her, she still rises above the racists and becomes a confident, successful Black girl. She avers in her poem *Still I Rise*:

You may shoot me with your words,
You may cut me with your eyes,
You may kill me with your hatefulness,
But still, like air, I'll rise.
(*The Complete Collected Poems of Maya Angelou* 163)

The love and affection of her family and relatives at different points in her life facilitate her growth from a scared, insecure girl—who wanted to be blond and have blue eyes to be loved—into a brave, confident young woman, capable even of getting a job as a conductor on the streetcars of San Francisco. Angelou "depicts how one can supersede the expected barriers and soar to new heights" (Gibson, *web.* 17 Oct. 2016). Her mother responds positively to her questions about her body and even lesbianism, opening the horizons for her.

Angelou graduates from high school at the age of sixteen and shortly afterwards gives birth to her son, Guy. Her mother accepts her pregnancy normally: "There was no overt or subtle condemnation. She was Vivian Baxter Jackson. Hoping for the best, prepared for the worst, and unsurprised by anything in between" (287). Daddy Clidell also assures her that she has nothing to worry about. Thus, with the support of her family, she swims through the hardships of life as an unwed mother. "Because of her firsthand knowledge of life during this time and because of her honesty in recording the settings and the events in her life, reviewers have said that she has used 'the clay of real life' in her writings" (Davis 2).

Angelou posits that the African American female adult is usually a formidable character, "an inevitable outcome of the struggle won by survivors and deserves respect if not enthusiastic acceptance" (272). She acknowledges that, being a Black female, she experienced "the tripartite crossfire of masculine prejudice, white illogical hate and Black lack of power" (272). Facing the hardships and colour-prejudices in life, she comes out victorious, becoming what she wants to be with courage, dignity, and endurance. She dedicates this book to Guy Johnson and all the strong Black birds of promise who defy the odds and gods and sing their songs. Thus, this text is for Black females to fight for their rights to set themselves free from the societal 'cages.' Her life is a source of inspiration and immense strength for women across the globe. "But most of all her story is the story of discovering who she is—of working her way through a multifaceted identity crisis" (Gale, *A Study Guide for Maya Angelou's I Know Why the Caged Bird Sings* 5). *I Know Why the Caged Bird Sings* exhibits that it is possible to prevail over obstacles as a successful, confident adult, regardless of the problems thrown en route. It illustrates how an innocent and naïve girl grows amidst the Great Depression and dons the role of an influential, powerful woman under a solid racist regime that dictates white Western society as the norm. Angelou confronts her own life with dignity and proves that despite the racist conditions in the 1930s–1950s, a young Black girl has survived successfully. She embraces the experience of growing up courageously and confidently as her family regards her worthy of it. She rises from humble beginnings and severe psychological trauma to a position of impressive leadership in race relations. Joanne M. Braxton is right in calling Maya Angelou "America's most visible Black female autobiographer" (*Black Women Writing Autobiography* 4).

Charlayne Hunter-Gault, in *In My Place*, recounts how she becomes a national figure by fearlessly enduring harassment and hostilities to become the first Black woman to attend the University of Georgia. Her family teaches her the inner strength and endurance needed to face the brutally racist treatment at the University of Georgia. She states in the prologue, "*In My Place* is above all the story of the people and their values that nurtured and sustained me and, in the process, provided me with the suit of armor and determination that I needed as I began my journey to the horizons" (3). Mary Carroll, in *Booklist Review*, projects, "Eloquent family tribute as well as intimate social history, *In My Place* is a useful addition to civil rights movement collections" ("In My Place," web. 16 Jan. 2017). It is a testament to the strength of family love, self-reliance, and self-esteem. The reserves of courage, resilience, and conviction instilled in her help her to be one of the two students to desegregate the University of Georgia. The strong values passed on to her during the formative years helped Hunter-Gault to achieve her goal with resilience and pride.

Her teachers, Victoria Sutton and Elsie Foster Evans, inspire confidence in her and nurture her passion. They develop her interest in journalism by making her an advisor for the student newspaper *The Green Light*, and she gets involved in it by volunteering to proofread articles for Mrs Evans. Along with her family and teachers, Robert F. Kennedy, an American politician from Massachusetts who fought against crime and worked for civil rights for African Americans, being a committed advocate of the poor racial minorities, and Martin Luther King, an American Baptist minister and activist and a leader in the Civil Rights Movement best known for his role in the advancement of civil rights using nonviolent civil disobedience, encourage her to be actively involved in the Civil Rights Movement for the freedom and equality of Blacks. "The Civil Rights Movement is probably the quintessential example of public-spirited collective action in our time. Not only did it spark radical changes in American society, it also served in subsequent years as the inspiration and model for a host of new public concerns. The student movement, the peace movement, the women's movement, the homosexual rights movement and other social movements are all to a significant extent riding on the coattails of the civil rights movement" (Chong 1).

In May 1961, Robert F. Kennedy visits the University of Georgia Law School as the keynote speaker for the National Law Day. Hunter-Gault, along with Hamp, goes to the auditorium to listen to the Attorney General. He states that we cannot live together without rules that help us distinguish between right and wrong. Law enables men to live together and create order out of chaos. The courts have an important role in safeguarding the rights of men, so we should follow and respect the decisions of the court, adding that, "respect for the law – in essence, that is the meaning of Law Day – and every day must be Law Day or else our society will collapse" (210). He talks about the challenge of international communism and civil rights, and points out that "50 percent of the countries in the United Nations are not white . . . people whose skins are a different color from ours are on the move to gain their measure of freedom and liberty." He adds, "In the worldwide struggle, the graduation at this university . . . of Charlayne Hunter and Hamilton Holmes will without question aid and assist the fight against Communism, political infiltration, and guerrilla warfare" (210). Earlier, Hunter-Gault is happy to get into the auditorium and hear him speak, but now she wants to meet this man, shake his hand, and let him know that she is the one going to defeat Communism. The speech draws a standing ovation, and after that Hunter-Gault goes to the Continuing Education Building, where the Law Day Committee is holding a reception for the Attorney General, who recognises her before she introduces herself and congratulates her for her achievement.

One day, as she is walking up Auburn Avenue, she meets Martin Luther King for the first time. She is very excited and calls out to Dr King, telling him her name. He grabs her hand, saying that he is so proud to meet her, for she is doing a splendid job in Georgia. He goes on to talk about the importance of education to people and why her case is so important in the struggle, saying that education is the key to their freedom. He thanks her again and wishes her success in life. "It is axiomatic that if we do not define ourselves for ourselves, we will be defined by others – for their use and to our detriment" (Lorde, *Sister Outsider* 45). Hunter-Gault defines her place and succeeds in her endeavour.

Charlayne Hunter-Gault ends with the chapter entitled "In Our Place," in which she shares her experience of returning to the University of Georgia after twenty-five years, on 11th June 1988, "as the first Black person to deliver the graduation address in the school's now 203-year history" (247). Hunter-Gault is asked to deliver the commencement address at the University of Georgia in fitting recognition of her contribution to the social, economic, and political advancements that the people of colour have made in the United States over the past few decades. In an interview with *Southern Living*, Hunter-Gault said, "I knew that we had really reached a significant milestone in the reconciliation between the Georgia we entered and the Georgia that I wanted it to be" (Young 78–83). The university now has a chair in honour of Hamp and Hunter-Gault, where once a year a distinguished speaker is invited to speak on some issue related to civil rights or race relations. The audience includes many of the professors who had taught her, Judge Bootle, whom she personally invites, and people from Atlanta, as she thinks after all these years it is time to pay gratitude to everybody. She starts her address by greeting everyone, "It's good to be back home again. In a place that I have always thought of as 'our place'" (248), adding that today she is going to recall memories. She remembers the day she sat in the audience to receive her graduation diploma twenty-five years ago and thanks her mother, their legal team, Hamilton Holmes and his family, for their support and encouragement, which helped her to be a graduate from the University of Georgia.

Reminiscing on the times which have been the driving forces for her, she feels grateful: "Those were times of testing and, yes, of triumph. Of pioneering and legend-building. Of armor-building… of character building… of charting new courses" (249). She remembers that out of sixteen hundred students in the graduating class, she was one of the two Blacks. She was a curious, inquisitive Black girl who once dreamt of being Brenda Starr and finds the University of Georgia the place to fulfil that dream, and her journey to this place is no casual undertaking. She remembers the white people, the members of the faculty and administration, some fellow journalism students, her loyal friend Marcia Powell, and her companion and friend Walter Stovall. She also remembers that twenty-five years ago the Southerners were treated bitterly with "denial, hatred, and violence" (253). The lessons she learnt on this campus stayed with her for life and helped her fight disharmony and intolerance.

Fifteen new Black faculty members are added for the upcoming academic year, and Hunter-Gault is convinced that "the presence of more faculty members here will not only attract more Black students to this campus, but their presence, along with those other Black students, will move this place, our place, to a new phase in its pioneering history. A place that could be a model for a more perfect union. A place in which people of color are on the ascendancy" (256). She celebrates this happy moment with all present and asks them to join her in their continuing journey in search of justice, equity, and love. As recounted in *The Atlantic*, Hunter-Gault's address to the university stressed the need for "acknowledging the guiding principles of fundamental human decency and then living by them" in "a waiting and needful world" (151).

In an interview in May 2000, Hunter-Gault voices her disappointment that the University of Georgia has not completely fulfilled its obligation to Blacks: "I think that Hamp had made his peace with UGA. As for me, I thought for a long time that I had; I certainly moved in that direction after making the graduation speech in 1988. And I took a few more steps over the years as I began to make more appearances on the campus. But I don't think I will ever make my peace with that institution until Black students and Black professors there are as comfortable as whites are, and until I'm convinced that they [university officials] have made every effort to ensure that. But from what I can tell, that's not yet happened" (qtd. in Pratt 156).

In My Place is a coming-of-age story set during the turbulent 1960s, wherein Hunter-Gault underlines harassment in those dramatic years, as well as her growth as a journalist, her public speaking tours, and even her romance with a white Southerner. It is an inspiring, informative, historical journey and a compelling documentation of the ugly turmoil of the times. *In My Place* is "a remarkably generous, fair-minded account of overcoming some of the biggest, and most intractable, obstacles ever deployed by southern racists" ("In My Place by Charlayne Hunter-Gault," web. 12 Sept. 2016). Defining her place was an essential task for Hunter-Gault, and a vivid feeling of place and directness pervades her life writing. Generous, witty, warm-hearted, and dynamic, it is the journey of a remarkable woman.

Zora Neale Hurston's *Dust Tracks on a Road* is a candid, funny, bold, and poignant work—an imaginative and exuberant account of her rise from childhood poverty in the rural South to a prominent place among the leading artists and intellectuals of the Harlem Renaissance, a social, cultural, artistic, literary, and intellectual flowering that fostered a new Black cultural identity in the 1920s–30s. *Dust Tracks on a Road* is a rare treasure from one of literature's most cherished voices, full of wit and wisdom, by a proud, spirited woman who started off low and attained great heights. In this book, Hurston plays the role of the storyteller as in her fictional works, but here she tells the story of her own life. Her self-portrait offers a compelling, revealing, often audacious glimpse into the public and private life of an extraordinary artist, anthropologist, and chronicler of the Black experiences in America. *The New Yorker* declares *Dust Tracks on a Road* as "warm, witty, imaginative, and down-to-earth by turns. This is a rich and winning book by one of our few genuine, Grade A folk writers" (79). Her writing emphasizes her fighting spirit in the struggle to achieve the education she desperately aspires for.

Dust Tracks on a Road is an encouraging, enjoyable, and inspiring story for any member of the human race who will be proud to have more members of the calibre of Zora Neale Hurston. It "is a fascinating exploration of her life and provides us with a sense of what shaped Hurston as a person and artist. It is a complex account of her life as she desired her readers to perceive it. In effect, she becomes the manipulator and crafter of her life story" (Jones, Sharon 42). She chooses to write the version of life, and through her rendition, one learns that the author is born to roam, listen, and narrate a variety of stories. "She searched for freedom as an artist. She searched for how to be Black without limitation, and how to be a woman without constraints" ("African American Women Writers: Zora Neale Hurston – Author, Anthropologist And Folklorist," PDF). At the beginning of her writing endeavour, she uses all the sights she sees, all the people she encounters, and the exploits she survives. She describes herself as aggressive, intelligent, and obstinate. She says that the nicest people she meets in her life are whites who show kindness right from the time she is about to come into this world.

In this work, Hurston presents herself as having interracial contacts at a very young age. One man who pleases her always is the white man who helped her come into the world. When she was small, he teases her and then praises her for not crying. When she is old enough to do things, he takes her fishing, and while fishing he talks to her as if she is a grown-up girl—and she likes this. He tells her funny stories, makes her tell him about her doings, and tells her what to do about things. He calls her "Snidlits," explaining that Zora was a hell of a name to give a child (30). Repeatedly, he reminds her, "Snidlits, don't be a nigger" (30)—"nigger" meaning not a race but a weak and contemptible person of any race, as weak people always lie. He teaches her to speak the truth and gives her lessons for life. These wise talks go on until she is ten, when the white man dies after falling from a horse. He frequently gives money to Black schools, takes care of his family as a good provider, and nobody finds any fault with this man as he is a wonderful human being. Hurston is confused by contradictory pieces of advice from the adults she respected most: her father, a brave and successful man, ordered her to be meek and self-effacing in order to placate the whites. Her trusted white friend, on the other hand, urged her to stand up for herself and fight for what she believed in (Witcover 35). As she grows up, she absorbs both these philosophies without truly integrating them ever.

A year before his death, Hurston happens to meet two white women. The whites who come down from the North are often brought by their friends to visit the village school. They are always sympathetic, kind, and curious, as a Negro school is something strange for them. Whenever a visitor is expected, the schoolroom is set in order, the children are cautioned to put on shoes, comb their hair, clean their ears and fingernails, a close inspection of each one of them is done in the morning, and they are advised to behave properly in front of the white visitors.

One afternoon, two young ladies come to the school without any prior notice. Mr. Calhoun is agitated and confused, but tries to put up the best possible show. He dismisses the class he is teaching and calls the fifth grade—Hurston's class—for a reading session. The story that they read is new and hard for the class in general, but not for Hurston, as she had already read her reader in the first week when her father had bought the book for her. She is fifth or sixth in line to read, and after counting the number of children ahead of her, she knows which paragraph she will have to read. So she does not concentrate on reading; rather, she observes the visitors, having shiny brownish hair, gold chains, and finger rings. But what fascinates her the most are the long, thin, white fingers of the ladies with which they hold the book. On her turn, she reads so well that Mr. Calhoun, with a proud smile, nods her to go on reading till the end.

At the dismissal of the class, Mr. Calhoun calls Hurston. She is worried she will be whipped in front of the visitors because she is barefoot; her feet and legs are dusty, her hair is not properly combed, and her nails are not clean. But Mr. Calhoun pats her shoulder, and the ladies smile and hold out their "flower-looking fingers" (37) towards her to shake hands. They ask her if she likes school, and she tells a lie that she does like school, though she only likes geography, reading, and playing at recess break. Later, Mr. Calhoun tells Hurston that the two ladies, Mrs. Johnstone and Miss Hurd, like her and she is to go to meet the ladies at the Park House the next afternoon, a hotel in Maitland. He asks her to tell her mother to clean and brush her from head to toe and make her wear shoes and stockings, and advises her to put on her best behaviour in front of the ladies.

The next day, she is allowed to leave school an hour early to go home to get ready for the meeting. Her elder brother John accompanies her up to the gate of the hotel. The ladies serve her well and ask her to eat anything that she wants. They show her their Japanese dolls and hand her a copy of *Scribner's Magazine*, and ask her to read a specific portion. After a paragraph or two, they ask her to stop reading, with smiles on their faces. They take a picture of her on the ground under the palm tree and hand her a gift tied with a ribbon, asking her not to open it until she is back home. Hurston and her brother hurry home to see what the gift is; she is full of joy to find one hundred gold new pennies roll out of the gift in the shape of a cylinder. She is moved by the beauty of the thing and plays with them for a while. Then her mother asks her to keep them safe. This being just the beginning, the next day she receives an "Episcopal Hymn-Book bound in white leather with a golden cross stamped into the front cover, a copy of *The Swiss Family Robinson*, and a book of fairy tales" (38). She at once sets out to read them in a rhythmical manner.

After a month, the two ladies send her a huge box packed with books and clothes. The clothes are not new, but they are very good, and Hurston shines like a morning sun in them. The books, however, give her more pleasure than the clothes, and she reads them all. Reading so many books contributes to Hurston's early exposure to literature and opens up a new world of fantasies to her. Through her mother she learns to read the Bible; one day, her mother whips her, locks her in a room, and the Bible is the only thing there. After reading much in childhood, she is happy only in the woods and loves the plants and animals and is not afraid of anything. "The mother/daughter relationship is one fundamental relationship among Black women. Countless Black mothers have empowered their daughters by passing on the everyday knowledge essential to survival as African-American women. Black daughters identify the profound influence that their mothers have had upon their lives" (Collins 112).

Hurston gathers reflections of life around her on her own and absorbs them as per her instincts. Joe Clarke's store is the heart and spring of the town, as men sit on boxes and benches and gossip about everything that anyone can think of. The store porch is the most interesting place for Hurston. She is not allowed to sit there, but whenever she is sent there to get something, she hears occasional gossip. bell hooks shares, "Within the world of my childhood, we held onto the legacy of a distinct black culture by listening to the elders tell their stories… I can recall sitting at Baba's (my grandmother on my mother's side) at 1200 Broad Street – listening to people come and recount their life experience" (*Talking Back* 158).

Hurston really loves to listen to the folktales that men narrate; one explains the origin of different racial groups and how Blacks obtained dark skin. One day, God gets clay and hardens it the way He wants. Another day, He cuts out human shapes and leaves them to dry, and the next time, when He finds time, He adds life to them. After that, from time to time, He calls everybody to give them spare parts like feet, eyes, toenails, etc. One day, He informs them that the next morning, sharp at seven, He will provide colour, so everybody should be there on time.

The next morning, God sits on His throne and looks at the multitudes of human shapes standing in all directions. He looks over to His left and moves His hand over the crowd and gives them yellow colour. Then He moves His hand over another crowd and gives them red colour, and similarly, white colour to another crowd.

All of them thank God and leave after getting their colour; however, the people are missing on the right side of God's throne. Tired of waiting, He sends Gabriel, His messenger, to find them and ask them to hurry up. Gabriel finds the missing multitude lying asleep by the sea. He wakes them up and asks them to go to the throne and get their colour; otherwise, God will not give them any. After hearing this, the multitudes go running towards the throne and shout to get the colour. The first ones try to be polite, but there is so much pushing from behind that they get all squeezed up against the throne till the throne tilts over to one side. God asks them to get back, which is misunderstood as "get black," and thus they get black colour.

"Hurston was exposed to the Black storytelling tradition. In fact, the shop owned by Joe Clarke proved invaluable for Hurston, as the stories she heard told there would plant the seeds for her later work" (Jones, Sharon 36). Hurston hears dozens more tales in one way or another. Her father and his preacher associates tell the best stories of the church. These tales of God, the Devil, animals, and natural elements seem normal to most of the people in the village, but they stir up fancies in Hurston.

"Likewise, Hurston relates her own 'prevision' childhood abilities to animate thoughts, words and actions, to animate the inanimate" (Rodriguez 39). It does not surprise her at all to hear that the animals can talk. She picks up brief details out of what she hears and stores them to use later. It seems to her that the tree is talking to her and telling her things. She herself does not know when she started making up stories. From one fancy to another, she adds more and more detail, until they seem real. She tells her made-up stories to her mother, who sometimes listens to her tales and sometimes does not, but never seems displeased.

"When inanimate things ceased to commune with me like natural men, other dreams came to live with me. Animals took on lives and characteristics which nobody knew anything about except myself. Little things that people did or said grew into fantastic stories," (58). Her fantasies keep fighting against the facts. "As a child, the author communicates with and exists within those worlds in ways which escape her in the analogous world of dreams, the world that sustains her experience of the visions.... That the author communes with the dreams that she animates contrasts sharply with her powerlessness against the dream visions" (Rodriguez 39).

Apart from these influences, Dwight O. W. Holmes, English teacher at the night school, gives her the key to certain things; his very presence kills dullness and discouragement in her and assures her that things can be done. One day, he stops Hurston after class and compliments her on her work, "No matter about the difficulties past and present, step on it!" (124). He never asks anything, but Hurston feels that he knows all about her, the way he speaks to her. Hurston offers a glimpse into her mindset and the multiple influences on her creativity, which include her family, her physical environments, and her relationships with other people.

Her first publication is on the blackboard in the assembly hall at Morgan College, where she writes an allegory using the faculty members as characters. The two years at Morgan pass happily. Every new thing she learns in school makes her happy, for at last, she is doing the things she wanted to. "Certainly for Black women, our struggle has not been to emerge from silence into speech but to change the nature and direction of our speech, to make a speech that compels listeners, one that is heard" (bell hooks, *Talking Back* 6).

She plans to stay at Morgan College, but there is something else in her destiny. Mae Miller, daughter of the well-known Dr. Kelly Miller of Howard University, comes to Morgan to spend the weekend with her cousins, Hurston's classmates. They get together, and after a few hours of fun, Mae tells Hurston that she is Howard material and should join Howard. As everyone knows, "Howard University is the capstone of Negro education in the world. There gather Negro money, beauty, and prestige. It is to the Negro what Harvard is to the whites" (129). Hurston had heard about Howard and knew that she could never make it. She tells this to Mae, who offers her to stay at their house in Washington to save the room rent and suggests she try for a job to manage the tuition fees.

Hurston moves to Washington and gets a job as a waitress in the exclusive Cosmos Club downtown and later as a manicurist in the G Street shop of George Robinson, a Negro, the owner of a chain of white barber shops in downtown Washington. She manages money for her first quarter's tuition and goes to Howard to get registered. At Howard, she meets Dwight Holmes, who saves her spirits again. She is short of money and is just about to give up when she has a talk with Dwight Holmes, who encourages her, and finally, she is registered at Howard. Sitting in the chapel of that great university, in her first college assembly, Hurston feels dignified, "You have taken me in. I am a tiny bit of your greatness. I swear to you that I shall never make you ashamed of me" (130). She is careful to do her classwork and be worthy to stand there under the shadow of the hovering spirit of Howard. "She learned to be sure of herself and proud of her personal worth" (Porter 9).

Robinson manages that Hurston works from three-thirty every afternoon to eight-thirty. This way, she is able to support herself. As most of the customers know that she is a student, they give her tips that help her make twelve to fifteen dollars a week. The shop is frequented by bankers, senators, cabinet members, congressmen, and gentlemen of the press, who talk of world affairs, national happenings, personalities, secret love affairs, and so on and so forth. They speak about anything and everything in the world in front of Hurston, having faith in her that she will keep the secrets to herself.

One afternoon, a Negro comes to the shop for a haircut and shave, and Banks, the manager, tells him that Robinson has a fine shop for Negroes on U Street, but he insists on being served there according to the Constitution of the United States. They ask him to leave, but he does not listen and is carried and thrown into the middle of G Street by barbers, customers, and porters. He tries to lie there and be a martyr, but the roar of the oncoming cars makes him jump and hurry off the place.

Hurston does not participate in the uproar, but she too wants him to be thrown out as her business was threatened. She realises "how theories go by the board when a person's livelihood is threatened" (134). In bed that night, she analyses the whole thing and realises that she is giving sanction to Jim Crow, which theoretically she is supposed to resist. "But here were ten Negro barbers, three porters, and two manicurists all stirred up at the threat of our living through loss of patronage" (135). This is the first time she pays attention to the fact that self-interest rides above everything else. The fifteen Negroes working in the shop should have felt the racial thing and served him, as he was one of them, but serving him would have ruined Robinson — another Negro — who had got what he had after facing a lot of difficulties by the dint of hard work. All his shops would have been forcibly closed, turning his life into a tragedy — a person who had always helped Negroes, whatsoever the circumstances. "She argues that taking care of oneself would be more important than offering support or encouragement to this victim of discrimination. Her commentary reveals the many complexities of civil rights issues for the black community" (Jones, Sharon 37).

At the university, Hurston gets on well with her class and friends. The teacher who influences her the most is the head of the English Department, Dr Lorenzo Dow Turner. Inspired by him, she decides to be an English teacher. She does a year and a half at Howard University but is not able to complete her two years on account of her illness, and now she does not have money for her fees. She joins Zeta Phi Beta Sorority and takes part in all the literary activities on the campus and forms a small literary society on the hill, "The Stylus," and names the student paper *The Hill Top* (138). Her joining "The Stylus" influences her later moves. On account of a short story in the magazine, Charles S. Johnson, founder of *Opportunity* magazine, writes to her for material, explaining that he is writing to all the Negro colleges with the idea of introducing new writers and new material to the public. "This move on the part of Dr. Johnson was the root of the so-called Negro Renaissance" (138) — a historical phase of cultural and political development leading to the maturation of blacks in the United States. Johnson, director of research for the league, had single-handedly turned *Opportunity* into an expression of 'New Negro' thought. 'New Negroes' were black people who made it clear that they would not accept a subordinate role in American society, and Johnson believed that "young writers like Zora Neale Hurston would help prove the cultural parity of the races" (Hemenway 9).

Hurston sends him a short story, "Drenched in Light," and he publishes it. Later, he publishes her second story, "Spunk." He writes a kind letter and urges her to write and to go to New York. Being out of school for lack of funds and wanting to be in New York, Hurston decides to go there and tries to get back into school in that city. "So the first week of January, 1925, found me in New York with $1.50, no job, no friends, and a lot of hope" (138). She comes to New York through *Opportunity*, and through it, to Barnard. "She was confident of her ability to survive in the big city; she had been on her own since the age of fourteen. Brown-skinned, big-boned, with freckles and high cheekbones, she was a striking woman; her dark brown eyes were both impish and intelligent, her voice was rich and black" (Hemenway 9).

She wins a prize for her short story at the first Award Dinner on 1st May, 1925, where Fannie Hurst offers her a job as secretary and Annie Nathan Meyer offers a scholarship for Barnard. Her record is good, and she enters Barnard in the fall, graduating in 1928 — an achievement few black women would have had the opportunity to make at that time. She joins Fannie Hurst as secretary and lives at her apartment, and things are fine. At Barnard, she works under the guidance of Dr Gladys Reichard and presents a term paper that draws the attention of Dr Franz Boas. She has the same feeling at Barnard that she had at Howard; she feels that she is highly privileged and is determined to make the most of it. She shifts from being in the majority at Howard to being in the minority at Barnard College. Thus, Hurston successfully navigates both the black and the white worlds. She sets out to maintain a good average and graduates entirely satisfied with a B record.

Two weeks before she graduates from Barnard, Dr Boas tells her that he has arranged a fellowship for her to go south and collect Negro folklore. Shortly before that, she is admitted to the American Folk-Lore Society. Later, while she is in the field, she is invited to become a member of the American Ethnological Society and the American Anthropological Society. "Booker T. Washington said once that you must not judge a man by the heights to which he has risen, but by the depths from which he came" (141). These honours may appear insignificant to the world, but to Hurston, they mean a lot. "It was a long step for the waif of Eatonville. From the depth of my inner heart I appreciated the fact that the world had not been altogether unkind to Mama's child" (141), and thus she gets on the road to success.

Hurston is extremely grateful that Dr. Franz Boas trusted her to go south to do research in folklore. With the study of the folklore of her people begins her lifelong interest in Black folk roots. The first six months of research are disappointing for her, not because of a lack of research aptitude but because of the wrong approach. Mrs. R. Osgood Mason, Hurston's godmother and a wealthy white woman, set aside two hundred dollars a month for two years for Hurston's writing, research, and travel. They are thousands of miles away, yet they can read each other's minds; Hurston shares everything with her – the tales, the songs, the dances, the sayings, and the doings of the Negroes when she is out researching their folklore.

"Hurston's relationship with Mason illustrates the politics of white patronage and Black artistic production during the Harlem Renaissance. Often, whites with preconceived ideas about Blacks funded projects; this allowed Black artists to create, but this state of affairs arguably compromised some of their material out of a need to satisfy the expectations of their patrons" (Jones, Sharon 38).

Her search for knowledge takes her into strange places, full of adventures. Her life is in danger several times; she could have been killed any day during her research work, as "primitive minds are quick to sunshine and quick to anger" (146), but she learns how to take care of herself in these circumstances. At times there is nothing personal in the killing — the killer wishes to establish a reputation, and the one who is killed serves as a sample.

Hurston recounts almost being killed by a woman named Lucy, who does not appreciate her collecting the songs from Slim, "who used to be her man back in West Florida before he ran off from her" (152). He is a valuable source of material to Hurston. She buys him drinks and lets him ride in her car. Lucy finds out where he is after a year and follows him to Polk County, but Slim ignores her, and Lucy tells everyone that Hurston is responsible for their breakup. As a result, she wants to kill Hurston, who is lucky to befriend Big Sweet, Lucy's enemy.

Big Sweet helps Hurston collect material without any idea of why it is needed. She sees to it that Hurston gets what she wants. She recommends people who know songs and stories and organises storytelling contests. When Big Sweet comes to know that Lucy is threatening Hurston, she warns Lucy. Several weeks later, Hurston goes to the jook alone and Big Sweet arrives later. Lucy tries to kill her, thinking Big Sweet is not around. When she intervenes, Lucy is surprised to see her. A sort of battle starts, with everyone fighting. Amidst the chaos, Big Sweet tells Hurston to run away. She runs to her room, throws her things in the car, and leaves for New Orleans.

She decides to go to South Florida again and to the Bahamas, as she is fascinated after hearing some Bahaman music and seeing a Jumping Dance in Liberty City. Hurston believes that the music of the Bahaman Negroes is more original, dynamic, and African than American Negro songs. Without giving Godmother a chance to object, she sails to Nassau to know more about them, and she loves the place the moment she lands there. She goes to every Jumping Dance she hears of, learns to "jump" (158), collects more than a hundred tunes, and resolves to reveal them to the world.

On her return to New York in 1932, she introduces Bahaman songs and dances to a New York audience at the John Golden Theatre. "I aimed to show what beauty and appeal there was in genuine Negro material, as against the Broadway concept, and it went over" (158) — both the songs and the dances — and the concert achieves its purpose. Since then, there is a trend towards genuine Negro material and primitive Negro dancing, and her group is invited to perform at different places. She has no intention of doing concerts; she wants to show the wealth and beauty of the material to those who are in the field, and therefore she feels that her job is done.

She enjoys collecting the folktales and believes the people from whom she collected them enjoy telling tales just as much as she enjoyed listening to them.

Of her research in the British West Indies and Haiti, her greatest thrill is coming face to face with a zombie and photographing her. This act of taking the picture has never happened before in history. In *Tell My Horse*, Hurston writes about all that she knows on this subject, which is also published in England under the title *Voodoo Gods*.

In 1929, when she is in the research field, the idea of *Jonah's Gourd Vine* comes to her, wherein she tells a story about a man as per her reading and observation. "Negroes were supposed to write about the Race Problem" (171), but she is thoroughly sick of the subject and her interest lies in what makes a man or a woman do what they do regardless of their colour. She is afraid to tell the story the way she wants.

"Black people were able to create with their music an aesthetic community of resistance, which in turn encouraged and nurtured a political community of active struggle for freedom. Spirituals, blues, jazz, rhythm and blues, and progressive hip-hop all form part of a 'continuum of struggle which is at once aesthetic and political'" (Davis, Angela 201).

Hurston collects a mass of work songs, blues, and spirituals in the course of her research and offers them to two Negro composers, who refuse on the grounds that white audiences will not listen to anything. She decides to see if this is true. "LET THE PEOPLE SING" (172) is her motto, and she resolves to see what will happen. She borrows money and puts on a show at the John Golden Theatre on 10th January 1932, and tries out her theory. The performance is well received by both the audience and the critics. She neither loses money nor makes much, but she is satisfied to prove her point and is happy to see the effects of that concert in all the Negro singing groups since then.

"Traditionally, blues assumed a similar function in African-American oral culture to that played by print media for white, visually based culture. Blues was not just entertainment; it was a way of solidifying community and commenting on the social fabric of working-class Black life in America" (Collins 116). The lyrics sung by many of the Black women blues singers challenge the externally defined controlling images used to justify Black women's objectification as the 'Other.' Sara Martin's "Mean Tight Mama" rejects the cult of true womanhood and its confining images of beauty:

Now my hair is nappy and I don't wear no clothes of silk
Now my hair is nappy and I don't wear no clothes of silk
But the cow that's black and ugly has often got the sweetest milk. (Harley 69)

The primitive Negro dancing gets tremendous impetus, and work songs are taken on. In the performance, Hurston introduces West Indian songs and dances that have taken an important place in America. She is not upset by the fact that others make something out of her things but is glad that she brought beauty to the attention of those who can use it. Katie Geneva Cannon writes about Hurston in *Journal of Feminist Studies in Religion*: Of all the women in the Black women's literary tradition who have contributed to the concrete depiction of Black life, Zora Neale Hurston (1901–1960) is "par exemplar." As an outstanding novelist, journalist, folklorist, anthropologist, and critic, Hurston possessed a sharp accuracy in reporting the positive sense of self that exists among poor, marginal Blacks, "the Negro farthest down." The primary impetus for all her writings was to capture the density of simple values inherent in the provincialism of Blacks who worked on railroads, lived in sawmill camps, toiled in phosphate mines, earning their living as common labourers. Hurston's extreme closeness to the sensibilities of her unlettered characters, along with her meticulous collection of folklore, legends, superstitions, music, and dance of the common people, enabled her work to serve as "a rich repository of resources helpful in delineating the moral counsel cultivated throughout the various periods of Black history in the United States" (37).

Zora Neale Hurston, in *Dust Tracks on a Road*, throws light on the slavery prevalent during her time. As an anthropologist, while collecting folktales, she does a little research jointly in Mobile, Alabama, for *The Journal of Negro History* and Columbia University; her research brings her into contact with Cudjo Lewis, a former slave, whose African name is Kossola-O-Lo-Loo-Ay. In 1859, when the fight between the South and the Abolitionists was heading towards the Civil War, he arrived on the last load of slaves run into the United States and was the only Negro alive who came over on a slave ship. Hurston finds him a cheerful, poetical old gentleman in his late nineties who can tell a good story; he details to her the circumstances in Africa that brought him here. Finding the slave trade so profitable, the powerful kingdom of Dahomey abandons farming, hunting, and all other activities to capture slaves to stock the barracoons on the beach at Dmydah to sell to the slavers who came from the ocean.

The able-bodied, who are captured, are marched to Abomey, the capital city of Dahomey, and are brought before the King, then put into the barracoons to await a buyer. The too old and too young, the injured in battle, are instantly beheaded, their heads dried and carried back to the King; he pays off on heads, dead or alive. The skulls of the slaughtered are not wasted either, as the King has his famous Palace of Skulls. The palace grounds have a massive gate of skull-heads, and the wall surrounding the grounds is built of skulls. The Kings of Dahomey are truly great and mighty, and a lot of skulls are bound to come out of their ambitions.

One thing that impresses Hurston immensely from her three-month association with Cudjo Lewis is: "The white people had held my people in slavery here in America. They had bought us, it is true, and exploited us. But the inescapable fact that stuck in my craw was: my people had sold me and the white people had bought me" (165). It impresses upon her the universal nature of greed and glory, as civilised money stirred up African greed. The wars between the tribes were often stirred up by the white traders to provide more slaves in the barracoons, but the African princes could have prevented it. Hurston posits, "my own people had butchered and killed, exterminated whole nations and torn families apart, for a profit before the strangers got their chance at a cut" (165). Cudjo's eyes are full of tears and memory of fear when he tells Hurston of the attack on his city and its capture.

His nation, Takkoi, is attacked at dawn as they are getting out of bed to go to their fields. He recalls, "A whooping horde of the famed Dahoman women warriors burst through the main gate, seized people as they fled from their houses and beheaded victims with one stroke of their big swords" (166). He was nineteen years old then. They take him and tie him, and he has no idea where his people are, as he never saw them anymore. Their King was captured, and his head was struck off and his highly polished skull was mounted in a beautiful ship-model and treated with great respect; no one of royal blood was sold into slavery, so he was killed. After the fall of Takkoi, they were yoked by forked sticks and tied in a chain to march to Abomey. The heads of the victims who cause trouble are cut and hanged on long poles. With a trip across the ocean in the *Clotilde*, a fast-sailing vessel, finally the cargo arrives in Mobile, where they are unloaded up the river and more than a hundred Africans begin a four-year life of slavery. Cudjo's great sorrow in America was the death of his favourite son, David, who was killed by a train, and his other great sorrow is that he lost track of his folks in Africa, who do not know what has become of him. After seventy-five years, he still had that tragic sense of loss and the yearning for blood and cultural ties.

Hurston discusses race issues and reflects on the Black utterance, "My People! My people!" noting the ways in which it is used, especially as an expression of disapproval of others' actions. Hurston notes that "Blacks are not a monolithic group and that darker-skinned Blacks, especially females, are often given trouble by other Blacks" (Jones, Sharon 33–34). From her childhood, Hurston often hears the traditional cry of "My people! My people!" (177) from the Negroes forced outward by pity, scorn, and hopeless resignation. The observations of one class of Negro on the doings of another branch of the brothers in Black calls forth such a cry. The well-mannered Negro is embarrassed by the crude behaviour of the other Negro, as he sets himself to measure up to what he thinks of as the white standard of living. The humble Negro does not resent a white man looking down on him, but he resents any line between himself and the wealthy, educated ones of his own race.

She hears of "Race Prejudice" (179) as something bad that makes white people feel superior to blacks and denies justice to Negroes. "Race Pride" makes Negroes feel themselves superior to whites if they have it. "Race Man" is somebody who always keeps the glory and honour of his race before him and is ready to defend the Negro race from hurt, harm, and danger. "Race Consciousness" is a plea to Negroes to bear their colour in mind at all times, and as such, no Negro in America forgets his race. "Race Solidarity," which actually does not exist, is something the "Race Leaders" cry over. These phrases Hurston listens to as a child, but with growing years, they fade away like mirages. Racial and class discrimination are useless, Hurston writes; she does not view blacks as superior or inferior. Preferring to focus on individual rather than group progress, Hurston does not want to accept responsibility for thirteen million people, and she critiques the idea of "Racial Solidarity," citing diversity. Hurston sees race consciousness and racial pride as barriers for white people as well as for black people, even if they advance group solidarity.

Hearing things since her childhood, she is curious about her race. What falls in her ears from time to time confuses her more than it clarifies things, because of contradictory viewpoints expressed by the same persons at different times. In the tales Hurston hears, a Negro is at times considered a genius and at times a monkey eager to copy the white man and then make a great mess of things. "Perhaps it was an acknowledgment of our talent for mimicry with the monkey as a symbol" (183). She finds jokes being made on the Negro, the blackest ones, and particularly on black women. Born in the all-black township of Eatonville, Florida, she grows up in an atmosphere remarkably free of the racial prejudice and violence faced by most southern blacks. In Eatonville, Hurston wrote later, she had learned, "that I did not have to consider any racial group as a whole. God made them duck by duck and that was the only way I could see them" (Witcover 14–15).

There are differences within the blacks themselves, and it is believed that nobody can bring them together, not even God. Even a child in the first grade can see this from what happens in the classroom and during school programmes, as the light-skinned children are always the angels, fairies, and queens of school plays. Hurston realizes that the Negro race is not one band of heavenly love, and there is stress and strain inside as well as outside the race. Therefore, she does not have to consider any racial group as a whole. She learns that skin is no measure of what is inside people: "So none of the Race clichés meant anything anymore. I began to laugh at both white and black who claimed special blessings on the basis of race. Therefore I saw no curse in being black, nor no extra flavor by being white" (191). She neither considers it an honour nor a shame to belong to a particular race. "Hurston knew that African Americans were different, not inferior" (Porter 9).

Alice Walker, in *In Search of Our Mothers' Gardens*, depicts Hurston as the black woman's voice, as the prime symbol of "racial health; a sense of black people as complete, complex, undiminished human beings, a sense that is lacking in so much black writing and literature" (85). Race consciousness is completely absent from her work, as she feels that "nigger" is a matter of character rather than colour. She does not refer to the race riots and other atrocities of her times, and there is little discussion of the issues of race and segregation. She does give her opinions about race relations, both within and outside the African American community, but that is not her focal point. Being a master of self-representation, Hurston fashioned the narrative of her own history to present herself as the product of a rich African American cultural heritage. Despite the widespread racial and gender discrimination of the era, the story of her life continues to serve as an inspiring example, marked by a determination to succeed as a writer.

In May 1932, the Depression does away with money for research. Hurston decides to write, using the huge mass of material she is carrying around with her, to be laid in some sequence. Back in her native village, she writes *Mules and Men*, which is published after her first novel, and she gives three folk concerts under the influence of the faculty members at Rollins College, Winter Park. Then she writes a short story, "The Gilded Six-Bits," published in the August issue of *Story Magazine* in 1933. Four publishers write to her and ask her if she has anything of book length, and the very next week she moves to Sanford and sits down to write *Jonah's Gourd Vine*. Her financial condition is not good, yet she manages to complete the book in three months and gets it published. The producer Arthur Hornblow takes her to lunch; she is jubilant, and by then her five books have been accepted. Twice she has been a Guggenheim Fellow and has spoken at three book fairs with all the literary greats of America and abroad. "Alice Walker's efforts to have Zora Neale Hurston's unmarked grave recognized parallel her intellectual quest to honour Hurston's important contributions to Black feminist literary traditions. Reclaiming Black women's ideas also involves discovering, reinterpreting, and analyzing the ideas of subgroups within the larger collectivity of U.S. Black women who have been silenced" (Collins 16).

Hurston receives a Guggenheim Fellowship, sails off to Jamaica, and works hard on her research for writing *Their Eyes Were Watching God*. In Haiti, she writes the novel in seven weeks under pressure. Later, she regrets all her books and says, "It is one of the tragedies of life that one cannot have all the wisdom one is ever to possess in the beginning … the force from somewhere in Space which commands you to write in the first place, gives you no choice. You take up the pen when you are told, and write what is commanded," (175). She wishes she could rewrite them. Hurston writes *Dust Tracks on a Road* in California, where she goes on an invitation from her friend, Katharane Edson Mershon. *Dust Tracks on a Road* chronicles her growth and development as a writer, as well as her many migrations throughout the South, the North, and the Caribbean. Sonia Sanchez points out, "I've always known that if you write from a black experience, you're writing from a universal experience as well.... I know you don't have to whitewash yourself to be universal" (qtd. in Tate 142).

Fanny Hurst and Ethel Waters are the two friends who mean a lot to Hurston. In her undergraduate days, Hurston is secretary to Fanny Hurst, who amazes her with her mood swings, sometimes serious and immediately turning into a childish gaiety. She likes Hurston to drive for her, and they enjoy several tours together. Hurston wants to know Ethel Waters, a popular singer-actress, as she senses a great humanness and depth in her soul and wants to know someone like her. She writes letters to Ethel, which she ignores. Then they meet at a dinner party and get friendly, and Hurston gets to know her so well that she voices her sentiments. At the age of thirteen, Ethel went on stage for the first time, and at fifteen she introduced the *St. Louis Blues* to the world. She is gay and serious by turns, and they love talking about life and their experiences. Hurston is grateful for the friendship of Fanny Hurst and Ethel Waters and concludes that no one can live without friends. "Hurston explores race dynamics at the interpersonal level, notably with her friends Fannie Hurst and Ethel Waters" (Jones, Sharon 38).

Hurston discusses love, and what she has learnt about it both in books and real life. She marries a man whom she meets in college, but soon has second thoughts. Wanting to resume her research, she urges her husband to move to Chicago, but he ends up with another woman. Later, she meets an affectionate but poor man, whom she refers to as P.M.P., who has a deep impact on her. The two have a tumultuous relationship, as he does not want Hurston to continue with her profession. Commenting on the themes and works of African American women writers, Mary Helen Washington writes, "What is most important about the black woman writer is her special and unique vision of the black woman. Since *Iola Leroy*, the first novel written by a black woman writer, has been the black woman herself – her aspirations, her conflicts, her relationship to her men and her children, her creativity" (x). Hurston's experience with religion includes questions about God. She enjoys revivals and the preacher's behaviour during these events. Hurston sees purpose in religion: "People need religion because the great masses fear life and its consequences" (225).

On recollecting the things in her life, she realizes, "I have been in Sorrow's kitchen and licked out all the pots. Then I have stood on the peaky mountain wrapped in rainbows, with a harp and a sword in my hands" (227). She means that she endured sorrows in her life, the most hurting being the death of her mother. After that, she faced various hardships in her life courageously and came out victorious in every pursuit of life. In 1831, Maria W. Stewart questions, "How long shall the fair daughters of Africa be compelled to bury their minds and talents beneath a load of iron pots and kettles?" (Richardson 21). Orphaned at age five, bound to a clergyman's family as a domestic servant, Stewart struggled to gather isolated fragments of an education when and where she could. Many Maria Stewarts are there in the form of African American women whose minds and talents have been suppressed by the pots and kettles, symbolic of black women's subordination.

Hurston believes that God is too great an artist for the folks on her side of the creek to be all of His best works. "Some of His finest touches are among us, without doubt, but some more of His masterpieces are among those folks who live over the creek" (228). She yearns for universal justice and tries to make the day at hand a positive thing and realizes the uselessness of gloominess. She does not like thinking about the past, loves to live in the present, and does not know anything about the future. She hopes that the future will be full of work because through experience she knows that she can find happiness in work. She wants a busy life, a just mind, and a timely death. She summarizes life as, "tears and laughter, love and hate, make up the sum of life" (265). In this account of her life, Zora Neale Hurston meditates on race, class, gender, religion, migration, and the quest for self.

She even has plans for a long life, that is, she will write for herself and will read, enjoying coffee and liquor, which she has never used till date. She thinks kindly of the world because, "I think I can be like that because I have known the joy and pain of deep friendship. I have served and been served. I have made some good enemies for which I am not a bit sorry. I have loved unselfishly, and I have fondled hatred with the red-hot tongs of Hell. That's living. I have no race prejudice of any kind. My kinfolks, and my 'skinfolks' are dearly loved" (231). She sees the same virtues and vices everywhere; she extends her hand of fellowship and love and expects the same from others. She wishes to remember everyone in her good thoughts and implores others to do the same, not only for her but for everyone, even "those who walk in the dust" (232). She believes that tolerance and patience can create a noble world in a few hundred generations or so. Her writing presents a complicated view of race, and she celebrates the connections with people from different racial and ethnic backgrounds. Her analysis of the dynamics of race relationships in the past and her own reality provides an insight into the social climate of the day.

In her introduction to the 1991 edition of *Dust Tracks on a Road*, noted poet and author Maya Angelou states, "It is difficult, if not impossible, to find and touch the real Zora Neale Hurston" ("Zora Neale Hurston and the Post-Modern Self in *Dust Tracks on a Road*," web. 15 Sep. 2016). Hurston's writing certainly reveals many gaps and silences that raise many questions about her life. "While her narration is written in an informal, conversational style, and her point of view is definitely feminist, or, according to fellow African American writer Alice Walker, 'womanist.' The womanist stance in Hurston's works is an inspiration and a model for a new generation of African American women writers in the last quarter of the twentieth century" ("*Dust Tracks on a Road* Analysis: Form and Content," web. 17 Jan. 2017). According to Walker, to be womanist is to be responsible, independent, to act as a grown-up, to speak her mind, and thus be her own mouthpiece. In her foreword, Angelou has written, "*Dust Tracks on a Road* is written with royal humour and an imperious creativity. But then all creativity is imperious, and Zora Neale Hurston was certainly creative" (xii). Her life is a dramatic adventure, and she proves herself to be a survivor, essentially. "Far too many African-American women intellectuals have labored in isolation and obscurity and, like Zora Neale Hurston, lie buried in unmarked graves" (Collins 4).

Triangular Road, an account of self-discovery written by Paule Marshall, is her coming of age as a writer. It is a tribute to Langston Hughes, the charismatic Harlem Renaissance icon, and other influences on her; it honours family and mentors. Explaining the phenomena of the Harlem Renaissance, Sharon L. Jones writes, "The Harlem Renaissance, also known as the New Negro Movement, began in the early 1900s, and ended around 1940. Coinciding with modernist trends, the Harlem Renaissance was an interdisciplinary cultural movement that reflected literary, musical, dance, artistic, and dramatic developments in African American expression. Additionally, the civil rights movement and the rise of organizations for social justice also brought much to bear upon the Harlem Renaissance. This movement would have a wide-ranging impact on American literature, changing the growth and direction of what was valued and what was not" (227).

The first chapter of *Triangular Road* offers an affectionate tribute to Langston Hughes, who introduced Marshall to the world of European letters during a cultural tour of the continent. The subsequent chapters are adapted from the 2005 lecture series that Marshall delivered at Harvard University on the theme "Bodies of Water," with the titles "I've Known Rivers," "I've Known Seas," and "I've Known Oceans" referring to the specific rivers, seas, and oceans and their profound impact on Black history and culture in America. She borrows a metaphor from her mentor Langston Hughes's poem "The Negro Speaks of Rivers," wherein she traces her personal cultural development through several bodies of water that played key roles in African American history. In *The New York Times* book review, Blake Wilson writes, "This book, based on a series of lectures … in places reads more like a notebook than a polished work. But it's a lovely example of a mature writer's voice, as well as a record of how she found it" (BR21).

The first section is a "Homage to Mr. Hughes" that paints an appealing portrait of Langston Hughes, the tireless champion of young African American artists who made the African American experience the subject of his writings. It begins with an official letter that she receives in early May 1965 with the return address "United States Department of State, 301 Fourth Street, SW, Washington, D.C. 20547" (1). She registers only the words *State Department* and instantly panics as she anticipates the worst — bad news of some sort in the letter. As the Civil Rights Movement is at its height, she thinks she is summoned for her involvement in the northern front of the struggle. Finally, she manages to open the letter; its contents prove altogether different: "Rather than a dire summons, it turned out to be a once-in-a-lifetime plum of an invitation" (2). She stands mesmerised for a long time with the invitation in her hands.

The letter informs her that the world-renowned poet Langston Hughes is going to conduct a one-month cultural tour of Europe for the government. During the tour, he is supposed to give a series of readings as well as talks on African American literature. On a number of occasions, Langston Hughes had done this for the State Department in other parts of the world. This time, he insists on two young writers of his choice to be included in the tour, and Paule Marshall is one of the writers he wishes to include. She is surprised to know that the Poet Laureate has chosen her to accompany him on the cultural tour of Europe. "Me, a mere fledgling of a writer, with only one novel and a collection of stories published to date! Why would someone of his stature so much as consider a novice like myself?" (3). Soon, she realises that she should not be surprised, as Langston Hughes is known for the support and encouragement he extends to the generation of young writers like her who began publishing in the 1950s and early 1960s.

At the launch of her first novel in 1959, Langston Hughes had been kind enough to attend the book party in a Harlem storefront: "The poet who had long been a literary icon, come to celebrate with me, come to congratulate me on the favourable reviews my novel had received, there to beam at me like a *paterfamilias* whose offspring had done him proud" (4). To add to the celebration, Marshall was eight months pregnant at the time, and Hughes congratulated her for the book and the upcoming baby in the same year.

On the publication of her second book in 1961, the collection of stories entitled *Soul Clap Hands and Sing*, she receives a postcard from Langston Hughes stating that he has just received the book and looks forward to reading it. This way, he shows his thoughtfulness and support for her second book. The collection wins a modest award from the American Academy of Arts and Letters. Hughes is the first person to congratulate her at the award ceremony. She believes that maybe he recommended her collection to the academy's selection committee and must have been instrumental in the award. He continues to keep her in mind, now by inviting her to travel to Europe with him.

Back in New York, Paule Marshall quickly sets out making arrangements for her young son and puts aside the work on her second novel for some time. She takes along her first novel that Hughes had helped to launch, to find a European publisher for it. On the appointed day, she takes a taxi to Kennedy Airport along with William Melvin Kelley, the other fledgling writer chosen by Hughes for the tour. Hughes promoted Bill Kelley's work as well and had even hired him as a research assistant when he left Harvard to write full time. He greets both of them at the station with a paternal smile, and Marshall feels like bowing before his royal presence.

Marshall describes Langston Hughes being "open to people and parties" (27). Once the official day is over and they are done with their dinner and wine, Hughes recreates for Marshall the glory days of the Harlem Renaissance: "The writers, musicians, painters, philosophers et al. who were among his circle of friends; the small magazines in which he first started to publish — one called *Fire* that lasted all of one issue, and *The Crisis*, the magazine of the NAACP, which is still in existence today. He told riotous stories about the Harlem literati and 'niggerati,'" (28) a group of African American young men and women who were artists and intellectuals during the Harlem Renaissance. He spends the better part of the night educating Marshall about a period of their history that had been omitted in the standard textbooks, passing down Black American culture and history. He talks freely with her about literature, life, and Black American cultural history.

Hughes tells her stories from his travels around the world. He has written two travel memoirs, *The Big Sea* and *I Wonder as I Wander*. Marshall had read *The Big Sea* as a teenager and had privately vowed to follow the example of the author; she had decided to become a writer and a travelling woman as well. She does not accompany Hughes to Berlin on the tour, as she had to return home for her son and her novel that she had put aside to join the tour. Her friends inform her that massive demonstrations are being planned to pressurise the Congress and the President again to pass the Voting Rights Bill before the end of the year. The Voting Rights Act, signed into law by President Lyndon Johnson on 6th August 1965, "aimed to overcome legal barriers at the state and local levels that prevented African Americans from exercising their right to vote under the 15th Amendment (1870) to the Constitution of the United States. The act significantly widened the franchise and is considered among the most far-reaching pieces of civil rights legislation in U.S. history" ("Voting Rights Act," web. 31 May 2017).

Langston Hughes understands her dilemma and decides to complete the State Department tour on his own. He leaves two parting gifts for Marshall at the hotel's reception desk: flowers, grapes, and a note saying that it was fun travelling with her and he would like to do it again. Marshall never gets the opportunity to travel with him again, but he continues to support her work. He sends her notes and postcards from his travels and also calls her off and on to check her progress in writing. He is not pleased with the snail's pace at which she is working, taking so long to produce so little, and is concerned about her career. For her, "he was a loving taskmaster, mentor, teacher, griot, literary sponsor and treasured elder friend" (33). He died in 1967. The sense of loss continues, and she still misses him.

In addition to Langston Hughes, her mother, Adriana, also influences her in literary pursuits. Her parents are able to lease an old Victorian brownstone on Hancock Street No. 501 uptown, where Adriana remains busy in the large kitchen on the ground floor, entertaining her friends — part-time day-workers like her — and all the women from home, Barbadian immigrants. She is elated talking to her friends from home about everything under the sun and having an opinion about everything. Marcia Ann Gillespie shares in the foreword to *Life Notes*, "Some of the memories I hold dearest are of the times spent in the company of women, when we drop all pretence and the talk gets to the bone. Times of tears and laughter, when the silences that choke us are breached, when we speak about our fears and deepest secrets, when we let go and get free and simply say what's really in our hearts and spirits, and on our minds. Reflective, hesitant voicings of thoughts and feelings long held but priorly unspoken. We share our secret longings, let go of things held close in fear of reprisal, in fear of being ridiculed, or being held in contempt. Unedited, uncensored womantalk. Earthily sexual, downright raunchy sometimes. Other times a bearing of wounds and hurts that have lain festering for too long:

spiritual boils in need of lancing. Tears too long dammed. Feelings of shame and blame, of inadequacy, of frustration and rage. Unveilings of secret joys, forbidden pleasures, unresolved mysteries, and hidden dreams. From these woman-sharing talks, from peeling back the layers and exposing our secret pleasures and pains, our uncertainties and doubts, our angers and despair have come transformation, empowerment, community, activism" (13).

Marshall loves the sayings and Bajan proverbs that are part of their endless talk, which she does not understand fully but still loves. They are all master storytellers as well, and Marshall believes that she has her first lessons in the art and craft of writing while being forced to listen to Adriana and her friends; they develop in her a keen ear for dialogue and narrative. Decades later she christens them the "Mother Poets" (89) and pays grateful homage to them in "The Poets in the Kitchen," which is published as part of a series on the "Making of a Writer" in *New York Times Sunday Book Review*. In her autobiographical essay, "From the Poets in the Kitchen," Marshall describes the aesthetic roots of her fiction. "The group of women around the table long ago. They taught me my first lessons in the narrative art," she recalls. "They trained my ear. They set a standard of excellence. This is why the best of my work must be attributed to them; it stands as a testimony to the rich legacy of language and culture they so freely passed on to me in the wordshop of the kitchen" (Gale, "Marshall, Paule 1929 – *Contemporary Black Biography*," web. 14 Jan. 2017).

Marshall writes her first novel without telling anyone and starts contacting publishers. Her editor at Random House, Hiram Haydn, tells her that he likes her six-hundred-page manuscript and thinks it will sell. He suggests *Brown Girl, Brownstones* as the title of her first book and asks her to get back to work: "It is for you to take this swollen, overwritten baby tome of yours and to extricate from it the slender, impressive first novel that's buried there" (96). Along with the changes, he attaches a list of suggestions that might result in a really worthy work. Seeing her disappointed after listening to him, Hiram Haydn advises her to leave New York and go to Barbados to revise her manuscript with the advance for the book. Living in her parents' birthplace might help her understand them better, and Marshall goes to her apartment in Manhattan, buys two cheap extra-large suitcases, and starts packing for the trip.

Marshall is married by then. Both the sisters were driven into early marriage by their mother, but marriage does not pose any hindrance to her proposed stay in the Caribbean. Her husband is also from the Bajan Brooklyn, where his family owns several brownstones. They married in their early twenties: "Ours was a mutual apostasy that also rejected traditional marriage, so that while we lived together, slept together, we essentially led fairly independent, unfettered lives" (98). Finally, after nine years, they have a child, but the settled, stay-at-home married life does not suit Marshall and eventually ends in divorce. Barbara Christian believes that Marshall's persistence in writing, "despite strains on her familial relationships … indicates her strong determination to be her own woman and to do what she needed to do" (Gale, "Marshall, Paule 1929 – Contemporary Black Biography," web. 14 Jan. 2017).

Marshall quickly finds a room in a newly built manor-style house near the capital, Bridgetown, Caribbean. The owner of the house, Mr. Watson, an old Bajan, used his life's savings "to build this replica of a white planter's great house" (100), draining all his savings in the process. In his youth, he would have gone to a house as he now possessed to beg for a job as a yard boy. Marshall plans to write a story about old Mr. Watson and his house, "his colonial showpiece" (100). It is part of the collection of stories about old men called *Soul Clap Hands and Sing*, the title taken from a poem by W. B. Yeats on the subject of aging.

Paule Marshall settles down to revise and improvise "the bloated baby tome of a novel" (100), using her own instincts as well as the notes and suggestions by Hiram Haydn. Removing highly decorative prose, overwhelming style, and excess details helps her shape the novel. With time she learns the painful but necessary lesson of every novice: "that writing is rewriting, is honing, pruning, refining, is becoming, essentially, one's own unsparing editor" (101). To have a break from the routine and loneliness, she goes to Mr. Watson's plantation house for swimming—or, as the local folk call it, "a sea-bath" (101)—which they believe has the power to heal any disease. Marshall thinks that she could have used these healing powers years back when, at Hunter College, she suffered from tuberculosis because of taking a full academic program while working two part-time jobs and eating only sandwiches—hurriedly, at that.

In Barbados, she spends time at the Museum and Historical Society, reading the early history of the island as a relief from writing. For company, she spends time with a small group of friends after settling there. They are all part of the pro-independence movement, who had won scholarships to study in England and returned home radicalised, eager for change. Listening to their long, heated discussions, Marshall thinks of them as "Black people who could actually anticipate taking charge politically" (103). After nine years, in 1966, Barbados finally achieved independence. Twice a month, Marshall travels up to the remote hilly district called Scotland, where Adriana was born, to visit her eldest sister, Branford Catherine—the only one of the Clement children who still remains on the island—for she defied her mother M' Da-duh and refused to emigrate, and, to her mother's shame and disgust, chose to become a common hawker. Marshall even makes a futile attempt to track down her father's family and birthplace in Barbados.

Finally, she completes revisions in ten months and feels that she has achieved "a tighter, more focused, less self-indulgent manuscript" (118). Eager to show Hiram Haydn what she has accomplished and to begin the new novel she has in mind, she prepares to leave for home. The day before her flight, she goes to Scotland to say goodbye to her aunt. On the last day in town, she goes for a long sea-bath in the afternoon and a farewell dinner with her pro-independence friends in the evening, as she feels relieved for the first time in months.

Brown Girl, Brownstones, the first novel of Paule Marshall, wins the prestigious prize after the famous Pulitzer—the Guggenheim Award. The first thing Marshall does is call Hughes and thank him again for having written one of the letters of recommendation that helped her secure "such a bonanza of a grant" (120). She immediately makes preparations to head back down to the West Indies, the best and cheapest place to write, this time choosing the island of Grenada, which is even farther down and smaller than Barbados. Grenada is a beautiful island and seems like "the Eden the world had once been" (121). Having substantial money in her purse this time, Marshall rents a house—a completely furnished old-style Creole country house with large airy rooms, tall windows, and a spacious veranda overlooking the garden. She hires a housekeeper, a cook, and a cook's helper to do daily marketing. Three times a week, Mrs. Bishop comes to do laundry, and Marshall hires her husband as a handyman, yardman, and gardener, for he could not find steady work as a carpenter.

After interviewing a number of aspirants, she finds a suitable nanny for her son—Mrs. Charles, a pleasant and efficient old woman. She has a grandson of the age of her son, who is like a playmate for him. Her son is now three years old and has been travelling around the island with her since birth. Before the divorce, her husband occasionally visited them in the West Indies. Odessa Gittens—or Miss 'Dessa, as she is called—a friend in Grenada, helps her settle down on the island. She is in her fifties and had long worked as a health and social service officer in the underserved little villages of upcountry Grenada. Having seen Marshall's name and brief bio in the "Visitors to the Island" column in the local newspaper, where Marshall is described as "an American writer of Barbadian parentage" (124), she comes to meet her.

Marshall creates her own workspace, independent of the house, in the servant's room at the back. Mr. Bishop transforms the dark, cell-like room, with its one window and miserly cot, into a bright, airy, freshly painted workspace. For Marshall, it is like Virginia Woolf's "room of one's own" (125), to which every woman writer is entitled. As Woolf says in her essay *A Room of One's Own*, "… a woman must have money and a room of her own if she is to write fiction" (6). In no time, Marshall has a functioning office, dominated by a large new desk purchased in town, and the latest model of a new Royal portable she had bought just before leaving the States. The drawers of the desk are filled with enough writing supplies to last for the year that she plans to spend in Grenada. On top of the desk, she keeps the steno pads containing the research material she had spent months collecting—her most valuable possession for the book she intends to write. She plans to write a historical novel set in the present; the characters will be modern-day folk of various races and backgrounds, yet their lives, situations, relationships, thinking, and politics will reflect the past four hundred years of the hemisphere's history and its continuing lingering influence.

For the Guggenheim Fellowship, she is required to submit a summary of the proposed novel. In a short time, everything is set for writing, but she suffers from the "writer's block" (127), more massive than she had suffered before. The moment she sits down at the desk every morning, she feels a sort of paralysis, unable to write. She thinks the subject is too large and complex for someone like her to attempt, for she still is a novice with only one novel and a collection of short stories. She feels money has killed her creativity, as the checks in thousands of dollars come regularly from New York with no requisition of a progress report. She believes that the paralyzing guilt has to do with her being away again from the ongoing struggle at home. There were plans to organize another massive campaign to spur the Voter Registration Drive in the Deep South, especially in Mississippi. She thinks she should have been on one of the buses heading southward or back to New York raising funds to support the campaign through the Artists for Freedom Organization and other support groups she is associated with. Guilt over her absence from the movement might have been responsible for the present impasse.

To break the paralysis, she employs different strategies, but to no avail. She tries the "throw-away writing" (128), that at times offers a word, a phrase or even a sentence for a breakthrough, but nothing of the sort happens. Then she tries another tactic that comes from Mrs. Woolf's manifesto: "The female writer must be allowed to sit and stare, and for however long she chooses" (128–129). She believes that the act of simply sitting and staring into space allows important ideas, information, inspiration, and direction to emerge from the subconscious. "Creative writing is, after all, both a conscious and an *unconscious* act, the two spheres of the mind working in concert to create the novel, the story, the poem" (Italics original 129). Marshall tries this and at times simply sits and stares, waiting to be rescued by the deeper level of the self. Toni Cade Bambara, editor of the anthology *The Black Woman*, in her groundbreaking essay, "On the Issue of Roles," emphasizes, "revolution begins with the self and in the self" (qtd. in bell hooks, *Talking Back* 30). She also searches the stack of steno pads containing her priceless research notes. She goes through the material for hours, thinking that she might come across something that will lift her paralysis and initiate her into writing, but only to land in disappointment. In the afternoon, Marshall spends some time with her son every day at a nearby beach, Grenada's magnificent Grand Anse, known to be one of the truly great beaches in the world, as a short relief from the torture of Virginia Woolf's room. Her son helps her recover from the uncreative workday, but only for a while.

Heather Chambers, another close friend in Grenada, teaches literature in the Secondary School in St. George's. She has the passion of a devotee when it comes to "the Big Drum/Nation Dance ceremony held every year on Grenada's tiny satellite island of Carriacou that was mere two hours away on the local schooner" (140). Every year, her friend joins these Carriacou people in Grenada who faithfully return home for the event. This time, she invites Marshall to accompany her, as she insists that a history lover like Marshall should not miss the Nation Dance. Her friend, Miss 'Dessa, also insists she go, for a change will be good for her, as Marshall is not making any progress in her writing, and Miss 'Dessa promises to take care of her household and her son while she is away.

The Big Drum/Nation Dance is held at various sites across the island. The one Marshall's friend attends each year takes place in a small inland village her father would have immediately described, as he used to describe his birthplace, "a place forgotten behind God's back, with its little tin-roofed chattel houses, its depleted-looking fields and bare dusty gathering place at the center of the village where the yearly event was held" (142). The men play the drums and the women dance. The drummers are elderly men with work-swollen hands to beat the drum, and the old women dance to the beat. It is not a single dance but a number of separate and distinct dances, each signifying a different nation.

This reminds Marshall of James Weldon Johnson's memoir *Along This Way*, which she had read as a teenager. It had been on the list of books by coloured writers that she had boldly demanded at the local library. In the memoir, Johnson describes a circular dance called the "Ring Shout" that the old folk in his segregated neighbourhood of Jacksonville, Florida, performed nearly every night at their meeting hall. Moving in a tight circle or ring around the hall, they would sing, dance, and shout. Johnson's "Ring Shout" and the "Big Drum/Nation Dance" seem similar to Marshall, except that no drums were allowed at the "Ring Shout," as at that time drums in the hands of Black folk were considered "weapons" (145) for stirring rebellion.

The dancers acknowledge their nations and repeatedly honour them through songs and dances. Marshall thanks her friend for insisting she attend the festival. This overnight trip gives Marshall the idea for a novel that she will write decades later. "In it, a well-heeled Black American widow, an unapologetic bourgeoise, given to her yearly Caribbean cruise, recovers something of her true-true self after experiencing the Carriacou Big Drum/Nation Dance" (147).

Praisesong for the Widow is to be the name of her forthcoming novel. On the morning after the trip to Carriacou, back in the Virginia Woolf room, Marshall purposefully gathers up the stack of steno pads containing her research notes and respectfully deposits them in the storage closet in one of the expensive suitcases. Back in her room, she starts writing, understanding that as a fiction writer, a novelist, a storyteller, a fabulist, her responsibility first and foremost is to the story, and the historical truths will come through if she crafts her tale honestly. All of it will be there for those capable of reading between the lines. She understands that writing fiction is a wonderfully conscious and unconscious act. With this, her writing paralysis breaks, and she writes nonstop until it is time for her to go to Grand Anse Beach with her son. She puts her trust in her instincts, and the revelation frees her to write fiction that sings with authenticity at the best.

Enumerating the importance of Marshall's works, Harihar Kulkarni writes, "Marshall is a woman writer and therefore thinks that inherent in the process of recovery of self is also creation of feminine aesthetic which involves twofold responsibility: to break the patriarchal imperialism of representation and to celebrate womanhood. She, therefore, challenges woman's text and hegemonize or totalize 'female culture'…. While she affirms liberation from racial and gender oppression, she treats both of them as equally liberating points from which to create a literature that is political in form as well as in subject matter" (220).

In the last chapter, "I've Known Oceans: The Atlantic," she calls the Atlantic "an entire ocean permanently sitting shivah," apparently referring to the death toll of the trans-Atlantic slave trade. In this section, Marshall details FESTAC'77, the unofficial name of the

Second World Festival of Black and African Arts held in Lagos, Nigeria, in 1977. FESTAC'77 is, for Marshall, the second major plum of a cultural conference overseas with all expenses paid to come her way since the State Department Tour of Europe with Hughes a decade earlier. This particular plum is an almost month-long festival of arts by the Nigerian government. Its purpose is to celebrate the ending of colonialism by bringing together artists, writers, and scholars from the entire continent. It is to be "nearly four weeks of performances, recitals, readings, exhibits, concerts, colloquiums, forums and the like; nearly four weeks, moreover, of meeting, conversing and interacting with fellow artists in a spirit of confraternity" (152). Hours before the event is due to begin, the stands are packed inside the city's huge National Stadium.

The opening ceremony is modelled on the Olympic Games' grand parade, with each country clearly determined to outshine all the others both in spectacle and patriotic zeal. The hours-long procession is an endless display of national flags, national dresses, along with large photographs of the national leaders adorned on huge banners held up in the air, as well as on the marchers' matching outfits. Each country's troupe of drummers, dancers, and musicians is accompanied by a large corps of singers repeating the national anthem nonstop, "all the while waving mini versions of the national flag – a veritable blizzard of the little flags – up at the stands" (155). The parade of the Egyptians, with the largest number of delegates, is the most spectacular one.

The delegation of Marshall, of eighty or more, is positioned near the end of the massive line-up, as per the alphabetical order of the march. Their parade is totally lacking in spectacle – with no matching clothing or costumes, no marching order, no well-rehearsed troupe of entertainers, no horses of any kind, no banners or flags – unlike other parades. They are totally unprepared for an Olympics-style display, as most of them came from widely different parts of the States and arrived a day or two before the opening ceremony, with no time to organise a parade. Among them are people of differing politics, ranging from the revolutionary black nationalists to the moderate NAACP types. Their parade reflects their divisions: some sing the old Amen hymn (Marshall's seventeen-year-old son is a part of them), while the others sing the Negro National Anthem, "Lift Every Voice and Sing."

Marshall, being a part of all this, thinks, "My People. My People. Unprepared. Unrehearsed. Improvised. Disorganized" (158). But the crowd loves them. From the moment the name "The United States of America" is announced from the loudspeakers situated around the stadium, everyone present stands and welcomes them with huge applause.

The applause continues throughout their march around the field. The nonstop applause is pure "Omowale joy – Omowale meaning, in the Yoruba language, 'The child has returned'" (158). There is joy at their return and at their presence amongst them. There is also a large, discernible measure of pride that "the displaced child" has returned representing the wealthiest and most powerful "high muck-a-muck" nation in the world. There is admiration at how the Omowalies, often mistreated in what is now their home, continue to agitate for their full rights as citizens in the form of sit-ins, jail-ins, marches, rallies, protests, boycotts, demonstrations, the court battles, and the leaders, heroes, and foot soldiers who have been sacrificed for the cause. The applause is a praise song to all of them. Marshall believes that the excessive length of the praise song is partly due to a large measure of guilt and sorrow, as there is the old, shameful history between the Omowalies marching in disorder around the stadium and the people in the stands applauding them: "Because hadn't their forebears been complicit, some of them, in the nefarious trade that had reduced ours – the forebears of the present-day Omowalies – to mere articles of trade, commodities, merchandise, goods, cargo, chattel cargo! to be bought and sold and whipped and worked for free!" (159).

This commerce continued for five centuries, leaving their descendants, the Omowalies, as permanently displaced persons. Marshall feels this way at times and believes that guilt, shame, and sorrow emphasise the excessive welcome accorded to them. Arthur Monroe writes about FESTAC'77 in the journal *The Black Scholar*, "A 500 member U.S. contingent was organised by the U.S.A. committee and took part in every aspect of the festival. Indeed it was at times difficult for Africans to distinguish them from Guineans, Senegalese, Brazilians, or even Nigerians. It was the largest group of African American artists ever to return to Africa as a single group. In its deeper reflections there could not have been a festival without them" (34).

There are many other instances of reconciliation and forgiveness in the midst of the endless round of cultural events during the next three to four weeks of FESTAC. The members of their delegation are constantly claimed, reclaimed, and embraced – including even those who are far more white than black in appearance. Their African colleagues are desperate to make amends for the past. They often find themselves as the objects of heated debates among them, so as to determine their possible ancestry. FESTAC'77 ends with a palm-wine gala on the roof terrace of the National Theatre. Marshall reassures her friends among the African writers that this will not be her sole visit to the continent.

Her life, as she sees it, is a thing divided in three: "There was Brooklyn, U.S.A., and specifically the tight, little, ingrown immigrant world of Bajan Brooklyn that I had fled" (163). Once she started writing, the Caribbean, its conga line of islands, was home off and on for many years. "While all the time, lying in wait across the Atlantic, in a direct line almost with tiny wallflower Barbados, had been the Gulf of Guinea and the colossus of ancestral Africa, the greater portion of my tripartite self that I had yet to discover, yet to know" (163). Three years after FESTAC, the Kenyan government invites a group of Black American artists and writers, including Marshall, to visit the country with all expenses paid. On her own, she includes a side trip to Uganda, which proves to be an unwise choice at the time. She also tries but fails to enter Tanzania as well as Zambia. She plans to write about this limited and frustrating East African experience, and then is back to write a novel or a short story – her primary love.

Triangular Road recounts her beginning as a writer and how the search for her own voice took her to distant places. She talks about history and the present, race relations, colonialism, writing and diaspora, and how people find their place in the world despite seemingly unbeatable and unbearable odds. She recounts powerful first-hand stories of her family and travels. Her writing is as much about her work as it is about her life. It portrays a great writer who feels the same anxieties and uncertainties that any professional encounters as a writer. In *The Washington Post Book Review*, Jonathan Yardley writes, "Though fiction may have a pride of place in her heart, *Triangular Road* reveals a strong gift for self-scrutiny made all the more revealing by quiet humour and what appears to be complete honesty" (165).

African American women writers have created literature not for success, fortune or financial rewards, but to tell their stories and personal experiences: "In these lives, written by women who are marked by race and gender as objects and symbols of oppression, there is much to be learned, by women of other races and by all men, about the nature of survival – the principle of life itself" (Bell-Scott 413). They show how African American girls develop a self-resilient spirit in order to cope with an adverse external environment. They have brought a change in the way of thinking in the lives of African American people, especially African American women. Most importantly, twentieth-century African American women writers have broken new ground, created new literary canons, and paved the way for the writers of the twenty-first century. Bell hooks wishes to help make a world "wherein scholarship and work by black women is valued so that we will be motivated to do such work, so that our voices will be heard. I wish to help make a world where our work will be taken seriously, given appreciation, and acclaimed, a world in which such work will be seen as necessary and significant" (*Talking Back* 48).

In life writing, each particular incident, encounter and experience has its own story in the shape of a particular memory in the conscious and the unconscious mind; it is a liberating act of bringing it into the open by speaking out. Black women transcend the confines of intersecting oppressions of race, class, gender and sexuality. "How have African-American women as a group found the strength to oppose our objectification as 'de mule uh de world'? How do we account for the voices of resistance of Audre Lorde, Ella Surrey, Maria Stewart, Fannie Barrier Williams, and Marita Bonner? What foundation sustained Sojourner Truth so that she could ask, 'Ain't I a woman?' The voices of these African-American women are not those of victims but of survivors. Their ideas and actions suggest that not only does a self-defined, group-derived Black women's standpoint exist, but that its presence has been essential to U.S. Black women's survival" (Collins 108–109). The creation of independent self-definitions becomes essential to survival when Black women's very survival is at stake.

According to African American writers, the power to save the self lies within the self, no matter how oppressed an individual may be. In this journey towards personal empowerment, other Black women may assist a Black woman, but the ultimate responsibility for self-definitions and self-valuations lies within the individual alone. The act of acquiring a voice through writing, of breaking silence with language, eventually moves her to the action of talking with others. Self-definition is the quest to move from silence to language, to individual and group action. In this quest, persistence is a fundamental requirement for the journey. Black women's persistence is fostered by the strong belief that to be Black and female is valuable and worthy of respect. Her beliefs in self-definition, self-valuation and self-reliance that stem from her struggles to survive apprise the world of her worldview.

Chapter 4

Racial Segregation: Race against Racism

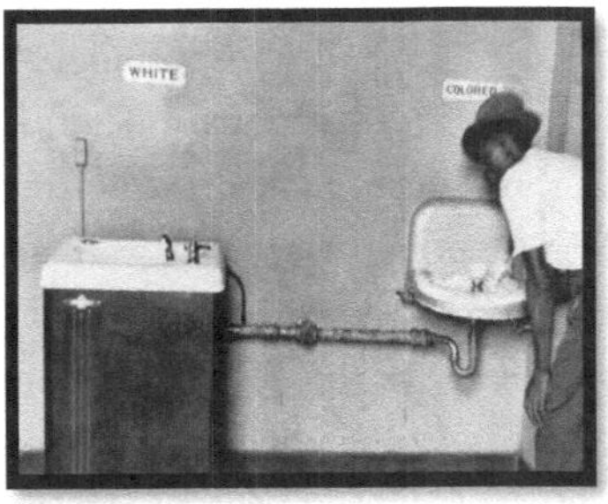

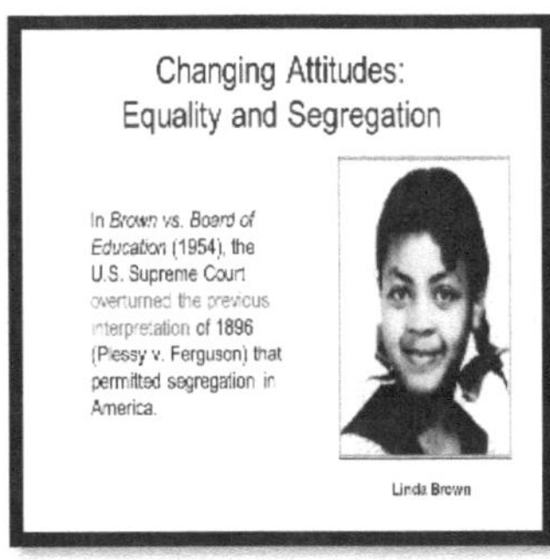

Reality can be (re) created by one who writes.

–Bell-Scott 25

Race as a mechanism of social stratification is of paramount significance in human history. The historical records show that neither the idea nor the ideologies associated with race existed before the seventeenth century. "In the United States, race became the main form of human identity, and it has had a tragic effect on low-status 'racial' minorities" (Smedley 690). Racial segregation in the United States encompasses the segregation of facilities, services, and opportunities in housing, medical care, education, employment, and transportation. It is the separation of humans into ethnic or racial groups, operative in almost every sphere of life, like eating in a restaurant, drinking from a water fountain, using a public toilet, attending a school, watching a movie, riding a bus, hiring a rental accommodation, or purchasing a house. The expression most often refers to the legally or socially enforced separation of African Americans from other races, followed by the general discrimination against people of colour by white communities, as well as physical separation and the provision of so-called "separate but equal" facilities, which are rarely equal. Racial segregation immensely affects the lives of African Americans, for they are not treated on humanitarian grounds.

The Congress passed the Reconstruction Act of 1867, and the ratification of the Fifteenth Amendment to the United States Constitution in 1870 provided the right to vote. The Civil Rights Act of 1875 forbade racial segregation in accommodations. As a result, the federal occupation troops in the South assured the right to vote to elect their political leaders. The Reconstruction amendments established the supremacy of the nation-state and formal equality under the law. However, they did not prohibit segregation in schools. By the early 1870s, the North lost interest in further reconstruction efforts, and with the withdrawal of federal troops in 1877, the Republican Party in the South split and lost support, while the conservatives took control of the Southern states.

Jim Crow segregation started in the 1880s and the disfranchisement of the blacks in the 1890s. Jim Crow laws were local state laws that enforced racial segregation in the Southern United States after the Reconstruction period. These laws remained operative until 1965, enforcing segregation in public schools, public places, public transportation, public restrooms, restaurants, and even drinking water.

By 1910, segregation was firmly established across the South and in most of the border region, and only a small number of black leaders were allowed to vote across the Deep South. "Poor educational opportunities, severely limited employment options, and segregation, as well as white violence and intimidation, all worked to keep blacks in an inferior social position and to persuade many that they were indeed inferior" (Megna-Wallace 19).

The legitimacy of laws pertaining to the segregation of blacks was upheld by the U.S. Supreme Court in the 1896 case of *Plessy vs. Ferguson*, 163 U.S. 537. The Supreme Court sustained the constitutionality of a Louisiana statute that required railroad companies to provide "separate but equal" accommodations for white and black passengers and prohibited whites and blacks from using railroad cars not assigned to their race. *Plessy* thus allowed segregation, which became the standard throughout the Southern United States and represented the institutionalisation of the Jim Crow period. Everyone was authorised to receive the same public services, but with separate facilities for each race. In practice, the services and facilities reserved for African Americans were almost always of lower quality than those reserved for whites; for example, most African American schools received less public funding per student than nearby white schools. All black students attended schools that were nearly all-black, with black teachers and only black students.

In My Place is a stirring story of Hunter-Gault's journey from a world of segregation — attending schools in the South where children often had no textbooks — to a world of international exposure, covering events of worldwide impact for a major news show" (Gale, "Hunter-Gault, Charlayne 1942 – Contemporary Black Biography," web. 15 Jan. 2017). Charlayne Hunter-Gault's *In My Place* throws light on the segregation prevalent in schools. "Her book gives a personal view of the turmoil and rage resulting from the Supreme Court's famous 1954 decision, rendered in *Brown vs. The Board of Education*, which ended school segregation" ("In My Place Summary," web. 16 Jan. 2017). The school where Hunter-Gault's mother teaches is several miles outside the town and befits Calhoun's description of coloured schools in Due West. Donald W. Calhoun describes the coloured school in Due West four years before Hunter-Gault is born: "It exists, and that is about all. The facilities consist of a large frame building, probably used in the pre-Civil War days, which contains rooms bereft of blackboard facilities to speak of and blessed by only the roughest of seating arrangements. The windows are mostly conspicuous by their absence, and the roof undoubtedly leaks. As to the type of instruction afforded, I do not have any specific information, but if it is influenced by the environment, it is poor indeed" (*In My Place* 12).

In 1940–41, the WPA (Works Progress Administration) built a new school named after George Washington Carver, improving upon the physical features of the old "coloured school" (13), but not the facilities. Five years later, in the town of Summerton, Reverend J. A. Delaine and a group of black parents filed a petition to their local all-white school board to simply get a bus so that the black children, like the white children, could have an easier time travelling the long distances to their little country schools. The school board turned it down, and they went to court asking not just for a bus but for education equal to the whites — services and school buildings. Hunter-Gault recalls, "It was to be the first in a long series of steps that would lead to the United States Supreme Court's decision that not only outlawed such segregated and unequal school systems but provided still another road leading me to my place in American society" (13).

Hunter-Gault, five years old, is the youngest and the tallest of all her friends but is not old enough to go to school. She decides to accompany Betty, her best friend, to the Washington Street School just to see what it is like. Nobody minds it, so she keeps going every day, and as a result, at the end of the first term, she gets her report card stating she is promoted to second grade. Washington Street School is the only school for black children in Covington, representative of how black schools are treated by the all-white school boards under their control. Few blacks are able to afford college, so classes are large, and the teachers have to carry a heavy load. There is no science or laboratory equipment, no playground equipment, barely a playground other than the gravelly expanse of red clay in front of the school on Washington Street. There is no lunchroom even, and sometimes, when the white schools have surplus orange juice, they give it to the black children to take home in jars. "Segregation had a profound impact on the quality of the education available to African Americans in the South" (Megna-Wallace 43).

The school does not have money for other things like crayons, art materials or even books for the library, but there is an active Parent-Teacher Association, and Hunter-Gault's mother gets involved, especially when it comes to raising money for the school. Every year there is a contest: the student who raises the maximum money is crowned as the queen of the school. There is a big program at night, and no one knows right up to the last minute who is going to be the queen, as the counting goes on up to the last minute. Hunter-Gault is the new queen as her mother raises $113 and a few cents, far more than the other contestants. Like the teachers, Black adults are aware that there is a difference in the distribution of teaching equipment and library materials. The teachers of the Black school work hard to teach students, prepare themselves, and give their best with the available facilities. Teaching is a mission for them; they see to it that their children learn and do not feel as if they are missing out on something, and they always teach their students to believe in themselves. After schools are desegregated, the Black teachers have more access to information. They find out that many of them are better qualified than the white teachers.

"Racial prejudice is an insidious moral and social disease affecting peoples and populations all over the world. It is diagnosed by the cataloguing of its various symptoms and manifestations which include fear, intolerance, separation, segregation, discrimination, and hatred" ("Racial Prejudice," web. 8 Sept. 2017). During Hunter-Gault's years at Washington Street School, the children tease her about her colour. This is her first encounter with racial prejudice, for she is mocked by other Black children for having a light complexion. After school, the girls from Short Street, "a rough part of town where people were always fighting, stabbing, or shooting somebody, especially on Saturday nights" (36), shout at her, call her "white girl," and push her into a circle to fight with another girl. She hates to fight, hates these scenes, and does not hit the other girl. She usually ends up getting hit by the other; however, her mother and grandmother never have such problems in Covington or in Short Street.

Hunter-Gault is enrolled at the E. R. Carter Elementary School when her family shifts to Atlanta. It is named after Reverend E. R. Carter, the author of *The Black Side* and other works, and a prominent A.M.E. minister whom Bishop Henry McNeal Turner calls "a preacher of the gospel [who] has few equals" (75). Reverend Carter is called a Race Man, a supporter of Black nationalism, for these Blacks are engaged in contributing and promoting the general advancement of Black people. The children learn Black history regularly from the teachers, who understand that while it is not within their power to give first-class citizenship legally, they can prepare them by transmitting a heritage that they can be proud of. The public school system does not provide schools with books or other materials that contain Black history, as they provide the white schools with books that contain mocking depictions of it. Eldridge MacMillan, who once taught at the Atlanta public school, tells Hunter-Gault of a discovery he makes after he is assigned to the former white school that has just been passed over to the Blacks. In the library, he sees some books lying over in a corner, one of which has a poem with illustrations of Blacks "looking like minstrels in raggedy clothes, croaker sacks, looking shiftless and lazy" (75):

"Nigger, Nagger, Ragger, Tagger
Going to the Mill
Up the Hill,"

This is what the white children are taught about the Blacks.

By the end of her first year in school, many Black families move to their new neighbourhood and many white families move out from there, and it is announced that the elementary school in the district will be given to the Blacks in the fall. "Racial segregation in urban housing became so entrenched that the majority of African-American women lived in self-contained Black neighborhoods where their children attended overwhelmingly Black schools, and where they themselves belonged to all-Black churches and similar community organizations" (Collins 12). Hunter-Gault is seriously disappointed to know that she will not be going to E. R. Carter, because by now she was quite comfortable with Carter and was sure to be with her friends in the seventh grade. Most of her close friends remain at E. R. Carter, while she and a few others from her neighbourhood start hoping about going to the white school that fall.

The white school is a beautiful school at the top of a hill overlooking Mozley Park. It also has a swimming pool, a large clubhouse with showers, and a beautiful hardwood dance floor. It draws crowds of young Black people, as nowhere else in Atlanta are better facilities than here. By the end of summer, Hunter-Gault is ready to go back to school. As she climbs the hill and walks through the doors for the first time, there is nothing white in sight: "only the ghost-whites that I conjured up as I climbed the stairs to my classroom and as I sat down in one of 'their' seats for the first time. It was a strange experience, being in one of 'their' schools. It even smelled different. Not better or worse, just different" (83). The only thing the whites leave is the school name—Frank L. Stanton—named after the poet laureate of Georgia, from whose poem the school song "Sweetes' Li'l Feller" is adapted, which they have to sing at assembly time. At first, none of them wants to learn this white song with the dialect which seems to mock them, but as the teachers insist on learning it, without any alternative, they sing it as their own. Hunter-Gault has a good year at Stanton; she adjusts herself quickly and gets involved in school activities, making herself worthy of the teachers.

During her final year in elementary school, the Supreme Court hands down its landmark Brown decision on 17th May 1954, "unanimously ruling that racial segregation in the nation's public schools was unconstitutional. The 'separate but equal' formula and farce that started with the 1896 Supreme Court Plessy vs. Ferguson ruling that mandated racially 'separate but equal' railroad carriages, and that, as the venerable *Atlanta Constitution* columnist Ralph McGill puts it, by the thirties had become 'a heavy weight on the nation's conscience,' was now to be consigned to ignominious history" (84–85). The case has its roots in several states, including Hunter-Gault's native place, South Carolina. It bears the name of Linda Brown, the schoolgirl from Topeka, Kansas, whose father, Reverend J. A. Delaine, an A.M.E. minister, files the case on her behalf that ultimately leads to the Supreme Court's order to outlaw segregated schools.

Like thousands of young Blacks all over the South, five-year-old Linda Brown had to pass a white school and ride a bus all the way in order to get to the Black school on the other side of town. There comes a time when Reverend Brown decides that little Linda has travelled long and far enough, so he offers his daughter as a test case, hiring the NAACP Legal Defense Fund to help her out. It was clear that none of them was in a school that was anywhere near equal to the white schools. Hunter-Gault recalls, "Even as late as 1960, in one of the most comprehensive studies ever done on Black Atlanta – 'A Second Look' – the Atlanta Committee for Cooperative Action revealed that Black students, who on average lagged two years or more behind their white counterparts, have been known to attend classes for weeks without being able to secure textbooks required for their courses; meanwhile, the practice continues of supplying Negro students with used or outdated texts discarded by Atlanta's white students." The study also pointed out that "many Black students had to travel ten miles a day to reach a school that will admit them; [and that] double sessions continue in about half of the Negro public schools'" (85). Hunter-Gault believes that she is probably better off in Atlanta than she would have been in the small town of Covington. Realising the rising court challenges to Jim Crow education in the South, the white establishment starts upgrading or building new Black schools all over the state.

The Black teachers discuss the Brown decision to understand exactly what it means and its consequences, such as whether they will have to compete with white teachers, who have power, if not superior training, and whether it will offer better opportunities to the students. "Henry McNeal Turner High School was probably one of those schools built by the white establishment to help them defend against integration" (87). It handpicks its faculty and administration and is far superior to Booker T. Washington, the only Black high school in Atlanta, and later the David T. Howard School. By the fall of 1954, Turner has the reputation of being the school for the Black *crème de la crème*—it means the best of the best in French. The school is named after Henry McNeal Turner, another A.M.E. bishop, originally from South Carolina, who had served as a chaplain in the Union Army and then in the Reconstruction Legislature of Georgia, with a distinction that earns him great enmity among whites. Hunter-Gault loves the high school as it is different from the elementary school and she feels grown-up suddenly.

She has just settled at Turner when very soon her mother gives news that they are going to Alaska. She is very upset to know this, as she does not want to go to Alaska, leaving behind the wonderful new world of Turner High School. The school she gets enrolled in, in Alaska, is called Ursa Major, after one of the two great northern constellations, also known as the Great Bear. Soon she meets her first disappointment when she gets to know that eighth grade is still elementary school. "I had lost not only my place but my freedom, too. It seemed as if I had been demoted" (93). In addition to this, she is the only Black student in the white school, with the inhibition of being inferior to the whites: "We were no longer taught by people who spoke our language, who understood our culture; we were taught by strangers. And further, we were dependent on those strangers for evaluation, for approval. We learned not to challenge their racism since they had power over us. Although we were told at home that we were not to openly challenge whites, we were also told not to learn to think like them" (bell hooks, *Talking Back* 99).

Hunter-Gault manages to catch up academically because "the South was behind" (97). Soon, her mother starts worrying about her grandmother and how her health might be failing. Her father remains busy from sunrise to sunset, coming home for dinner and then leaving for the servicemen's club. In late spring, at the close of school, she has a feeling that she is attending her last class in Alaska, and they leave for home without her father, who is to join them later. The distance created by earlier long separations from their father could not be bridged by staying together for nine months, but she is very happy to go home and be back at Turner High School in the fall.

At Turner High School, she realises that she has advanced academically and intellectually beyond the ninth grade. She joins clubs, the basketball team, and starts singing in the chorus. Victoria Sutton, her homeroom and English teacher, after seeing her excellent performance in tests and writing assignments, understands that she needs more of a challenge than what the classroom offers. Mrs Sutton believes in hard work, homework, and discipline, and is extremely protective towards Hunter-Gault. Another English teacher whom she admires is Elsie Foster Evans; her husband, Gilbert, is a Hampton graduate who works in a post office. Regardless of their qualifications, "Black men were shut out of the white world and its professions by rigid segregation, and unless they were self-employed, most of them ended up either teaching or working at the Welfare Department or in the post office" (108). Hunter-Gault enjoys the loving relationship of her teacher and her husband and wishes longingly for her parents to be like them.

At Wayne State University, she joins journalism, and here her roommates are two white girls from small towns in Michigan, Alpina and Dowagiac, who are not hostile towards her; it is a new beginning for her. At Frosh Weekend, a place away from campus where freshmen are required to come for orientation, she meets Kathi Fearn, a reserved Black girl from Washington, D.C., who is the only other Black fresh entry. They soon realise that their dormitory is quite segregated, with the whites on the right side of the corridor and all the Blacks on the left, with the exception of Hunter-Gault, as the authorities consider her white because of her light skin and never notice that she has come from a Black school. There is hardly any communication between the Blacks and the whites on the floor, except for Hunter-Gault and her roommates, and they live in two separate worlds in the "separate but equal" (133) dormitory. As in the dormitory, there is racial division on campus, which can best be observed in the dining hall during lunch, when one can see mostly all-white tables and all-Black tables.

Annie Adams, a Southern Black woman, describes how she became involved in civil rights activities: "When I first went into the mill we had segregated water fountains.... Same thing about the toilets. I had to clean the toilets for the inspection room and then, when I got ready to go to the bathroom, I had to go all the way to the bottom of the stairs to the cellar. So I asked my boss man, 'What's the difference? If I go in there and clean them toilets, why can't I use them?' Finally, I started to use that toilet. I decided I wasn't going to walk a mile to go to the bathroom" (qtd. in Byerly 134). Adams finds the point of view of the boss inadequate, develops her own, and acts on it. Her actions illustrate the connections among her lived experiences with oppression, her point of view concerning her experiences, and her acts of resistance leading to empowerment. "For U.S. Black women as a collectivity, the struggle for a self-defined Black feminism occurs through an ongoing dialogue whereby action and thought inform one another" (Collins 34). Speaking for oneself and crafting one's own agenda is essential for empowerment, for which Black women intellectuals from all walks of life must aggressively push the theme of self-definition.

One day, in a coffee shop at the Continuing Education Center of the University of Georgia, a guy dressed in army khaki trousers approaches Hunter-Gault and asks if he can join her for lunch. Walter Stovall is from Douglas, a small South Georgia town, fresh from the army and also in the Journalism School. Occasionally, the two meet and end up talking; Hunter-Gault finds him different, and they enjoy each other's company. One day, he invites her to the first football game at the university. They take their seats in the student section, from where they can see "the Black citizens of Athens who had come to the game and still had to sit in the segregated section known as the 'crows' nest'" (238). Hamp has interest in football, but the dean refuses, telling him that anyone from the two teams may try to kill him, as there is strong opposition from the whites.

Walter Stovall and Hunter-Gault spend time together, and she finds him increasingly appealing, with a great sense of honour: "To him, being unfair was dishonourable, and he saw clearly that segregation was, above all, unfair," and he treats her "like a desirable human being" (238). At Christmas, she gives him a copy of *John Brown's Body*, inscribing on it one of the verses they loved: "From a Brown Girl Bearing an Idle Gift" (239). They both decide to spend the rest of their lives together, as an act of love and defiance, "not as concubine and master, but as every segregationist's nightmare, husband and wife – only we couldn't tell anybody yet, because such marriages were illegal in the state and also unacceptable at the university," (242). Still, they live up to their beliefs and get married. Walter Stovall stops going to the movies because she will not get a seat in the segregated theatres, and also avoids the Varsity shop, as they will not serve her. They get married because they love each other. Despite the uproar they know it will initiate, they continue to be best friends. "What Hunter-Gault achieves in this extraordinary memoir is to convey the omnipresent daily textures of racism, and the strength and vitality of the Black culture that defied and transcended racism's seemingly unalterable codes" (Trachtenberg, web. 16 Jan. 2017).

In *I Know Why the Caged Bird Sings*, Marguerite and Bailey are amazed at the fast, noisy city life of St. Louis, which is in marked contrast to Stamps. They get enrolled in Toussaint L'Ouverture Grammar School, where they are shocked at the ignorance of their schoolmates and the rudeness of their teachers. The teachers in St. Louis "talked down to their students from the lofty heights of education and whitefolks' enunciation" (64), but in Stamps the teachers came from Arkansas Negro colleges and were friendlier than the formal teachers at St. Louis. The two learn to adapt to the new place, new school, new teachers, and new classmates in their own ways. She finds herself unable to settle in the high school, an institution for girls, as the young ladies are more prejudiced than any she had met at Lafayette County Training School. bell hooks also shares her experience:

"During my graduate school years, I dreaded talking face-to-face with white professors, especially white males. I had not developed this dread as an undergraduate because there it was simply assumed that black students, and particularly black female students, were not bright enough to make it in graduate school. While these racist and sexist opinions were rarely directly stated, the message was conveyed through various humiliations that were aimed at shaming students, at breaking our spirit. We were terrorized. As an undergraduate, I carefully avoided those professors who made it clear that the presence of any black student in their classes was not desired" (*Talking Back* 56).

The graduation day ceremony also brings forth the segregation and racial discrimination in schools. Marguerite is excited, as this is her eighth-grade graduation. She gets gifts from Bailey, Momma, and Uncle Willie as a token of encouragement, for she is one of the top students of the graduating class. She even likes her dress stitched by Momma for her graduation: "My dress fitted perfectly and everyone said that I looked like a sunbeam in it" (176). She hopes that the memory of that morning would never leave her, as everything is simply beautiful.

During the ceremony, Mr. Edward Donleavy, the white guest speaker from Texarkana, delivers the commencement speech. The white man who accompanies Mr. Donleavy to the stage takes the seat of the principal. Mr. Donleavy talks of the accomplishments of white schools in the area. He promises a paved playing field in exchange for votes in the elections. He speaks of a black individual's limited potential in the racist society and embarrasses the entire black community. He not only informs the black children of limited opportunities but also emphasizes the superiority of the white kids:

> "The white kids were going to have a chance to become Galileos and Madame Curies and Edisons and Gauguins, and our boys (the girls weren't even in on it) would try to be Jesse Owenses and Joe Louises" (179).

The black boys are considered fit only to be athletes or wrestlers, while the black girls fit nowhere in society; and the higher level of intellectual activity is reserved for the whites, the superior species. Everyone present listens to Mr. Donleavy's stereotypes of how white children could be thinkers and black children can only be athletes. A black mother in the South wrote to a national magazine in 1904:

"I dread to see my children grow. I know not their fate. Where the white girl has one temptation, mine will have many. Where the white boy has every opportunity and protection, mine will have few opportunities and no protection. It does not matter how good or wise my children may be, they are colored. When I have said that, all is said. Everything is forgiven in the South but color" (Lerner 158).

The proud graduating class of 1940 drop their heads, and "On the dais, the ancient tragedy was being replayed" (180). Mr. Donleavy awakens the graduating children with the bitter truth of their existence: "We were maids and farmers, handymen and washerwomen, and anything higher that we aspired to was farcical and presumptuous" (180). Hazel Carby suggests that the objective of stereotypes is "not to reflect or represent a reality but to function as a disguise, or mystification, of objective social relations," and that these controlling images are designed "to make racism, sexism, poverty, and other forms of social injustice appear to be natural, normal, and inevitable parts of everyday life" (qtd. in Collins 76–77).

Mr. Donleavy's supposed-to-be sincerely encouraging speech turns out to be another racist, stereotypical speech. After his address, which discourages the graduates and shows how inferior they are, Mr. Donleavy leaves the ceremony with the attitude that the graduation ceremony at Lafayette County Training School has been a mere preliminary, and now he is off to something really important. One of the most tragic manifestations of the pressure black people feel to assimilate is expressed in the internalization of racist perspectives. bell hooks shares:

> "I was shocked and saddened when I first heard black professors at Stanford downgrade and express contempt for black students, expecting us to do poorly, refusing to establish nurturing bonds. At every university I have attended as a student or worked at as a teacher, I have heard similar attitudes expressed with little or no understanding of factors that might prevent brilliant black students from performing to their full capability" (*Talking Back* 80).

Angelou writes, "It was awful to be Negro and have no control over my life. It was brutal to be young and already trained to sit quietly and listen to charges brought against my color with no chance of defense. We should all be dead.... As a species, we were an abomination" (180–181). Marguerite thinks about the colours she hates, "ecru, puce, lavender, beige and black" (182). Henry Reed, the class valedictorian, is not disheartened by the speech of Mr. Donleavy. He decides to renew the enthusiasm of the whole gathering of black people present at the graduation ceremony and delivers his valedictory speech, "To Be or Not to Be" (173), and suddenly he turns towards the proud graduating class of 1940 and sings the Negro National Anthem by James Weldon Johnson:

Lift ev'ry voice and sing
Till earth and heaven ring
Ring with the harmonies of Liberty. (183)

The anthem fills the blacks with pride and love for their race and promise for a better future. It demonstrates the great pride blacks have in their heritage. Angelou remembers, "I was no longer simply a member of the proud graduating class of 1940; I was a proud member of the wonderful, beautiful Negro race" (184). Thus, Henry Reed dilutes the negativity brought by the white speaker and glorifies the beautiful Negro race. Donleavy's stereotypical views of African Americans challenge Angelou's sense of pride in her academic achievements and upcoming graduation. The anthem renews her sense of accomplishment in making her aware of the struggles and achievements of her ancestors. "Angelou's description of her reaction to Edward Donleavy's speech at her graduation clearly demonstrates her personal opposition to Donleavy's belief that African Americans might only aspire to be athletes, domestics, or manual laborers" (Megna-Wallace 77). In each situation, individually or with the entire black community, Marguerite overcomes racism and proves that the blacks are not below the white race in any case.

In the 1940–1950s, before Anne Moody joins the civil rights movement, "African Americans lacked essential rights, such as the right to obtain an education equal to those offered to white children, and were often unable to exercise those rights they had, such as the right to vote" (Gale, *A Study Guide for Anne Moody's Coming of Age in Mississippi* 18). The African Americans of Mississippi face racial injustice in different ways including low pay, menial jobs, violence, and farmers not being allowed to produce enough on their land to make a decent living, followed by inadequate facilities in schools. Anne Moody, in *Coming of Age in Mississippi*, recounts her Willis High School, "the only Negro school in Centreville" (27), through which segregation in schools is brought to the fore. As a result of the 1954 Supreme Court decision, Wilkinson County, where Moody grows up, is a recipient of one of the new "Separate but Equal" (229) schools built throughout the South. It is constructed in Woodville on a fifty-two-acre plot. All the Negro high schools in Wilkinson County will consolidate into the new school, and it is supposed to be the largest new school in the state. Principal Willis is chosen by the state board as the head for this school, for he is considered the biggest "Uncle Tom" in the town: "Uncle Tom, which carried with it the recognition of complicity and internalized racism" (bell hooks, *Talking Back* 113).

Moody's class is to be the first to graduate in the new school building, and most of her classmates are excited about this—except Moody. While most of them think how good the white folks are to give them such a beautiful school, she thinks how dumb they are to accept it. According to her, the only reason the white folks are being so nice is that they are protecting their own schools: "Our shiny new school would never be equal to any school of theirs. All we had was a shiny new empty building, where they always had the best teachers, more state money, and better equipment" (229). The movement to end segregation prompts the government to build new, better schools for black students, but Moody is firm that they should not settle for anything less than complete equality, as represented by integration. She gets angry when she sees the "doctrine of 'separate but equal' for what it was: separate and inferior, with leftovers used to furnish African American schools, cast-off texts to educate African American students, and sometimes ill-qualified teachers forced through fear into passing along the safe doctrine of 'go along, don't make waves, stay alive'" ("Coming of Age in Mississippi: Researchomatic," web. 19 Jan. 2017). Moody is excited about graduation only for the fact that she is finishing high school and will be able to leave Woodville. She finally completes her graduation from Johnson High School. Neither Diddly nor Emma attend her graduation ceremony, but in the auditorium she sees her mother and blames herself for leaving her, who has grown very weak and looks too old.

After much persuasion by her mother, she agrees to spend a few days with her, and then she plans to go to New Orleans and get a job at a restaurant. She does not earn much from the business at the restaurant. She spends all her little savings while living with her father, as she was afraid to work for the whites in Woodville, and she just lived off her savings. She intends to join college but does not have a sufficient amount to pay for it. She calls her basketball coach, who helps her to get a basketball scholarship to Natchez College, a small college in Mississippi. She gets very disappointed to see the college in an old two-storey red brick building, and moreover, she does not like the food. She finds out that all students on full scholarship have to work part-time, and she gladly joins the kitchen, thinking she will improve the quality of food. But very soon she realizes she cannot make any improvement with whatever is provided, and she cannot even stand the cook, Miss Harris. She asks for another assignment and starts working as an assistant librarian.

Moody gets in an argument with Miss Adams, the Dean's secretary and the coach of the girls' basketball team. One day, as she is not well, she stays in bed for the day, and the next day she is given the assignment of washing the windows in the library by Miss Adams, for she thinks Moody had company during study hour in her room the previous night. Moody refuses to accept the punishment, for she has not done anything to be punished for. Miss Adams first calls the Dean and then President Buck to complain about Moody. The President agrees with Moody in the dispute, as he himself realizes that Miss Adams has silly rules for basketball girls, and he refuses to follow her rules. After this, Miss Adams makes life miserable for Moody. Still, she shows her strength and courage by always standing up for what she thinks is right, never caring about the risk involved.

After two months of college, Moody gets completely fed up and feels like a prisoner, as she cannot go out anywhere alone or without permission, and if they do not return by the time specified by Mrs. Evans, the matron will go in search of them. Her mother never questions her, not even when she leaves home and goes alone to Baton Rouge or New Orleans in search of a job, and here she is questioned for everything. Being a conservative Baptist school, there are so many restrictions on the girls. At the end of the school term, she is so sick of Natchez that she decides not to return for the next term; the schools in New Orleans cost a lot of money, and she returns for the next term also.

One day, maggots are found in the grits served to the students. Miss Harris, the cook, is a nasty old woman who knows that the grits are spoiled because of the leakage in the kitchen, yet she does not care and serves them to the students. Moody boycotts the school cafeteria—her first act of political activism—and the protest reaches the President. As the President is away for some work, Moody spends her savings to buy enough food to last for a couple of days. On his return, the President listens to the whole story from Moody and soon the leakage is fixed, the spoiled grits are thrown away, but Miss Harris is not removed from her job. For want of money, the students start going back to the school cafeteria, but Moody keeps her stand. She writes to her mother, who brings her canned food to last for the remaining semester. It is Moody's first experience in organizing a group of individuals to launch a structured revolt against the practices of an established institution, and this protest is a prelude to the sit-ins in the movement. She graduates with all A's and the highest average in the class, and this really impresses the President. The President recommends her name for a scholarship at Tougaloo College, the best senior college in the state for Negroes. She clears the test for the scholarship and receives a full-time scholarship. Her life writing is the story of her unbreakable spirit and character, and how she manages to excel in unthinkably odd conditions.

After learning of her scholarship, one of her friends at Natchez tells her that Tougaloo is not for people of colour. She asks what she means. She replies, "Baby, you're too black. You gotta be high yellow with a rich-ass daddy" (259). On hearing this, she fears going to Tougaloo College, because there the students are mostly lighter-skinned, who will look down upon her. Moody thinks of joining some other school in New Orleans, but by then it is too late to register in any of the schools, and so she heads for Tougaloo. On reaching the girls' dormitory and the room assigned to her, she finds that she has to share the room with "white-looking girls" (261). This disappoints her, but the next morning when she gets a glimpse of the campus, she feels happy, as it is beautiful, large, and spacious. For the new students' talent show, Moody, Freddie, and Paul perform tumbling and win the first prize; everyone is impressed by her, including the Dean of the College.

As classes begin, Moody discovers that she has only one black teacher for the semester, and this scares her, for she had never had a white teacher before. She remembers the whites in her hometown, "those that had Samuel O' Quinn murdered, those that burned the entire Taplin family, and those I worked for who treated me like a secondhand dirty dish towel" (266), but her roommate, Trotter, reassures her by telling her that the teachers on campus are all from the North and none from the South. "Northern whites have a different attitude toward Negroes" (267). The text is a presentation of Moody's constant struggle for survival against racism. It shows the amount of hate and rejection that blacks faced during those times. She creates "an unforgettable image of the inequities and violence that characterized southern society" (Gale, *A Study Guide for Anne Moody's Coming of Age in Mississippi*, 4).

In *In My Place*, Hunter-Gault remembers Reverend B. J. Glover, the preacher who tells her mother about the teaching job—a social activist who uses his pulpit as a platform for social reform. Black folks are not allowed to vote, and Reverend Glover comes to Due West on public agenda. In the late thirties, he attempts to register at the Abbeville County Courthouse, the county where Due West was situated, but even after passing the literacy test, the clerk dismisses him, saying that he cannot register him, without giving any explanation. The next Sunday, Reverend Glover rises to his pulpit and talks about black people registering to vote and the unfairness of his Abbeville courthouse experience. It draws the attention of the whites, including the Ku Klux Klan, a gang of white men who wear white sheets and come out in the dark and lynch any black person they can lay their hands on. One day, a group of white men stop him between Due West and Greenwood, take him in a car out of the county, strip him, ill-treat him, and beat him for five to six hours till he can no longer fight, and leave him to die in the woods. They call him a "nigger," (14) tell him to leave things as they are and not to act smart, but Reverend Glover survives, and his assaulters are never punished by justice.

In the early 1900s, many people in the United States saw African culture as something to be overpowered. Black people were said to be capable of working for white people only. The existence of African societies and traditions was unknown to many people: "European society was thought to be the best in the world, and surely everyone wanted to be like the best. So people who did things differently were backward. Many African Americans were ashamed of their colour and their African heritage... Black people were killed for all sorts of reasons, from being successful in business to talking back to a white person. Many victims were tortured; some were burned alive" (Porter 8–9).

Turner High seems "an idyllic island in a sea of segregation" (114), as Hunter-Gault states: "We were protected and isolated from most of the worst manifestations of segregation, hardly ever encountering overt hostility from whites" (114). There is a difference between the way most of the stores and restaurants treat Blacks and the way they relate to whites. From time to time, things happen that break their protected reality. One such instance is the murder of Emmett Till in August 1955—the first time Hunter-Gault and her friends know about the death of a young person—when they are in the eighth grade. He is shot to death for whistling at a white woman in a grocery store, and his mutilated body is dumped into Mississippi's Tallahatchie River. "Most of us had heard our parents, grandparents, or some Black adult talk with fear and/or bitterness about the Ku Klux Klan... and about lynching" (115). There has been nothing as dramatic as the murder of Till, and they can never forget the pictures of his limp, water-soaked body in the newspapers—worse than any image in a horror movie. "The whole spotted fabric of lynching has one thread running through it: The Negro must be kept in his place. Lynchings and threats of violence are but the more extreme expressions of the white man's determination to continue his exploitation of the Negro, which is most thorough when the Negro knows that he chooses between subservience and annihilation" (Megna-Wallace 28).

Angelou, in *I Know Why the Caged Bird Sings*, observes the happenings in the Store owned by Momma Henderson. Her insights into the visit of Mr Steward, the past sheriff of Stamps, to the Store and the activities of the Ku Klux Klan are those of a much more mature child than the one who first arrived in Stamps. She describes Mr Steward as "the quiet, bitter man who owned a riding horse… The used-to-be sheriff sat rakishly astraddle his horse. His nonchalance was meant to convey his authority and power over even dumb animals. How much capable he would be with Negroes. It went without saying" (17). This highlights the caste and class system in the rural South and how the Blacks were treated like animals.

Marguerite witnesses the pain and fear of racism when Mr Steward informs Mrs Henderson that "A crazy nigger messed with a white lady today" (17) and warns Uncle Willie to hide that night, as some of the Klan boys will be in search of that nigger. One incident brings the wrath of the whites on the entire Black community. It is too humiliating for Marguerite to hear from Mr Steward how her "uncle and every other Black man who heard of the Klan's coming ride would scurry under their houses to hide in chicken dropping" (18). They hide Uncle Willie in the vegetable bins in the Store to save him from the Klan boys, and he moans all through the night as if he had been "guilty of some heinous crime" (18–19). This makes evident the tense racial situation in Stamps during the Depression era. "In *I Know Why the Caged Bird Sings* one sees the traumatic fear and humiliation the threat of lynching inspires, and one understands that to resist the racial status quo was to risk death" (Megna-Wallace 26). The life writing covers a period from 1931 to 1944, realistically portraying life during the Depression and the Second World War.

Mrs Henderson is the only Black woman in Stamps who is referred to as 'Mrs.' One day, she hides a man in the Store who is trying to escape from people, as he had assaulted a white woman. He is summoned to court, and the judge questions him about his movements on the day of the crime, to which he replies that "he took refuge in Mrs Henderson's Store" (48). Mrs Henderson is called to court; the judge, the bailiff, and all whites present laugh at a Black woman being called 'Mrs' by a white man who does not know "that a woman who owned a store in that village would also turn out to be coloured" (48). A white man "assaulting white womanhood" (47) is summoned to court, but if a Black man assaults a white woman, he is "killed by whitefolks and thrown into the pond" (37), with no action whatsoever. These incidents are examples of segregation and lynching prevalent in Stamps.

The horror of discrimination and racial violence in the 1940s in Stamps is also presented through the incident when Bailey is sent on an errand to the whitefolks' town. He comes back to the Store shaking. "His little face was no longer black but a dirty, colourless gray" (195). After recovering from the shock, he asks Uncle Willie "what coloured people had done to white people in the first place" (196). He then tells that he saw "a coloured man" dead and rotten: "The man was on his back but the white man stuck his foot under the sheet and rolled him over on the stomach" (197). He does not understand why the whites hate the Blacks so much that they treat even a "rotten dead Negro" (198) so badly. The 'colourless' dead person is pulled from the river, Bailey is forced to help with the body and is threatened with imprisonment in the calaboose; he is horrified to the core. He is "locked in the enigma that young Southern Black boys start to unravel, start to try to unravel, from seven years old to death. The humourless puzzle of inequality and hate. His experience raised the question of worth and values, of aggressive inferiority and aggressive arrogance" (198). It is at this time that Mrs Henderson decides to go to California. She asserts, "we were growing up, that we needed to be with our parents, that Uncle Willie was, after all, crippled, that she was getting old" (194), and that the children will be safer in California than in segregated Southern Stamps.

Jim Crow was in effect throughout the time period of *Coming of Age in Mississippi.* Anne Moody "shows how absurd and arbitrary racial distinctions are" ("Coming of Age in Mississippi: Popular Essays," web. 18 Jan. 2017). One day, Uncle Ed, who takes care of Essie Mae and her siblings, takes them to their grandmother's home, where Essie Mae comes across two white-looking boys, Sam and Walter, who are also her grandmother's sons. She is confused as she does not understand why her uncles look white while all others are Black. She asks the reason from her mother; she scolds her and asks her to keep quiet, for it is not important. For the first time in her life, she confronts the difference in skin colour, and her mother fails to satisfy her curiosity. She grows up in a household where her mother would suppress any idea of questioning the way things were or the concept of segregation. She enters high school with a fresh insight into the life of Negroes in Mississippi. She had heard of Negroes found floating in a river or dead somewhere with their bodies riddled with bullets, but she does not know the mystery behind these killings. Her mother always tells her that it is the doing of an evil spirit, and if she is not a good girl, the evil spirit will kill her too. Since the age of seven, she lives in fear of that evil spirit, and it takes eight years to learn what that spirit is. "Moody initially sees her mother as a strict disciplinarian, a woman who tries to protect her daughter by withholding information. But as Moody matures and better understands the domains of power in her community, her ideas change" (Collins 203).

From one of the high school boys, Moody learns about the brutal murder of Emmett Till, a fourteen-year-old boy, in Greenwood by some white men for whistling at a white woman. When Emmett Till was brutally murdered in Mississippi in the summer of 1955, his thirty-three-year-old mother, Mamie Till Bradley, found herself in the centre of a national controversy. She wanted the whole world to see what had happened to her son, insisting that his battered body appear in an open casket at the funeral. This issue really bothers Moody, and she is acutely conscious of the prevalent racial inequality. She talks to her mother about the murder, who scolds her and tells her not to speak about it with Mrs. Burke, her white employer. Before Emmett Till's murder, she knows the fear of hunger, hell, and the devil, but now she knows a new fear, "the fear of being killed just because I was black. This was the worst of my fears" (132), and she is not able to sleep or work properly for days after this.

After a few days, she goes to work at Mrs. Burke's house, who is having a guild meeting with the eight women who are there for tea. She hears them talking about "nigger," "NAACP," and "that organization" (133). Back home, she asks her mother about NAACP and gets no answer. The next day in school, she asks her teacher Mrs. Rice, who informs her that NAACP is a "Negro organization that was established a long time ago to help Negroes gain a few basic rights" (134). She further tells her that NAACP (National Association for the Advancement of Coloured People) is trying to get the right to vote for Negroes in the South and is doing a lot for the Negroes. She also talks about Negroes being butchered and slaughtered by whites in the South. She also gives her a lot of information about the state of race relations in Mississippi. After knowing this from Mrs. Rice, Moody feels "like the lowest animal on earth. At least when other animals (hogs, cows, etc.) were killed by man, they were used as food. But when man was butchered or killed by man, in the case of Negroes by whites, they were left lying on a road or found floating in a river or something" (135). Mrs. Rice is the first guiding light for Anne Moody to the Civil Rights Movement, but her family does not understand her growing interest in the movement. "Like Mrs. Bertha Flowers in Maya Angelou's *I Know Why the Caged Bird Sings*, Mrs. Rice plays a pivotal role in Moody's maturation" (Nelson 282).

Moody's life is shaped by prejudice and racial discrimination that African Americans face in the South. She is fifteen when she begins to hate people; she hates the white men who murder Emmett Till and all the other whites who are responsible for the countless murders that Mrs. Rice talked about. She also hates Negroes for not standing up and doing something about the murders. She has a strong resentment towards Negroes for letting the whites kill them and looks down upon Negro men as cowards. Emmett Till's murder arouses anger and excitement among whites in Centreville. Every evening, guild meetings are held; canvassing teams and telephone campaigns are organized to add new members to the guild, and soon the guild organises two-thirds of the whites of Centreville as its members.

The most talked about subject is the love affair of Mr. Fox, the deputy sheriff, and Bess, a Negro girl who does general housekeeping and nursing for Fox and his wife. "White housewives began firing their maids and scolding their husbands and the Negro communities were full of whispered gossip.... The young white housewife didn't dare leave one alone in the house with her loyal and obedient husband. She was afraid that the Negro girl would seduce him" (137). Every young white man in Centreville has a Negro lover, whereas every Negro is afraid to walk the streets, for they can be hanged only for looking at a white woman. Emmett Till's murder is proof that for a Negro man, it is a crime, punishable by death, even to whistle at a white woman in Mississippi. Nobody ever hears of a single affair in Centreville between a Negro man and a white woman. "It was almost impossible for such an affair to take place. Negro men did not have access to white women. Whereas almost every white man in town had a Negro woman in his kitchen or nursing his babies" (139).

The next thing that is heard in the Negro community is how some white men had caught Jerry and nearly beaten him to death, who had made calls to the white operator. Jerry is Moody's classmate. Sheriff Ed Cassidy gives him a lift on his way home; he is taken to the woods and beaten badly by the white men and is left on the ground naked and bleeding. His father is too scared to take him to the hospital in Centreville to the white doctors, and when they try to file a case, the white lawyer disappears from Centreville within a few days. All the Negroes are shocked at Jerry's brutal beating in the town.

The most shocking and unjust crime occurs a few months later, which is a "terrible nightmare" (141) for Anne Moody. A whole family of Negroes, the Taplin family, is burnt to death at night by the whites. The Negroes from the neighbourhood silently look at "this debris and the ashes that covered the nine charcoal-burned bodies" (143). There is an expression of hopelessness on the faces of the Negroes, and Anne Moody feels an inflicting pain inside her: "Those screams, those faces, that smoke, would never leave me" (143). Mr. Banks, a high yellow mulatto man, has an affair with a white woman—the mother of three children—whose husband had left her. He lives next door to the Taplin family; for this reason, their house is burnt. Mr. Banks and the white lady disappear soon after the burning, while nine innocent Negroes are burnt to death. All these incidents are pointers to how interracial relationships lead to violence.

Moody is seriously disturbed by the events at Centreville, and as a result, she can neither concentrate in school nor at work at Mrs. Burke's house. As school is about to end, she decides to go to Baton Rouge to her Uncle Ed, who is now married and living there with his family. She thinks she will get a job there and will be able to earn more. Moreover, she wants to go for a change, as she feels like choking to death in Centreville: "I couldn't go on working for Mrs. Burke pretending I was dumb and innocent, pretending I didn't know what was going on in all her guild meetings, or about Jerry's beating, or about the Taplin burning, and everything else that was going on. I was sick of pretending, sick of selling my feelings for a dollar a day," (147). So she leaves home for the first time at the age of fifteen. The life writing is a social commentary and an exposé of racism in the South.

Samuel O'Quinn, a black empowerment activist and NAACP member, is murdered. His plans were to organize the Negroes in Centreville, but before he is able to organize his first meeting, he is killed. "His death brought back memories of all the other killings, beatings, and abuses inflicted upon Negroes by whites" (202). Moody hates herself and every Negro in Centreville for not putting a stop to the killings or at least putting up a fight. She thinks of waging a war in protest against the killings all by herself. She will take her savings, buy a machine gun, and walk down the main street in Centreville, cutting down every white person she comes across, as she is full of anger—for the whites and the blacks as well. Later, it is known that Principal Willis, the principal of the high school, is involved in the murder, but it never comes out which whites are behind the killing. Whenever Anne Moody sees Principal Willis, she is full of intense hatred and dreams about killing him. Moody reminds us of the relevant ease by which segregation flourished in American life for so many decades.

On her twenty-third birthday, as they are having breakfast and listening to the radio, a special news bulletin from Birmingham informs that a church is bombed in Birmingham, Alabama, where many Sunday school students are killed. Everyone is shocked to hear this, and Moody rushes out of the house crying and goes to the graveyard to communicate with God. In childhood, she used to go to the Sunday school church and was taught how merciful and forgiving God is. She thinks that God must be white too—that is why He is so merciless towards the Negroes. She asks God to kill her in that graveyard: "Maybe that's where all of us belong, anyway. Maybe then we wouldn't have to suffer so much. At the rate we are being killed now, we'll all soon be dead anyway" (347).

This incident has a terrible effect on Moody and makes her question everything she believed in. She loses her faith in God and even in the nonviolence policy of Martin Luther King. She strongly feels that there should be some other way; otherwise, there will be no end to the misery that they encounter. She remembers the Washington March where 250,000 people walked together for freedom, and this bombing is Birmingham's answer to the march. She had been taught that God says, "Thou shall not kill, Thou shall not commit adultery, Thou shalt not steal, and a number of other shalt nots," (371), but since she has been part of the movement, she has witnessed killing, stealing, and adultery committed against Negroes by the whites throughout the South. God does not punish the whites for these acts. The Negroes in the South, who are humble, peace-loving, religious people, are the ones who are suffering, as if they themselves are responsible for the killings and other acts committed against them. It seems to Moody that there must be two Gods, many Gods, or no God at all. Her writing is a reminder of the abhorrent racial policies practiced throughout the United States. "*Coming of Age in Mississippi* is filled with examples of the hatred that existed between the blacks and the whites in the 1960s and 70s, not written by an individual simply analyzing the situation but by an individual exposed to racism firsthand throughout her life and having to live with the fact that if you are black, you are less than white" ("Aunt Moody and *Coming of Age in Mississippi*: Analysis," web. 20 Jan. 2017).

Segregation in the world of religion is also brought to the fore by Maya Angelou in *I Know Why the Caged Bird Sings*. During the Easter program, Marguerite forgets the lines of the poem she is to recite in the 'Colored Methodist Episcopal Church.' Hunter-Gault also throws light on the segregation prevalent in the church in *In My Place*. The African Methodist Episcopal Church was established in 1819, with Richard Allen as its first bishop. Allen, a former slave, breaks with the Methodist Church over their insistence that blacks sit in seats separated from the whites. In staging a walkout at the St. George's Church in

Philadelphia in 1787, Allen is widely credited with starting "the first protest movement by Negroes in America … the first attempt on the part of Negroes to strike for dignity and respect for personality" (29–30).

One of the major events of their high-school years is the decision of Carolyn, Wilma, and Hunter-Gault to convert to Catholicism. It starts almost casually when they occasionally attend Mass. Interest in the Catholic Church grows among Blacks by now, owing to a much more visible and aggressive Church presence in the Black community. On their side of town, the Catholic Church builds a new church and a hospital which offers better care to the Blacks. "In fact, a beautiful new hospital was a godsend, because Blacks were excluded from all of Atlanta's fourteen general hospitals. Of the 4,000 available hospital beds, there were fewer than 400 for Blacks, and those were at the aging Grady Memorial, the city hospital … There were also about 250 beds in three small private hospitals owned by Blacks" (116).

Hunter-Gault is attracted to the ritual and mystery of Catholicism; she seems to connect herself more directly, more personally, with the Deity. The services in the church get longer and longer, and the preacher is more concerned with raising money than saving souls. Her conversion comes as a shock to her father, who is now stationed at Fort Jackson, South Carolina. Conversion to Catholicism is her first serious act of defiance, which her father, though hurt, chooses not to challenge.

Her father is a preacher, and as such he loves the soldiers, and they love him as he boosts their morale, telling them that everything will be fine and things are going to be better. They meet her father, Chaplain Hunter, if they have any personal or other problem. Her father is called in when army officers establish a recreation club for the white enlisted men, and the Black soldiers pay the club fees but are not allowed to attend the club downtown in Pusan. After her father is called in to negotiate, a separate club is established in the Black work area. Chaplain Grey Johnson tells the soldiers, "Black men dying in the service of a country that didn't give a damn about them back home" (70).

It is a conflict unique to chaplains like Hunter-Gault's father, and they just get to the point where they cannot stand it. A soldier dies for freedom, for democracy, fighting for a country that still keeps him "in his place" (71). The soldier still fights and dies for the ideal of American freedom and equality—if not for himself, maybe for his children. Hunter-Gault gets a glimpse of the pain her father silently suffers when, preaching a guest sermon on Sunday morning, he brings the battlefield into the pulpit and talks of his experience reading from the Bible to a wounded young soldier before he dies.

One Sunday morning, a white soldier and his wife, both from Mississippi, attend the church for the first time since their arrival in Alaska. Hunter-Gault's father walks into the chapel, and it becomes difficult for the white woman to sit and listen to a minister "who was Black." She listens to the minister preaching the Bible with a terrific voice and realises that he is educated, as his sermon is well prepared. As weeks go by, the sermons of this "Negro" become a source of great strength, and she makes "the minister's color as minor as possible" (94). After some time, the woman's husband is to have surgery, and the minister does much more than his duty, voicing things which she holds unsaid in her heart. The lady then decides that "everyone should have the right to an education, be they white or Black, but they must 'earn position' after that. The chaplain 'earned position' with me," (94–95), and together they pray for her husband's recovery, which gives her strength.

Her father is able to transcend race as he relates with everybody at a human level, and his services are easily the most popular on the post, attended by all races and religions, as he makes no distinctions in his counsel or his ministry. In the time of "slow, begrudging racial transition, being able to appeal to such a broad cross section of the post population was one of the few tangible signs of progress and achievement for a Black officer" (103–104). He spends hours talking about the problems of Black people in the military and in the town. "The military had been on orders to desegregate 'as rapidly as possible' since 1948, after a historic executive order by President Harry Truman" (94). In Alaska, Hunter-Gault's father is the only Black chaplain and one of only a handful of Black officers.

Hunter-Gault's father takes her mother out to a dance at a battalion party. During the evening dance, one of the Black officers asks the wife of his friend, a white captain, to dance with him. The post commander sends word to the table and tells this captain that they do not allow whites dancing with Blacks, proving that the army people are not comfortable with the idea of desegregation.

Hunter-Gault also faces awkwardness on the social side during a formal dance party organised by the school, which involves partners, and she keeps sitting the whole evening as no one asks her to dance. By the close of the evening, her teacher, Fred Martin, asks her to dance with him. Everyone else in the room notices this, but it does not inspire anyone else to be her dancing partner.

On another occasion, she goes with a group of her classmates to a teenage club near the school, where the man in charge does not allow her to get in, saying that only members are allowed to enter the club. He thinks she is an enlisted man's daughter, and the club is for the children of officers. In anger, her father goes to the club. The man says that the chaplain's daughter can join and confesses that he was not aware that she is the daughter of the chaplain.

I Know Why the Caged Bird Sings "focuses on themes of oppression, racism and sexism and dismantles prevalent stereotypes of black women" (Sickels PDF). Angelou explicitly depicts racism and segregation in Stamps in *I Know Why the Caged Bird Sings* through the prejudices she experiences at the office of Dr. Lincoln, the white dentist, who refuses to "treat nigra, colored people" (188). Marguerite has a terrible toothache, and Momma is not able to cure it with her homemade remedies, so she decides to take her to the dentist. There is no black dentist in Stamps, and the nearest black dentist is twenty-five miles away in Texarkana. Momma visits the white dentist in Stamps, for he owed her a favour as she had helped him financially during the Depression. They reach Dr. Lincoln's clinic and knock on the back door; a young white girl opens it and is surprised to see them. Momma tells her that she wants to see the dentist and asks her to tell him that 'Annie' is there. It humiliates Marguerite to hear Momma describe herself as if she has no last name: "It seemed terribly unfair to have a toothache and headache and have to bear at the same time the heavy burden of Blackness" (187). Featherston recognises the fact of Blackness by pointing out, "color is the ultimate test of 'American-ness,' and black is the most un-American color of all" (iii).

Marguerite and her grandmother wait for an hour in the sun. Dr. Lincoln comes out of his clinic and refuses to treat her because he does not treat coloured people. Momma reminds him that he owes her a favour, to which he replies that he has paid back the money he owed her. He adds, "Annie, my policy is I'd rather stick my hand in a dog's mouth than in a nigger's" (189). He does not consider Marguerite a human being, for he does not even once look at her. Momma asks Marguerite to wait for her downstairs and goes inside the dentist's clinic. She pressurises the dentist to pay her an interest of ten dollars on the money she had lent him during the Depression, and with this amount, she takes Marguerite to the black dentist in Texarkana. The white dentist's evilness and hostility towards a black patient, that too a child, heightens the prejudice prevalent at that time. From rape to racism, Maya Angelou has experienced immense hardships in life.

Hunter-Gault is excited to go to the E. R. Carter Elementary School and be a part of Miss Quarterman's special class, but she is distressed to know that she is not a part of Miss Quarterman's class and starts getting physically sick with stomach pain almost every day. In the beginning, her mother suspects that it is a case of heartbreak over not being in Miss Quarterman's class, but when the problem persists, she becomes so worried that she takes her to the army hospital at Fort McPherson. The doctor examines her for appendicitis and other signs of infection and gives medicine for indigestion. The pain continues, and he asks her to open her mouth and is confused to see her teeth missing.

Her mother explains to the doctor that she had once taken Hunter-Gault to the dentist in Covington when she had a minor toothache. He was the only dentist in the town and was white, who saw black patients on a certain day when there were no white patients and treated them in a cramped little lab where he made dentures and cleaned his equipment. It was full of dirty instruments and plasters that emanated a bad smell. He did not consider filling the minor decay in her permanent teeth; instead, he pulled two each from both sides in one sitting. The dentist neither prepared them for the pain she would suffer following the extractions nor told them what they could do to lessen the pain. He never told her mother that these were permanent teeth and needed to be replaced with some kind of denture. After hearing her story, the doctor explains that she is having stomachaches as she is not able to chew her food. So he sends her to the dentist, who begins the lengthy process of replacing the empty holes in her mouth, and she starts feeling better after the treatment.

Angelou lives in the segregated town of Stamps, Arkansas, in the South of the United States, during a period when segregation was still sanctioned by law. Segregation is so complete in Stamps: the blacks are the poor, powerless, ragged workers who are treated like slaves by the rich, powerful, well-dressed whitefolks. Marguerite can neither force herself to think of whitefolks as people nor believe them to be really real. She feels such because of their too-small feet, too-white skin, and their way of walking like horses on their heels. She calls them "others, the strange pale creatures that lived in their alien unlife, weren't considered folks. They were whitefolks" (26). She considers people who live on her side of the town as people, though she doesn't like any of them. Crossing the black area of Stamps in childhood was like a whole world for Marguerite and Bailey. But on reaching the white part of the town, all their enthusiasm flies. They thought they were "explorers walking without weapons into man-eating animals' territory" (25). Angelou exhibits a strong feeling of separation and segregation between the "whitefolks" and the "black people," and the devastating effect on the minds of the innocent black children. bell hooks explains the predicament of black Americans: "For black Americans living in a small Kentucky town, the railroad tracks were a daily reminder of our marginality. Across those tracks were paved streets, stores we could not enter, restaurants we could not eat in, and people we could not look directly in the face. Across those tracks was a world we could work in as maids, as janitors, as prostitutes" (*Feminist Theory* xvi). In such bleak conditions, black women were at a triple disadvantage, which bell hooks tries to explain in her writings, with hope to bring about change in their lives.

The poor, dirty, ill-mannered white children, referred to as "the powhitetrash children" (28) by Angelou, live on Henderson's land and antagonize her. They have an acute sense of superiority over the Blacks and know the amount of power their colour can exercise over them. They imitate, mock, taunt, and try to agitate her, but she remains unperturbed by their behavior, never loses her composure, and faces the white society by singing hymns. Such incidents, subjecting her to insults and humiliations, are daily reminders of being born Black, which means being lowest of the low. Momma demands cleanliness and manners from her grandchildren. She believes that "cleanliness was next to Godliness, dirtiness was the inventor of misery. The impudent child was detested by God and a shame to its parents and could bring destruction to its house and line" (28). Only the Black children follow these "customary laws" (28), as the powhitetrash children are mannerless, impudent, and shameless. Momma triumphs over the dirty white children who disgrace the whole white society by choosing not to stoop down to the level of the powhitetrash girls. Momma resists racism in a dignified way by offering passive confrontation. Dolly A. McPherson, in her essay "Initiation and Self Discovery," notes Momma's triumph over the powhitetrash girls: "On the one hand, three white girls, attempting to use their race as an overbearing instrument of power, treat a Black woman like another child, practicing the rituals of white power with the full sanction of the white community and attempting to reduce the Black woman to their level. On the other hand, the Black woman chooses the dignified course of silent endurance" (29).

Momma tells Marguerite and Bailey that the less they relate to the whitefolks or the powhitetrash, the better. She intends to teach them the ways of life which she and her generation and all the Negroes had found to be safe. "She didn't cotton to the idea that whitefolks could be talked to at all without risking one's life. And certainly they couldn't be spoken to insolently" (47), and herein she is not being a coward but a realist. Marguerite and Bailey follow the advice of their grandmother and remain quiet and serious in front of the powhitetrash children, "but if one of the playful apparitions got close to us, I pinched it" (28). Marguerite does so out of anger, frustrated by their behavior towards Momma, and because she does not believe in the reality of their flesh, they being white. She gets angry to see that even after their misbehavior, Momma treats the powhitetrash with respect and calls them "Miz" (32), while they call her by name. This gives expression to the caste system in rural Stamps, where the white children do not recognize Henderson as a human being owing to her Black colour. In "Singing the Black Mother: Maya Angelou and Autobiographical

Continuity," Lupton notes, "To survive in a racist society Momma Henderson has had to develop a realistic strategy of submission that Maya finds unacceptable" (132). Angelou is always full of explosive ideas. Momma Henderson sticks to her "strategy of submission" almost through all her dealings with the whites.

The whites are so much prejudiced in Stamps that a "Negro couldn't buy vanilla ice cream ... he had to be satisfied with chocolate" (49). The prejudice on the basis of colour of the skin is to such a great extent that the Blacks could not have an ice cream of white colour. Angelou remembers that "A light shade had been pulled down between the Black community and all things white" (49). The whitefolks, their women, children, wealth, houses, cars, clothes make the Black people envy them. They do not understand how the whites got the right to waste money this way. Marguerite believes that God is also "white" but no one can make her believe that "He was prejudiced," as her grandmother "had more money than all the powhitetrash" (50). Racism is an inherent part of the lives of the Blacks, and no member of the community can escape the ugly truth of marginalization. Every white thing seems hateful or unattainable; the white God seems distant, white cotton balls are difficult to work on, and even white vanilla ice cream is denied to poor Blacks. This makes the Blacks "develop a fear-admiration-contempt for the white" (49) in the South of the 1930s. Angelou portrays the life of a young girl as she learns "what it is to be Black under a solid racist regime that dictates white western society as the norm" (Carvalho PDF).

The Blacks draw strength from their community bonding in spite of their troubles and hard life. "Whatever was given by Black people to other Blacks was most probably needed as desperately by the donor as by the receiver. A fact which made the giving or receiving a rich exchange" (49). The Blacks are ready to sacrifice anything for each other. Although the whites have money which they waste, the Blacks depend on the generosity of their fellow Blacks. In "The Black Writer and the Southern Experience," Alice Walker writes, "What the Black Southern writer inherits as a natural right is a sense of community. Something simple but surprisingly hard, especially these days, to come by" (17). A feeling of fellowship and common brotherhood prevails in the Black community, for they all suffer at the hands of the whites in one way or the other.

The preparation for life is given to Black Southern girls in the home of a white family as a working woman. At the age of ten, Marguerite becomes an employee of Mrs. Viola Cullinan: "a white woman's kitchen became my finishing school" (Angelou, *I Know Why the Caged Bird Sings* 105). Mrs. Cullinan first pronounces Marguerite's name incorrectly as 'Margaret' and further shortens her name to 'Mary': "That's too long. She's Mary from now on" (108). In the former case, Marguerite does not like her name being spoken incorrectly by a fat white woman, and in the latter case, she is enraged beyond words to let some white woman rename her for her convenience and to suit her preference. One of the most important aspects of a person is one's name, and it is a great insult for anyone to change the name without prior consent—especially due to a racist attitude. Miss Glory, the older maid, whom Marguerite refers to as "a descendant of slaves" (105), tells her that her original name is 'Hallelujah,' given to her by her mother, which was changed to 'Glory' by the mistress twenty years back. She likes her new name better because it is short. Miss Glory symbolizes the passive older generation who chooses to be subjugated and conforms to the old history of slavery.

On the other hand, Marguerite confronts it, as she knows how to resist and revolt when necessary and is determined to keep her own identity. According to her, "Every person I knew had a hellish horror of being 'called out of his name.' It was a dangerous practice to call a Negro anything that could be loosely construed as insulting because of the centuries of their having been called niggers, jigs, dinges, blackbirds, crows, boots and spooks" (109). She decides to teach Mrs. Cullinan a lesson; she drops and breaks to pieces Mrs. Cullinan's favourite chinaware—a casserole shaped like a fish and the green glass coffee cups—acting on the advice of her clever brother, Bailey. First, the enraged Mrs. Cullinan shouts at her, "That clumsy nigger. Clumsy little black nigger," and later says, "Her name's Margaret, goddamn it, her name's Margaret" (110). This act of revolt and the noise of the broken crockery make Mrs. Cullinan realise that Marguerite's name was not 'Mary.'

By breaking the crockery given to Mrs. Cullinan by her mother, Marguerite asserts her identity—that is, her name, which was also given to her by her grandmother—and she will not allow a white woman to belittle it as of no importance. She proves that, as a Black girl, she will not tolerate Mrs. Cullinan's discrimination and, as a result, she resists and fights against it. This act "foreshadows Maya's eventual inability to sit quietly and is very much an expression of her growing acceptance of her own self-worth" (Smith, *Where I'm Bound* 131). She enjoys the importance of her identity, while earlier she had been indignant about her Black existence; this is her first act of rebellion and resistance. "Once an oppression is expressed, it can be successfully fought" (Bell-Scott 410). Angelou opposes this undeserved discrimination and yearns for her beliefs in equality to be heard. She looks back in anger at the racism and rape she suffered as a child. The incidents she endures speak of the horrible nature of racism. Racism is an inherent part of the lives of the Blacks in America, but it goes to the credit of determined visionaries like Maya Angelou who fight to preserve the dignity of their race and ancestors. Speaking about changing perspectives on Black identity, writer Toni Morrison said in a recent interview, "Now people choose their identities. Now people choose to be Black" (qtd. in bell hooks, *Talking Back* 113).

Anne Moody, in *Coming of Age in Mississippi*, also narrates the jobs she does in order to earn well, to fight poverty, and to rebel and resist against her white employers. She starts babysitting for Mr. and Mrs. Jenkins, a young couple. Mrs. Jenkins, whose name is Linda Jean—a poor white woman—treats Essie Mae nicely and asks her to call her by her name, as there is not much age difference between them. But her mother, Mrs. Burke, insists that everyone, "especially Negroes, call her 'Mrs.'" (94) and gets very angry to hear Essie Mae call Linda Jean by name. Domestic work fostered Black women's economic exploitation, yet it simultaneously created the conditions for distinctively Black and female forms of resistance. Domestic work allowed African American women to see white elites, both actual and aspiring, from perspectives largely obscured from Black men and from these groups themselves. In their white "families," Black women not only performed domestic duties but frequently formed strong ties with the family and children they nurtured. On one level, this insider relationship was satisfying to all concerned. "Accounts of Black domestic workers stress the sense of self-affirmation the women experienced at seeing racist ideology demystified." But on another level, these Black women knew that they could never belong to their white "families." They were economically exploited workers and thus would remain outsiders. The result was being placed in a curious outsider-within social location—a peculiar marginality that stimulated a distinctive Black women's perspective on a variety of themes (Collins 13).

Linda Jean shifts to another house. Moody agrees to work for Mrs. Burke, for there is no other source of income at that time, and to stop working would mean starvation. Mrs. Burke, a racist, symbolizes the white supremacy over the blacks, who try to do everything to break her spirit and make her do things their way: "She was one of those whites who would let her dog occupy a seat at her dining table before she would a Negro" (119). The moment she begins working there, she realizes that only Mrs. Burke has a negative attitude towards blacks, while all other family members are good to her and treat her as equal. "White supremacy threatens our existence and well-being, and act in complicity by internalizing racism and denigrating and devaluing blackness" (bell hooks, *Talking Back* 65). Mrs. Burke tries to rule over her, while Moody has her own little ways to resist her rule and domination, and finally Mrs. Burke decides to let her do things her way, as she has no complaints as far as her work is concerned and lets her be. Working with her is a challenge for Moody, who persists in her struggle with Mrs. Burke, and with her strength and stubbornness, tires out Mrs. Burke. She does not allow anyone to dominate her and does not accept being an inferior African American to any white person. Her story is the story of her struggles and triumphs in rural Mississippi. Domination always involves attempts to objectify the subordinate group, as bell hooks asserts, "As subjects, people have the right to define their own reality, establish their own identities, name their history. As objects, one's reality is defined by others, one's identity created by others, one's history named only in ways that define one's relationship to those who are subject" (*Talking Back* 42–43). Many forms that objectification can take are exemplified by the treatment afforded to black domestic workers.

At Baton Rouge, she gets a job at Mrs. Jetson's, a poor white woman who pays her three dollars for a day's work. She does not pay her for a week, and the next week she shifts her house, owing Moody two weeks' payment. For Moody, she is the worst woman she has worked with—worse than Mrs. Burke. She decides to go back home, but her friend Susie is able to find a job for her. She tells her to lie to the employers that she is eighteen, not fifteen, and that she has finished school, otherwise they will not hire her. She gets the job for twenty-four dollars a week and is considered "a pretty little sweet colored girl" (152). After two weeks, in a friendly talk with the lady, she discloses that she is only fifteen and has not finished high school yet, and the very next day, she is fired.

She goes back to Centreville with sixty-five dollars in her pocket and new school clothes. On her way back home, she meets her classmate Doris, who tells her about Benty and Mrs. Rosetta—another interracial affair in the town. She is disturbed to know about it, as Benty is her cousin. She is very nervous, and on reaching home, asks her mother about Benty. She finds everyone behaving strangely, and her mother scolds her for being interested in things like that. Moody finds nothing wrong in talking about Benty, who is their relative. "Negroes are being killed, beaten up, run out of town by these white folks and everything. But Negroes can't even talk about it" (154). Moody recalls what Mrs. Rice had told her while talking about the NAACP—that she should find something to do to change her mind. She should have fun and enjoy her life and not concern herself too much about killings, beatings and burnings, as "The Negroes here ain't gonna do nothing about them" (155). She intends to join the band, play basketball and take piano lessons to keep herself busy, so that she does not think about the Taplins, Jerry, Emmett Till or Benty. As soon as she finishes high school, she will leave Centreville for good.

Mrs. Burke comes to her house to ask her to start working for her again. She agrees and even tutors Mrs. Burke's son, Wayne, and his friends in Algebra. Wayne starts to have a crush on her, and on realizing this, Mrs. Burke gets very angry and makes life difficult for her. She calls Junior to her house for some work and accuses him of stealing her purse, and an angry Moody eventually quits and gets another job. Bonnie Thornton Dill finds in her study that the domestic workers refused to let their employers push them around, as one respondent declares, "When I went out to work … my mother told me, 'Don't let anybody take advantage of you. Speak up for your rights, but do the work right. If they don't give you your rights, you demand that they treat you right. And if they don't, then you quit'" (qtd. in Collins 107). An equal relationship between a black female and a white male is virtually impossible. Mrs. Burke demonstrates how senseless and destructive the whites' prejudice is against blacks. The insistence that feminism is really "a white female thing that has nothing to do with black women" masks black female rage towards white women—a rage rooted in the historical servant-served relationship, where white women have used power to dominate, exploit and oppress (bell hooks, *Talking Back* 179). In spite of busying herself with extra-curricular activities at school, she finishes her tenth grade with all A's.

She plans to go to New Orleans to her mother's sister Aunt Celia, to find a job as a waitress in a big-time restaurant. She is told that a waitress can make as much as fifty dollars a week, and she has to save money for college. She wastes a whole month searching for the job of waitress, but to no avail. Finally, she is able to get a job in a chicken factory, where all workers are blacks, who look very tired: "Some of them looked as dead as the chickens hanging before them" (177). The chicken factory is like a slaughterhouse, where Moody works for a month, as they pay $9.60 per day and she cannot earn so much money anywhere else. Back at Centreville, she feels herself more mature than other kids at school, because of her life experiences and understanding of the world after working behind the picket fence in the chicken factory. She keeps herself busy with basketball, gymnastics, tumbling and the church. Within no time, she becomes a regular pianist at Centreville Baptist Church, and in addition, she continues working for Mrs. Hunt. At the end of the year, Gymnastics and Tumbling Night is organized for the first time in the history of the school. Mr. Hick, the new coach, sponsors the program, and Moody is the only girl tumbler. The program is a great success.

In the next vacation, Moody plans to go to New Orleans again, hunts for a job for three weeks, goes to the chicken factory but finds no vacancy. Her grandmother Winnie works as a dishwasher in Maple Hill, a little restaurant on Maple Street. One of the boys who used to wash dishes with her is sick and will not be working for the next two weeks; Winnie asks Moody to join the job for twenty-six dollars a week. There also, all the workers are blacks, and Moody is pained to see how the white folks throw away so much food while there are so many hungry people who get nothing to eat.

Seeing her grandmother Winnie working at this age, Moody is pained at her hardships: "her twenty-some years on Mr. Carter's plantation, thirteen children and no husband, and always the hope of something better. But now she'd ended up in Maple Hill Restaurant washing dishes" (191). Moody is a beautiful girl now, and all the boys find her very attractive. She is promoted from dishwashing to a waitress; she learns almost every aspect of the restaurant business, from cooking to managing money and leadership skills. Among her coworkers are two gay men, Lola and Lily White, whom she befriends. Lily White is a strip club dancer; Lola teaches her to dress nicely and set her hair, which changes her appearance for good; she learns a lot from the work at the restaurant and her coworkers.

"In theaters, concert halls, and public auditoriums of southern towns, the Negro is either excluded or permitted to occupy only some special section which he must usually reach through a side or back entrance. Rural communities seldom have even this provision for Negroes" (Megna-Wallace 48). Moody speaks about the segregation in movie theatres as well. On Saturday evenings, her mother takes them for movies: "The Negroes sat upstairs in the balcony and the whites sat downstairs" (*Coming of Age in Mississippi* 33). One Saturday, they arrive at the movie at the same time as the white children who live near their house and play with them. They are happy to see them, and they follow the white children to the downstairs lobby. Their mother is busy talking to someone, and when she sees them in the white lobby, she gets angry, drags them through the door, and takes them out crying. They hear the white children crying inside the white lobby, and after that, they are not allowed to watch the movie and are taken back home by their mother: "All the way back to our house, Mama kept telling us that we couldn't sit downstairs, we couldn't do this or that with white children. Up until that time I had never really thought about it. After all, we were playing together. I knew that we were going to separate schools and all, but I never knew why" (33).

Essie Mae confronts the issue of race from a very early age, but she never realises that in the movies sitting downstairs is any better than sitting upstairs, but now she realises that it was: "Their whiteness provided them with a pass to downstairs in that nice section and my blackness sent me to the balcony" (34). After this incident, the white children stop playing with them; after two weeks, they are there again to play with them, but things have changed. "The ensuing ruckus brought her the sad realisation that she was perceived as inferior to whites. Rather than railing at the unfairness of this perception, she became an observer, an inquisitor into the strange idea that skin colour had anything to do with who she was" ("Coming of Age in Mississippi: Researchomatic," web. 19 Jan. 2017).

Moody has never really thought of them as whites before: "Now all of a sudden they were white, and their whiteness made them better than me because they were white, but everything they owned and everything connected with them was better than what was available to me" (34). On thinking, she realises that the schools, homes, and streets of the whites are far better than that of the blacks, and it bothers her that the whites have all the nice things and they have nothing. "There is a secret to it besides being white" (34). She always remains confused about it, and whenever she asks her mother about white people, she is outraged. As a young child, she struggles to understand the inequity between the races, and she wonders if there is any real difference between blacks and whites, save for the fact that the black woman cleans the white woman's homes, indicating how dependent middle-class white families are on the blacks.

A glimpse of segregation in the Southern town of Stamps is given by Maya Angelou in *I Know Why the Caged Bird Sings* through the incident when Bailey goes to see a movie starring a white movie star, Kay Francis, who resembles their mother. It grows dark, and Bailey is not home; everyone gets worried. Marguerite describes her grandmother's worry: "The Black woman in the South who raises sons, grandsons and nephews had her heartstrings tied to a hanging noose. Any break from routine may herald for them unbearable news. For this reason, Southern Blacks until the present generation could be counted among America's arch conservatives" (114). They go out in search of

Bailey, and when they find him, he neither gives any explanation nor reacts to the beating given to him by Uncle Willie.

After a few days, he tells Marguerite that he got late for he saw a double show of the movie, for the white star in the movie resembled their mother, and he promises to take her to the movie when any other picture would come to Stamps starring Kay Francis. After two months, a movie starring Kay Francis is put up, and both children go to watch it. Marguerite finds a subtle depiction of racism propagated through cinema. In the movie, the beautiful white star's maid was 'Black' and her driver a 'Negro,' suggestive of the fact that all the menial jobs are meant for the blacks. The cinema affirmed the lowest rank of the blacks in the strata of American society. Segregation is operative in movie theatres too: "The whitefolks downstairs laughed … throwing the discarded snicker up to the Negroes in the buzzards' roost" (118). Marguerite is, however, happy, for the big movie star looked just like her mother. The white folks laugh every few minutes watching the movie: "I laughed too, but not at the hateful jokes made on my people. I laughed because, except that she was white, the big movie star looked just like my mother. Except that she lived in a big mansion with a thousand servants, she lived just like my mother. And it was funny to think of the whitefolks' not knowing that the woman they were adoring could be my mother's twin, except that she was white and my mother was prettier. Much prettier" (118–119). Marguerite also tells the story of the white woman who would not sit beside the "Negro civilian on the streetcar" (213), bringing forth the segregation present in the means of public transportation too.

Marguerite is aware of the harshness of racial discrimination and is afraid of the future of the black community. She describes the congregation of the black community around the radio in the store to listen to the boxing matches. Listening to the radio, she wonders whether the announcer knew the fact that "he was addressing as 'ladies and gentlemen' all the Negroes around the world who sat sweating and praying, glued to their 'master's voice'" (134). She further describes the pain and suffering of the black community and how the whites treat them: "My race groaned. It was our people falling. It was another lynching, yet another Black man hanging on a tree. One more woman ambushed and raped. A Black boy whipped and maimed. It was hounds on the trail of a man running through slimy swamps. It was a white woman slapping her maid for being forgetful." They accuse them of being lower types of human beings: "Only a little higher than the apes" (135). The blacks believe that God Himself hates them and ordains them "to be hewers of wood and drawers of water, forever and ever, world without end" (135).

In the boxing match, Joe Louis, a black boy, wins the heavyweight championship of the world. A black mother's son "was the strongest man in the world" (136); a black fighter dares to compete for the title of Heavyweight Champion of the World. "From Angelou's description it appears that the outcome of the fight has a direct correlation to her people's destiny and self-worth" (Megna-Wallace 123). As Joe Louis represents his people and wins, his triumph is for blacks everywhere, and some black people do not return home but stay overnight in town, as they are not afraid to be on a country road at night when Joe Louis has proved "we were the strongest people in the world" (136). Maya Angelou mirrors the American landscape, paving the way for a "firsthand experience with racism, single parenting, over-coming poverty, seeking higher education, creating wealth, living through and participating in the civil rights movement" ("Maya Angelou Leadership and Legacy," web. 20 Jan. 2017).

Paule Marshall's *Triangular Road* is a recollection of her quest as a young black female writer trying to find footing in the white patriarchal literature. She tells the story of her years as a fledgling young writer in the 1960s and her involvement in the civil rights movement. She receives a letter from Langston Hughes asking her to accompany him on a cultural tour of Europe, and if she is interested in joining the tour, she will have to go to Washington to be briefed beforehand. She takes the plane to Washington; her dossier is required at the State Department office where the briefing is held. Her dossier contains a detailed account of her involvement in every political organization that she has been a part of. The two organizations within the northern front of the Movement are AYD, American Youth for Democracy, the Communist Party fringe, and the Association of Artists for Freedom and Concerned Mothers for Justice. The principal activity of the two organizations was to support the voting rights efforts in the Deep South by raising funds. Her file also includes the transcript of every speech she had given against the government. On record is also the list of each rally, protest, meeting, demonstration, and march she had participated in, including the Anti-Vietnam War March, the first ever Joint Civil Rights March which had taken place in the previous winter at Times Square.

The government officer conducting the briefing turns out to be a matronly woman who, on seeing Marshall's dossier, says, "Seems you've been fairly active" (8). Putting the dossier aside, she begins the briefing by giving the history of the government's cultural programs around the world. She goes on to describe their particular tour, the various European cities they will be visiting, and the general nature of their activities: "The United States Information Service (USIS) people in charge of 'operations on the ground' in each city would have a detailed schedule of those activities" (9). On a lighter note, she talks about the places they will be visiting, informing her about the food and weather conditions there. Paris will be their base camp, as the tour will begin from there and they will regularly return after visits to other places.

The woman speaks for an hour but never again mentions Marshall's dossier, filled with her condemnation and actions against the government, lying between them on her desk. Her quarrel with the U.S. government is a matter of record, yet they are perfectly willing to send her on a trip to Europe for a month, paying all expenses. She is confused that the government, knowing she will be as outspoken abroad as at home, still agrees to let her accompany Langston Hughes. She concludes that her being openly critical of its policies can well serve as proof that the country is "truly a democracy committed to respecting the First Amendment Rights of even its most vocal detractors" (10–11). Every time she opens her mouth, Washington will come out the winner. The relegation of her dossier to one side by the civil servant implies that "The file might have been trotted out simply to put me on notice that Big Brother was watching and would continue to watch. So be it, then" (11). Marshall decides that, whatever the reason may be, she will definitely go on the tour with a world-famous writer and will speak her mind about the government when asked to: "Speaking out would be a way of making use of being used – if, indeed, such was the case" (11).

They reach Paris and stay in the California Hotel, with small, plain rooms. Marshall believes that the State Department people in Paris could have arranged far better accommodation for them. The first phase of the tour becomes "a busy round of lectures, readings, seminars, panels, panel discussions, colloquia, roundtables, roundtable discussions – and talks" (15). Each of these is followed by a reception and more talk at the end of the day. The subject of the events, as stated, is African American literature, but the question-and-answer sessions that follow the formal presentations are consistently more about the freedom struggle in the States and less about literature. The audience consists of progressive-minded young graduate students and scholars eager for firsthand information on the movement and the government's response to the mounting pressure for change.

Langston Hughes is the star attraction, but he tends to leave such discussions to Bill Kelley and Paule Marshall. As they are too willing to stand in for him, they describe in vivid terms the violence meted out to protesters in the Deep South: "The police dogs being sicced on them, the policemen's billyclubs beating them to the ground, the huge fire-engine water hoses turned on them full blast, and black children as young as twelve being thrown in jail" (16). They point out that in the Civil Rights Movement the primary issue at the moment is to give the green signal for a comprehensive voting rights bill. All efforts are focused on pressurising Congress to pass the bill this year in spite of fierce opposition from southern members in both houses, and this is seen as being misled or delayed on the president's part.

In the course of their lectures and talks in Paris, the audience repeatedly brings forth the subject of black-white relations and attendant racism. Marshall and Kelley, the other fledgling writer chosen by Hughes for the tour, do not hesitate to speak in detail about the lingering racist nature of American society, citing the political, social, and economic institutions – including government policies – that uphold and aggravate the problem. "For us, true speaking is not solely an expression of creative power; it is an act of resistance, a political gesture that challenges politics of domination that would render us nameless and voiceless. As such, it is a courageous act – as such, it represents a threat. To those who wield oppressive power, that which is threatening must necessarily be wiped out, annihilated, silenced" (bell hooks, *Talking Back* 8).

Marshall thinks that Hughes might have been remembering his own personal trials and tribulations at the hands of the U.S. government, so he usually maintains reflective silence. He is labelled as the most dangerous radical in America by the government. It is said that, to save his career, he had to deny his socialist and communist principles: "For this he had been severely criticized, even denounced by many in the black community: He had betrayed W. E. B. Du Bois; he had betrayed Paul Robeson – those two giants who had remained faithful to the cause" (18). Langston Hughes had endured all this only to be embraced again by black America, as well as called upon by the government to serve as the cultural ambassador of the world. The contradiction and the illogic of it account for the expression on his face that he cannot understand white as well as black folks.

London is the second city on their itinerary, and the African House in London follows the pattern established in Paris. Their talk on African American literature is largely supplanted by a discussion of the movement. The discussion takes an ugly turn, for a number of young British-born blacks in the audience attack Hughes personally. Marshall is ignored by them, and they level their criticism at him alone. After listening to the accusations against him, he speaks in an outraged voice. He informs the young critics that the revolution present in black America did not begin yesterday, nor will it end tomorrow. He and his generation have done their part: "marching, demonstrating, picketing; they had protested the horrendous lynchings and burnings of the 1920s and '30s; had defended the innocent – the Scottsboro Boys, 1931" (21). Nine young black men were falsely accused of raping a white woman, and the fight to free them, in which he had been deeply involved, had gone on for years. All this happened long before any of those present in the audience had been born. He subjects the young blacks to a crash course in twentieth-century African American history. He concludes that monumental work is still to be done, and instead of passing judgments, making comparisons, or taking a superficial view of people and events, it is for them to educate themselves and to understand the complexity of the struggle that fundamentally involves people of colour around the world. Racial segregation remains a fundamental feature of the U.S. social landscape, leaving many African Americans with the belief that "the more things change, the more they stay the same" (Collins 26).

In the second chapter entitled "I've Known Rivers: The James River," Marshall builds on the slave trade. Paule Marshall and her friend Virginia decide to spend part of their Labour Day holiday on the north bank of the James River, a major artery of the slave trade, close to where it flows through the heart of Richmond. The river courses east some three hundred miles across the state and reaches Jamestown, the first permanent English settlement in America, and so the James River is "America's most historic river" (36). They reach the beach and find an ideal spot to sit on a somewhat flat stone that calls to Marshall's mind the oversized ottoman under a tall oak tree with breeze blowing gently.

Marshall and Virginia have been friends since she came to live in Richmond twenty years ago. Both are travelling women who love to move around the world, and this is the cause of the immediate bond between them. Marshall comes to Richmond for a two-year contract job as Writer-in-Residence at Virginia Commonwealth University, and after completion of the two-year contract she is invited to stay on as a permanent member in the graduate creative writing program. Marshall and Virginia meet after a long time on Labour Day and share the latest happenings; Marshall tells her about the African American Writers' Conference in Paris, and Virginia tells her about the events in black Richmond that took place during her absence. They talk about their children, their lives, books, writers, and the morning passes in pleasant conversation.

On Labour Day, Marshall reflects upon the work done by the slaves, work neither recognised nor honoured in the great national holiday. James River brings her memories of the slave trade that was carried on during the night, as its tidewater offered "safe passage to the ships up from the Atlantic, with their chattel cargo, that made for the wealth and status the Old Dominion would enjoy for nearly two centuries" (45). The chattel, the black slaves, was brought into town only at night, marched chained together at the neck and legs along the riverbank over to the Mayo's Bridge, the first to link the river's north and south banks, which in turn collected them in Old Richmond Town on the north bank. At daybreak, in a place separate from the town called the Bottom, the shipment was put up for sale among a group of traders, agents, suppliers, exporters, commodities brokers, auctioneers, and scores of large and small independent buyers.

Richmond "was the principal port of entry for Africans brought to the New World in the eighteenth century" (47). Often the buying and selling took place on board the ship the moment it landed; the trade was so quick, and plenty of money was made out of it. At times, "scrambles" (47) were held in the small towns and villages along the James before the ships reached Richmond. In "scrambles," the chattel cargo was taken off the boat and put into a fenced-in yard with a locked gate. A crowd of eager buyers, each with a long rope, would be waiting outside. As the gate was opened, the "scrambles" began, with the buyers dashing about the yard, desperate to loop and enclose as many chattels as possible, ignoring their terrible condition. The demand was great, as they needed manpower to produce tobacco, the cash crop of all time, to which all Europe was addicted at that time. They also worked as "hired-out hands (their wages paid to their owners)" (50), in factories, mills, tobacco warehouses, and munitions plants that had made possible harnessing the falls of the James, and were also used as servants in the big houses that were soon made along the tidewater.

During her first week in Richmond, on a stroll downtown, Marshall encounters a group of women in full Scarlett O'Hara garb, accompanied by men in grey uniform with swords at their sides. No longer is she a published novelist and teacher living in the last quarter of the twentieth century. "For a hairbreath of a second, time reverses itself … I'm suddenly chattel cargo, merchandise, goods, a commodity to be bought and sold" (51). She quickly regains perspective and realises that she has encountered Civil War reenactors—people who choose, for a period of time and for various reasons, to relive an era when it was legal to own another human being.

In the weeks before the classes begin, Marshall takes a self-administered crash course on the Old Dominion, the early southern history. One evening, searching the stacks of books, she gets the despised Edict of 1808:

Be it enacted, by the Senate and the House of Representatives of the United States of America in Congress assembled, that from and after the 1st day of January, 1808, it shall not be lawful to import into the United States from any of the kingdoms of Africa any Negro with the intent to be sold or to be held to service or labour. (Italics original 53)

Bringing an end to the slave trade when there was still so much work to be done caused much uproar—work that was to be done only with the strength and muscle power of the African people. The purposeful breeding and sale of homegrown chattel was the quickly found way out to maintain the supply of African slaves and to add to it. It proved successful, and by the mid-1800s there was surplus chattel labour, which was again put by cart into Richmond Town and quickly sold in the Bottom. The river and the railroad provided the final solution for the surplus chattel labour.

Point Comfort was the name given in 1607 to the actual landing site of the first band of English settlers. After years, it became the place where the first "scrambles" (57) took place. More than twenty Negroes were put up for sale at Point Comfort, exchanged for sacks of corn, beans, and oats or meat, but not for money, and were quickly led to the work awaiting them, as were the eight million Negroes like them who followed over the centuries. Virginia's great-grandparents on her mother's side were also chattel labour, and once they were free of slavery, they became sharecroppers. "The vast majority of African-American women were brought to the United States to work as slaves in a situation of oppression. Oppression describes any unjust situation where, systematically and over a long period of time, one group denies another group access to the resources of society. Race, class, gender, sexuality, nation, age, and ethnicity, among others, constitute major forms of oppression in the United States. However, the convergence of race, class, and gender oppression characteristic of U.S. slavery shaped all subsequent relationships that women of African descent had within Black American families and communities, with employers, and among one another. It also created the political context for Black women's intellectual work" (Collins 6).

The Negroes who arrived at Jamestown's Point Comfort came by way of the West Indies rather than directly from Africa. Their island of origin might have been Barbados, "Barbados being, circa 1600, as important a holding pen and transshipment point as Richmond, Virginia, would become, circa 1820, owing to a surplus at the time of locally bred chattel" (61–62). It is the easternmost lonely island some distance out in the Atlantic, geographically the closest point in the Caribbean to West Africa. "Barbados, British-owned and colonized from the beginning, was a principal way station at the outset of the trade" (63). Barbados was the first small piece of land sighted on the long Atlantic run when the trade in chattel cargo began in earnest. "The island was at once landfall and a safe haven, with a natural harbour along its Caribbean coastline" (62). The chattel cargo who managed to survive the crossing were prepared for market at Barbados. They were cleaned and fed to put flesh on them, and then the better part of the cargo was transported from one ship to another for sale up and down the hemisphere. Those who were left behind were put to work on the tobacco fields and later on sugarcane estates. Marshall can feel her ancestors' torment acutely: "The history of colonization, imperialism is a record of betrayal, of lies, and deceits. The demand for that which is real is a demand for reparation, for transformation. In resistance, the exploited, the oppressed work to expose the false reality – to reclaim and recover ourselves. We make the revolutionary history, telling the past as we have learned it mouth-to-mouth, telling the present as we see, know, and feel it in our hearts and with our words" (bell hooks, *Talking Back* 3).

Virginia informs Marshall that while she was away, there was an official talk to put up a historical marker at the Manchester Docks, where people who resembled her were purchased like cattle for lifetime bondage. Marshall replies that it might take a long time to happen or may not happen at all, and Virginia agrees with her. With this, they gather up the things they had brought along and start climbing up the north bank, leaving behind the oak tree, the stone ottoman, and "the once-pristine but now shamefully polluted and ill-used river" (60). It is polluted by becoming a dumping ground for generations of human and animal waste, dangerous industrial contaminants, and tons of sulfuric acid from the Civil War arsenals, armouries, and munitions plants, and it was ill-used for the trading of Negroes as slaves, chained and kept like animals. Paule Marshall is "steeped in slavery's legacy; it permeates her work and her worldview" (Juris, web. May 2009). The title

Triangular Road also alludes to the Triangular Trade beginning in the seventeenth century, when raw materials were sent from the New World back to Europe, which produced goods that were shipped to Africa, where they were exchanged for human beings transported to America and sold into slavery. In *The New York Times*, Marshall opines, "This is my attempt to get a fuller picture. We need to see the triangular nature of our inheritance and our place in the world" (Lee C1).

One day, while in Grenada, Marshall sees a political rally of the long-standing chief minister, Eric Matthew Gairy, "a man disdained, even hated, by the white planters and the small Black and Creole bourgeoisie in town, while adored by the masses of poor Black country folk" (133). Marshall, without any hesitation, decides to attend the rally, takes some sandwiches with her, and sets off down the main road on foot, catching the bus in St. George's, "Grenada's pretty little colonial capital" (134). According to the bus driver, the rally is special and will be "held on the carenage, the local name for the long curving wharf that faithfully repeated the horseshoe outline of the harbour" (134). By the time Marshall reaches town, it is well past noon and the entire carenage is packed to overflowing with the chief minister's supporters.

The only standing room to be found is on a narrow roadway above the harbour, where Marshall joins a small group of onlookers from town already gathered there. What follows is an endless wait in the crucifying mid-afternoon heat. Finally, the distant figure of the chief minister on the deck of the sailboat is seen, dressed in white, only his face Black amid all the white apparel. He speaks about the many bills he is fighting to get passed in Parliament to improve the condition of his supporters. He tells them that only for their welfare is he in politics. He repeatedly reminds them of the upcoming general election. As always, he is depending on their votes. Another of his impassioned themes is full independence: "Finish with this so-called home rule! We want we own government, we own flag, we own anthem! And no more chief minister, but the Honourable Eric Matthew Gairy, Prime Minister, if you please!" (137). There is a roar of approval from the carenage.

An ordinary market woman standing near Marshall on the roadway suddenly gives an angry outburst: "Always a big show and a lotta big talk! Always fooling up the poor, ignorant country people. He ought be shame, oui!" (138). She abruptly turns and walks away; several others there join her, and shortly afterward, Marshall also leaves again on foot. But the bus comes along in due course and, within two hours, drops her home. She thinks whether the chief minister had made any provision to feed or give free bottles of sweet drink or just plain water to his ardent supporters during the day-long rally. It had been a mere circus without a breadcrumb; they were making no efforts to improve the condition of the Blacks. Like Moody, Marshall also realizes that the need of the hour is to improve the economic conditions of the Blacks.

Patricia Hill Collins, in *Black Feminist Thought: Knowledge, Consciousness, and the Politics of Empowerment*, defines racism "as a system of unequal power and privilege where humans are divided into groups or 'races' with social rewards unevenly distributed to groups based on their racial classification. The variations of racism include institutionalized racism, scientific racism, and everyday racism. In the United States, racial segregation constitutes a fundamental principle of how racism is organized" (300). Racism in the United States of America has always attempted to destroy the humanity of the African Americans. Racial discrimination ranges from political oppression to economic disempowerment. The United States of America, the land of opportunities, has remained, for all the reasons of racism, a land of oppression for the African American woman, as depicted in their life writings. bell hooks suggests, "Black women must identify ways feminist thought and practice can aid in our process of self-recovery and share that knowledge with our sisters. This is the base on which to build political solidarity. When that grounding exists, Black women will be fully engaged in feminist movement that transforms self, community, and society" (*Talking Back* 182).

Malcolm X is an important role model for those who wish to transform their consciousness, for he was engaged in ongoing critical self-reflection, in changing both his words and his deeds. He asserts, "It is our collective responsibility as people of color and as white people who are committed to ending white supremacy to help one another. It is our collective responsibility to educate for critical consciousness. If I commit myself politically to Black liberation struggle, to the struggle to end white supremacy, I am not making a commitment to working only for and with Black people. I must engage in struggle with all willing comrades to strengthen our awareness and our resistance" (qtd. in bell hooks, *Talking Back* 118). It is important that individuals work to transform their consciousness and strive to be anti-racist. It is equally important to remember that the struggle to end white supremacy is a struggle to change the system, the structure. The efforts to end white supremacy can be truly effective through individual struggle to change consciousness that must be fundamentally linked to collective effort to transform those structures that reinforce and perpetuate white supremacy.

Chapter 5

Civil Rights Movement: Desegregation

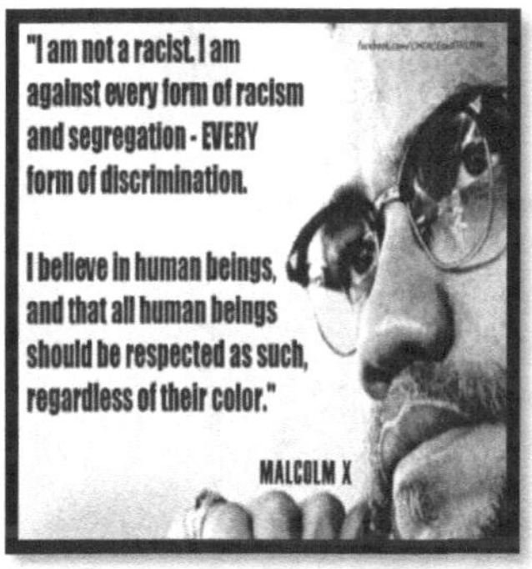

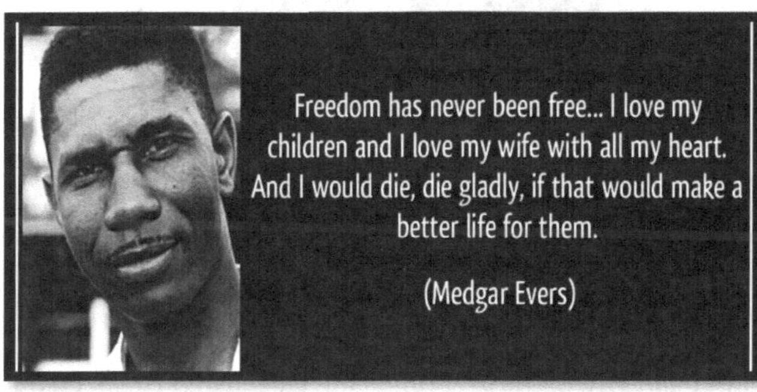

I want to write about that battle, the skirmishes, the losses, the small yet so important victories that make the sweetness of my life.

– Lorde,
The Cancer Journals 11

The American Civil War (1861–1865) is the greatest war in American history; it was a war for freedom wherein many people paid the price with their lives, for their desire for freedom ran deeper than the colour of skin. On 1st January 1863, President Abraham Lincoln issued the Emancipation Proclamation as the nation approached its third year of bloody civil war. It declares, "that all persons held as slaves" within the rebellious states "are, and henceforward shall be free" (Lincoln, qtd. in Berlin 49). Nearly a hundred years after the Emancipation Proclamation, African Americans in Southern states still inhabited a starkly unequal world of disenfranchisement and segregation, with various forms of oppression, including race-inspired violence. The local and state laws enforcing racial segregation in the Southern states, termed "Jim Crow," barred them from classrooms and bathrooms, from theatres and train cars, and from juries and legislatures.

The Civil Rights Movement encompasses social movements in the United States whose goal was to end racial segregation and discrimination against African Americans and to secure legal recognition and federal protection of the citizenship rights enumerated in the Constitution and federal law. In 1954, the U.S. Supreme Court struck down the "separate but equal" doctrine that formed the basis for state-sanctioned discrimination, drawing national and international attention to the plight of African Americans. In the turbulent decade and a half that followed, civil rights activists used nonviolent protest and civil disobedience to bring about change, and the federal government made legislative headway with initiatives such as the Voting Rights Act of 1965 and the Civil Rights Act of 1968. Many leaders of the African American community rose to prominence during the civil rights era, including Martin Luther King Jr., Rosa Parks,

Malcolm X, Andrew Goodman and many more who risked and even lost their lives for freedom.

The movements to obtain civil rights for Black Americans have special historical significance; such movements have not only secured citizenship rights for Blacks but have also redefined prevailing conceptions of the nature of civil rights and the role of government in protecting these rights. The important achievements of the African American civil rights movement have been the post-Civil War constitutional amendments that abolished slavery and established the citizenship status of Blacks and the judicial decisions and legislation based on these amendments, notably the Supreme Court's *Brown v. Board of Education of Topeka* decision of 1954, the Civil Rights Act of 1964 and the Voting Rights Act of 1965. These legal changes affected the opportunities available to women, non-Black minorities, disabled individuals and other victims of discrimination.

The *Brown* decision demonstrated that the litigation strategy of the NAACP (National Association for the Advancement of Colored People) could undermine the legal foundations of Southern segregationist practices, but only when Blacks, acting individually or in small groups, risked crossing the racial barriers. Thus, even after the Supreme Court declared that public school segregation is unconstitutional, Black activism was necessary to compel the federal government to implement the decision and extend its principles to all areas of public life rather than to schools only. The initial phase of Black protest activity in the post-*Brown* period began on 1 December 1955, with Rosa Parks of Montgomery, Alabama, refusing to give up her seat to a white bus rider, thereby defying a Southern custom that required Blacks to give the front seats in buses to whites. With her imprisonment, the Black community's boycott of the city's buses began and lasted more than a year, demonstrating the unity and determination of Black residents and inspiring Blacks everywhere. Her heroism was the first of its kind, a bold and dangerous act that inspired thousands of people, especially Martin Luther King Jr., to march, protest, demonstrate and speak out against discrimination.

Martin Luther King Jr., who emerged as the boycott movement's most effective leader, understood the larger significance of the boycott and quickly realised that the nonviolent tactics used by the Indian nationalist Mahatma Gandhi could be used by Southern Blacks. He explains, "I had come to see early that the Christian doctrine of love operating through the Gandhian method of nonviolence was one of the most potent weapons available to the Negro in his struggle for freedom" (qtd. in Herman 130). Although Parks and King were members of the NAACP, the Montgomery movement led to the creation in 1957 of a new regional organisation, the clergy-led SCLC (Southern Christian Leadership Conference), with King as the president.

King became the major spokesperson for Black aspirations, and as in Montgomery, little-known individuals initiated subsequent Black movements. On 1st February 1960, four freshmen at North Carolina Agricultural and Technical College began a wave of student sit-ins designed to end segregation at Southern lunch counters. These protests spread rapidly throughout the South and led to the founding of the SNCC (Student Nonviolent Coordinating Committee) in April 1960. This student-led group, even more aggressive in its use of nonviolent direct action tactics than King's SCLC, stressed the development of autonomous local movements in contrast to the SCLC's strategy of using local campaigns to achieve national civil rights reforms.

The SCLC protest strategy achieved its first major success in 1963 when the group launched a major campaign in Birmingham, Alabama. Highly publicised confrontations took place between nonviolent protesters, including school children, on the one hand, and police with clubs, fire hoses and police dogs on the other. The Birmingham clashes and other simultaneous civil rights efforts prompted President John F. Kennedy to approve the new civil rights legislation. By the summer of 1963, the Birmingham protests had become only one of many local protest uprisings that culminated in the 28th August March on Washington, which attracted at least 200,000 participants.

King's address on that occasion captured the idealistic spirit of the expanding protests: "I have a dream that one day this nation will rise up and live out the true meaning of its creed, 'We hold these truths to bc self-evident: that all men are created equal'" (Carson 85). Although some whites reacted negatively to the spread of the 1963 protests, King's linkage of Black militancy and idealism helped bring about the passage of the Civil Rights Act of 1964, which outlawed segregation in public facilities and racial discrimination in employment and education, also benefiting Blacks, women, and other victims of discrimination.

The SCLC focused its efforts in the urban centers, while SNCC worked in the rural Black Belt areas of Georgia, Alabama, and Mississippi, where white resistance was intense. Although the NAACP and the predominantly white CORE (Congress of Racial Equality) also contributed activists to the Mississippi movement, young SNCC organizers led the civil rights efforts in the state. Black residents in the Black Belt, many of whom had been involved in civil rights efforts since the 1940s and 1950s, emphasized voter registration rather than desegregation as the goal. The proponents of racial liberation often saw the African American freedom struggle in international terms, as a movement for human rights and national self-determination for all people.

The assassinations of Malcolm X and Martin Luther King, and the intense infighting within the Black militant community caused a decline in protest activity after the 1960s. The African American freedom struggle nevertheless left a permanent mark on American society. Overt forms of racial discrimination and government-supported segregation of public facilities came to an end, although segregation persisted in northern as well as southern public school systems and in other areas of American society. In the South, anti-Black violence declined; Black candidates were elected to political offices in communities where Blacks had once been barred from voting, and many of the leaders or organizations that came into existence during the 1950s and 1960s remained active in southern politics. Southern colleges and universities that once excluded Blacks began to recruit them. Despite the civil rights gains of the 1960s, racial discrimination and repression remain significant factors in American life. Civil rights advocates acknowledge that desegregation has not brought significant improvement in the lives of poor Blacks, but they are divided over the future direction of Black advancement efforts.

"With the outbreak of the Civil War, many African Americans deployed their pens and their voices to convince President Abraham Lincoln that the nation was engaged in nothing else than a war to end slavery, which Black men, initially barred from enlisting, should be allowed to fight" ("African American Literature: The Civil War and Reconstruction," web. 12 Jan. 2017). With the end of the Civil War, African Americans finally hoped to witness a new era of freedom and opportunity. Just as Black activists were pushing to end segregation and racism to create a new sense of Black Nationalism, so were Black authors attempting to address these issues in their writings.

Anne Moody is one of the many voices of the Civil Rights Movement who fights courageously to gain freedom and self-respect for herself as well as for the Blacks. *Coming of Age in Mississippi* is one of the most self-reflective accounts of the civil rights movement in America. Being a young Black woman living in a segregated world, Moody joins her fellow young African American civil rights activists to challenge the white supremacist system that relentlessly oppresses their lives. She reveals important roles that African American women played in the movement by being leaders and supporters. Her life writing covers a span of nineteen years, from four to twenty-three, including her involvement in the civil rights movement. Her personal evolution parallels and symbolizes the development of the civil rights movement. Her life writing is a story of how one young woman deals with the system and survives to become a civil rights activist by participating in sit-ins, demonstrations, rallies, and protests to achieve freedom and equality for the Blacks, and thus, she considers herself an activist, not a writer. "In the beginning, I never really saw myself as a writer. I was first and foremost an activist in the Civil Rights Movement in Mississippi" ("Anne Moody: Biography," web. 14 Aug. 2016).

Charlayne Hunter-Gault, in *In My Place*, recounts the memories of how she could enrol as the first African American woman at the University of Georgia, as well as be one of the first two African American students to break the colour barrier and integrate the schools in 1961. Her life writing is about an African American woman's lead role in the desegregation of the University of Georgia. It offers insights into the Civil Rights Movement and gives a moving account of the deeply painful individual sacrifices of people such as Hunter-Gault and Hamilton Holmes so that African Americans could enjoy equal rights under the law. "*In My Place* is the story of a young girl's entry into the Civil Rights Movement – a movement that permanently changed the status of Black people in America and altered the very structure of our society" (Trachtenberg, web. 16 Jan. 2017). Hunter-Gault underlines how racism persisted in society and the difficult fight that the Blacks waged to gain the rights denied to them as citizens. She holds her ground against racism to become a voice of consciousness in the field of American broadcast journalism.

One day during her senior year, in conversation with her counsellor about what she wants to do after graduation, Hunter-Gault confidently replies that she is going to study journalism. Even as a child, Hunter-Gault admires Brenda Starr, a reporter having a life full of adventure, mystery, and romance. She decides to study journalism in college in the hope of having an exciting career in the field. She is the editor of the student newspaper *The Green Light* for two years at Turner High School, being the first junior to be appointed to this position ever, and soon she becomes a full-fledged member of the *Green Light* staff. She starts her second year as editor of the paper and is made assistant yearbook editor by Mrs. Evans.

At Turner, her counsellors press her to make choices; she wants to join a university that has a journalism school or a strong department of journalism. From a former student at Turner who had gone to Wayne State University in Detroit, Michigan, Hunter-Gault learns that Wayne State University has a strong journalism department, and she proceeds to apply for Wayne as well as for a number of small Midwestern colleges. Even if she does not get scholarship money from Wayne, she will still be eligible for aid from the state of Georgia, by virtue of the fact that she wants to major in a field of study that is offered only in the white schools.

In order to discourage any possibility that a Black person will even think of applying to one of those white schools, the state provides funds for Blacks to study in those fields, at other institutions in other states where no one cares if Blacks go to school with whites. "Many a Black in Georgia was 'treated' to what probably amounted to an even better education than they would have gotten in the white state school by virtue of this segregationist policy and practice" (Hunter-Gault, *In My Place* 124). Keeping in mind the prospect of the state aid for her to study journalism anywhere but in the Georgia state system, Hunter-Gault decides that she will look for her place at Wayne State University in Detroit, Michigan. "Education is a political issue for exploited and oppressed people. The history of slavery in the United States shows that Black people regarded education – book learning, reading, and writing – as a political necessity" (bell hooks, *Talking Back* 98).

Moody's life writing is a civil rights testimonial that serves the role of informing people in contemporary times about the perseverance exhibited by the individuals involved in the struggle. "Moody, intimately involved in the civil rights movement in the first half of the 1960s, created an unforgettable image of the inequities and violence that characterized southern society" (Gale, *A Study Guide for Anne Moody's Coming of Age in Mississippi* 5). After graduating from high school, Moody joins Tougaloo College, where she meets Trotter, her roommate and the secretary of the NAACP chapter on the campus, who suggests she become a member as they are starting a voter registration drive in Hinds County and they need canvassers for that. A few weeks after Moody gets involved with the Tougaloo chapter of the NAACP, they organize a demonstration at the state fair in Jackson; four picketers are sent to the fair from Tougaloo, the demonstrators are arrested and bailed that night around eight. All of them await their arrival sitting outside on the dormitory steps. When the police cars come and the students get out of the cars, they congratulate them and sing, "We Shall Overcome" (Moody, *Coming of Age in Mississippi* 271).

Soon Moody becomes a part of the SNCC (Student Nonviolent Coordinating Committee) and agrees to canvass every weekend for them. She likes the SNCC workers, for she had never known people so willing and determined to help others. The SNCC boys have friends everywhere among the Negroes, while most of the whites are just waiting for a chance to kill them all. The threats do not stop them and they just keep going. When Hunter-Gault was asked on the NPR (National Public Radio) how she would like people in 2011, especially college students, to view the civil rights era, she avers, "I think that the thing that we learned back in the day of the civil rights movement is that you do have to keep on keeping on" (Chappell, web. 7 Jan. 2011).

On Saturdays, they spend all day canvassing and often at night they have mass rallies, which are poorly attended as many Negroes are afraid to come out. Most of them are old plantation Negroes who had never heard of voting or who think that only whites are supposed to vote. On Sundays, they usually go to Negro churches to speak to the people, but those who join them are fired from their jobs, thrown off the plantations, and rendered homeless. Moody feels that she is beginning to change. "For the first time I began to think something would be done about whites killing, beating, and misusing Negroes. I knew I was going to be a part of whatever happened" (276). One day, she goes to town shopping with Rose, a girl from the dorm. They had planned to split the cab fare back to campus, but they do not have enough money. As bus fare is less, they decide to take the Trailways to come back. When they reach the station, Moody suggests Rose take the white side and she walks in the white entrance. She asks the man at the ticket counter for two tickets to Tougaloo. He slaps the ticket down at the counter, throws the change at her that falls off the counter and rolls over the floor, and he laughs at them as they pick it up.

Another man gets on the phone and keeps looking at them while talking, as if he is reporting to the police what is taking place. They both sit opposite each other to wait for the bus so that they can see what is happening at the terminal. People come, stare, and laugh at them; a bunch of white soldiers sit with them and start talking. A drunken white man walks into the station and starts yelling at them. They miss the bus as there is no announcement, so they wait for the next bus. The drunken man curses them and, after throwing and breaking the bottle on the floor, goes away. One white bus driver comes to them and asks if they have come there for some entertainment. He starts making different kinds of facial expressions, and the rest of the whites at the bus station laugh at him. Amidst all this, they miss the second bus also, so they decide to leave as they can perceive that the crowd can be violent any minute. They get up and walk backward to the door. The crowd follows them and some threaten to kick them or throw them all the way to Tougaloo. Outside the station, they do not know what to do or where to run. Then a Negro voice from a car asks them to get in; the driver is a minister who works part-time at the bus station. He tells them not to sit in ever again without first planning it with an organization, as they cannot just go around doing things on their own. He drives them to the campus and makes them feel bad by telling them that he may probably be fired for helping them.

In many cases, Black women practiced individual protest against unfair rules and practices. In the drugstore cafeterias of Washington, D.C., Ruth Powell had her first encounter with Jim Crow. In the 1940s, when she was a law student at Howard University, her experience was devastating: "I sat there for about ten minutes watching the waitresses whizzing back and forth in front of me, when suddenly the awful truth dawned and I realized what was happening." She left the store. She knew that "I, alone, couldn't do anything concrete to revolutionize conditions," but she also believed "I had to do something to preserve what remained of my self-respect." Her "something" evolved into a one-woman campaign. She would enter cafeterias, politely ask for service, and, when refused, sit quietly, sometimes for hours at a time. During her sit-ins, she would pick out a waiter and stare at him for perhaps an hour or more. Powell maintains, "Whether I was finally served or not was unimportant. What I believed was that all these little bits of agitation would go toward that vital … awakening process" (qtd. in Murray 205). Her stance represents the action taken to change the rules.

The NAACP holds its annual convention in Jackson, and Moody is so excited that she sends one of the leaflets home to her mother and asks her to come, who forbids her to go to the convention as it will cause danger to her as well as to her family. Moody becomes active in the NAACP and the civil rights movement despite her family's impassioned pleas to quit. Being an active member in the Black empowerment movement gives a new meaning to Moody's life. She prefers to work in the movement where she can fight against racial inequality, so she is made the spokesman for a team of three members who will sit in at Woolworth's lunch counter. They enter Woolworth's and make small purchases from various counters and then occupy three seats at the previously segregated Woolworth's lunch counter.

First, the waitress ignores them, but as they start to write their orders down on their own, she realizes that they want service. She asks them what they want, and as they read from their order slips, she tells them that they will be served at the Black counter for Negroes, but Moody insists on being served in the white section only. Thinking that violence will break out, people start leaving without being served, while a crowd of cameramen and reporters gathers around, taking pictures and asking questions. Moody answers them that they are all students at Tougaloo College, they represent no particular organization, and all they want is service. In the afternoon, students from a nearby white high school come to Woolworth's. They are surprised to see Blacks in the white section and do not know how to react, so after some time, they start chanting anti-Negro slogans.

Violence breaks out when one man throws Memphis, a demonstrator, from his seat and slaps Moody. Another man who works in the store throws Moody against an adjoining counter. Memphis is lying near the lunch counter with blood running out of the corners of his mouth, and as he tries to protect his face, the man who had thrown him down continuously kicks him against the head. Finally, a police officer arrests Memphis and his attacker. Pearlena, the girl demonstrator who is thrown to the floor, gets back to her stool along with Moody. Some white Tougaloo teachers in the crowd ask them to leave as things are getting rough. Soon, Joan Trumpauer, a white student and SNCC secretary, joins them in the sit-in. She is lifted from the counter by her waist and carried out of the store. Two high school boys snatch Moody's stool and drag her thirty feet towards the door by her hair. They both get up and join Pearlena at the center of the counter. Lois Chaffee, a white Tougaloo faculty member, joins them. Now they are four: two Negroes and two whites, and all women. The mob starts throwing ketchup, mustard, sugar, pies, and everything on the counter at them.

John Salter, in charge of NAACP activities on campus, joins them, and the moment he sits down, he is hit on the jaw with brass knuckles. Blood gushes from his face, and someone throws salt into the open wound. New demonstrators join them, on whom the mobs spray paint from the counter. A high school student wearing a white shirt has the word "nigger" (290) written on his back with red spray paint. They sit there for three hours taking the beating, when the manager decides to close the store as the mob has begun to get wild with stuff on the counters. He begs everyone to leave, but no one moves. About ninety policemen standing outside the store keep watching the whole thing through the windows, but they do not go in to stop the mob or do anything. Dr. Beittel, the president of Tougaloo College, comes running as he hears about it. He takes all the demonstrators out and asks the police to protect them after they are outside the store. As they go outside, the policemen form a single line to block the mob from them, but they allow them to throw at them everything they had collected. The Woolworth's sit-in is an illustration of how Blacks and whites, male and female, join the movement. Their united determination in the face of violent adversity is compelling and demonstrates how dedicated they all are to the movement.

Reverend King, the civil rights activist, picks them up in his station wagon and takes them to the NAACP headquarters on Lynch Street. After the sit-in, Moody thinks of how sick Mississippi whites are; they believe so much in the segregated Southern way of life that they will kill to preserve it. Before the sit-in, she used to hate the whites in Mississippi, but now she knows, "it was impossible for me to hate sickness. The whites had a disease, an incurable disease in its final stage" (290). She recalls how many times the whites have killed; she knows that the killings have just begun and many more will die before it is over. She is disgusted that so many whites in Mississippi are holding on to racial inequality so violently.

At night, a mass rally is organized at the Pearl Street Church in Jackson, where Medgar Evers, a civil rights activist from Mississippi, introduces all the sit-inners and tells the audience that this is just the beginning of such demonstrations. He asks everyone present there to pledge themselves to unite against segregation in Jackson and throughout the state. The rally ends with the freedom song "We Shall Overcome" (291) and sends home hundreds of determined people. Moody imagines that Mississippi Negroes are about to get together at last; the Woolworth sit-in binds her to the Black empowerment movement.

On 1st February 1960, four Black students from North Carolina Agricultural and Technical College, the historically Black college, sit down at Woolworth's lunch counter in Greensboro, North Carolina, and refuse to move until they are served; the sit-in movement begins and the event makes headlines across America. The day after the first sit-in at the Greensboro Woolworth's, more students from North Carolina Agricultural and Technical College, that the original four attended, descend on the store. The local media covers the second sit-in, even though there are no confrontations. When the national media picks up the story, it strikes a chord with other students, who begin to duplicate the sit-ins in other locations.

"F.W. Woolworth's was a discount store that represented Americana. One of the nation's few chains, it helped create a national identity. The lunch counters at the front of the stores were popular meeting spots. Civil rights leadership recognized the symbolic power of Woolworth's and acted quickly to organize more sit-ins. Within two weeks, students in 11 cities had staged sit-ins at Woolworth's and S.H. Kress stores. To show their support, Northern students, both Black and white, picketed local branches of chain stores that practiced racial segregation in the South" (Penrice, web. 2 Feb. 2018).

Before the sit-in demonstration, Moody had written a letter to her mother, who writes back begging her not to take part in the sit-in. She knows the whites have already started threatening and intimidating her family, as she is the first Negro from her hometown who has openly demonstrated and worked with the NAACP. Whenever Negroes threaten to do anything in Centreville, they are either shot or made to run out of town. She waits to hear the news that someone in Centreville has been murdered, and she knows if anything happens, it will be her family member.

After the Woolworth's sit-in, Moody receives a letter from her mother telling her that the sheriff came to their house to enquire about her, and he told her mother that the whites are upset with her involvement in these things. She also gets a letter from her sister Adline, telling her how Junior had been cornered by a group of white boys and was about to be lynched, when one of his friends came in a car and rescued him, and adds that a group of white men had beaten old Uncle Buck. They are scared to death and cannot sleep for fear of night riders. She ends the letter by cursing Moody and saying that she is trying to get every Negro in Centreville murdered.

"Although this struggle for Black equality was fought on hundreds of different 'battlefields' throughout the United States, many observers at the time described the state of Mississippi as the most racist and violent. Mississippi's lawmakers, law enforcement officers, public officials, and private citizens worked long and hard to maintain the segregated way of life that had dominated the state since the end of the Civil War in 1865. The method that ensured segregation persisted was the use and threat of violence against people who sought to end it" (Austin, web. 2 Feb. 2018).

By 1959, many of Atlanta's young progressive Black professionals have been trying to figure out how and where to begin Atlanta's movement towards equality. They organize themselves into a group called the Atlanta Committee for Cooperative Action, which is known by its acronym, ACCA. Some of these leaders are involved in an earlier effort to desegregate one of the Atlanta-based colleges of the state university system, the Georgia State College of Business Administration, but they fail in their efforts. They are convinced that "if they could crack the lily-white system of higher education, then everything else would surely follow" (Hunter-Gault, *In My Place* 125).

The civil rights activists want to integrate all-white Southern colleges, for which they have to find two students who cannot be challenged by the state on moral, intellectual, or educational grounds, and the best place for this is the students at high school. Alfred Holmes, although not officially a part of this group, volunteers his son Hamilton Holmes, Hamp, who, after being pressurised by his father, agrees without much enthusiasm. A small committee from ACCA comes to Turner; they approach Hunter-Gault, who is ranked third in her class. She listens to them, finds the idea interesting but with remote prospects, and in the end has the same attitude as Hamp and replies, "Why not?" (126). Soon after the first meeting, members of the same committee, Jesse Hill and M. Carl Holman, take them to the campus of Georgia State in downtown Atlanta.

Hunter-Gault is curious to see what they have to offer in journalism training. Hamp's interest is in pre-med, as he wants to follow his grandfather's footsteps and become a doctor. Inside the registrar's office at Georgia State, people receive them pleasantly, as if this kind of thing happens all the time and they are prepared for it. They ask for the catalogue of courses and are surprised to find it very thin, and after opening it, they conclude that it offers very few courses, so they leave without waiting for any questions. They inform the adults who are accompanying them that the university has nothing to offer of their interest. Soon they say that they want to go to the University of Georgia. They get the applications through mail, and M. Carl Holman, English professor, ensures that their applications are filled properly. The local NAACP lawyer, Donald Hollowell, works on them, seeing that everything is certified and sent by registered mail. Their applications become a test of changing racial attitudes as well as of the growing strength of the civil rights movement in the South. "Struggle to resist white supremacy and racist attacks informed black attitudes toward education. Without the capacity to read and write, to think critically and analytically, the liberated slave would remain forever bound, dependent on the will of the oppressor. No aspect of black liberation struggle in the United States has been as charged with revolutionary fervor as the effort to gain access to education at all levels" (bell hooks, *Talking Back* 98).

The story of their plans to apply makes the Atlanta papers on 11th July, 1959. The headline on Raleigh Bryan's front-page story in *The Atlanta Constitution* is, "2 NEGROES TRY DOORS AT ATHENS" (129), wherein the registrar signals the approach the university will take for the next year and a half. Bryan writes, "Registrar Walter N. Danner said the university is full up and already is turning down would-be freshmen. He said that because dormitories are full the only freshmen he can admit are those who are bona fide Athens residents" (129). Meanwhile, according to their plans, Hamp goes to Morehouse and Hunter-Gault to Wayne. She is disappointed to know that Wayne will not allow any student to major until junior year and that no journalism classes are offered to freshmen. At Wayne, the black Greek organizations play an important role, as they are a virtual necessity on the campus with only twenty-five hundred blacks out of a student body of twenty-five thousand. In these organizations, the black students find respect and reinforce their identity.

During spring break, Hunter-Gault goes home and finds a dramatic change in her best friends, like "a final coming of age than a transformation" (139). Carolyn and Wylma step up to fulfill the historic mission of the talented tenth and join the largest and most impressive group of Negro students in the country, with some four thousand students in the Atlanta University Center. In simple terms, they start the Student Movement, which in time acquires the impressive title of the Committee on Appeal for Human Rights, with a plan to end segregation across Atlanta using the tactic of civil disobedience and the philosophy of nonviolence. The first official act of the group as a committee is the drafting of a document outlining their grievances, demands, and their manifesto called "An Appeal for Human Rights" (140). The manifesto says that the students join their hearts, minds, and bodies in the cause of gaining those rights which are inherently theirs as members of the human race and as citizens of the United States. Every normal human being wants to walk the earth with dignity and hates any ban owing to race or colour.

In the manifesto, they clearly state that they cannot tolerate the discriminatory conditions under which the Negro is living in Atlanta, being denied the rights, privileges, and joys of life in a nation professing democracy and among people professing Christianity. They hold that the practice of racial segregation is not in keeping with the ideals of democracy and Christianity and that it is robbing not only the segregated but also the segregator of his human dignity. The Negroes have not been accorded first-class citizenship, even though they fight and die for their country in times of war, and they do not enjoy participation in city, county, and state government at the level where laws are enacted. Segregation and prejudices impede the social, economic, and political progress of Georgia. The propagation of racial prejudice is unfair to the generation to be born and sets a poor example in the area of race relations for which America is fast losing the respect of other nations. It is unfortunate that the Negro is being forced to fight for what is due to him and is freely granted to other Americans. In spite of the fact that the world is fast moving towards an integrated humanity, some people hold on to the wrong idea of racial superiority.

In addition to this, the manifesto states that it is time for the people of Atlanta and Georgia to take a look at what is really happening in the country and stop believing those who tell them that the Negro is happy and satisfied and everything is perfectly fine. Their churches, which claim to be the houses of all people and are ordained by God, encourage racial segregation to the point of making Sunday the most segregated day of the week. The students of the Atlanta University Center call upon the people in authority, the leaders, and the public to affirm themselves and abolish these injustices. They plan to use legal and nonviolent means to secure full citizenship rights as members of this great democracy. On 9th March, 1960, the manifesto is published, and Carolyn and Wylma, along with four thousand students of the Atlanta University Center Colleges, march through the streets of Atlanta saying, "Our time has come" (143). A week later, the students hold their first sit-in to draw attention to their demands and get themselves arrested in order to make cases that will challenge "the Jim Crow laws that sent us to the separate 'colored' water fountains, that sent us to separate 'colored' toilets, or that kept us from eating at all" (143). The sit-in includes places like theatres and department stores. "Georgia student activists participated fully in the social and political upheaval that overtook the nation in the 1960s. Although often overshadowed by events in other parts of the nation, the Georgia student movement played an integral part in the story of the twentieth century's most turbulent decade" (Huff, web. 28 March 2017).

The Negroes had been protected and privileged within the confines of their segregated communities, but now the students leave the protective covering so that the blacks can see their past and future in a new light. They can see the past full of slavery, segregation, deprivation, and denial, with a system designed to keep them in their place and convince them that it is their fault as well as their destiny. Now they see themselves as the inheritors of the struggle that enables them to take control of their destiny. The young people demonstrating in one way or another throughout the South are not heroes; they are simply doing what they were born and raised to do. bell hooks states, "Often our elders would say that they were punishing us to teach us our place, to keep us in line, so that we would not be punished by white people, so that we would not be destroyed. Such attitudes have had a profound impact on the way black children are raised, on our capacity for creative expression" (Talking Back 162). Hunter-Gault resents the whole colour issue and strongly feels that black people should not be guilty of the very thing that the countless black students throughout the South are fighting to overcome.

A six-man delegation of Negro ministers is chosen to meet Mayor Thompson. They present the demands on behalf of Jackson Negroes. Their demands include the hiring of Negro policemen and school crossing guards, removal of segregation signs from public facilities, improvement of job opportunities for Negroes on city payrolls, encouraging public eating establishments to serve both whites and Negroes, integration of public parks, public schools and libraries, the naming of a Negro to the City Parks and Recreation Committee, and forcing service stations to integrate restrooms. After this meeting, Reverend Haughton, the minister of Pearl Street Church, commits that the Mayor is going to consider all the suggestions, but the next day Thompson denies making any promises and says that the Negro delegation got carried away following their discussion with him. They decide to prove to Mayor Thompson and the white people of Jackson that they mean business, and, as a result, demonstrations, sit-ins, and pickets follow, wherein eighty-eight demonstrators are arrested.

During the demonstrations, Moody helps in conducting several workshops to teach potential demonstrators—high school and college students—how to protect themselves. She joins the pray-in on the post office steps with Reverend King and a group of ministers. There are fourteen of them, seven whites and seven Negroes, and all of them are arrested. The jail is also segregated. Moody tells, "Here we were going to school together, sleeping in the same dorm, worshipping together, playing together, even demonstrating together. It all ended in jail. They were rushed off by themselves to some cell designated for whites" (296). The Negro cell does not even have a curtain over the shower. They are glad to know that over four hundred high school students had been arrested, and they sing freedom songs until the jailer threatens to put them into solitary chambers if they do not stop singing.

Within four or five days, Jackson becomes the "hotbed of racial demonstrations in the South" (299). The mass rallies become a nightly event, and after one such rally, Medgar Evers is shot dead. No one is able to believe it, and the NAACP organises a protest march at Medgar's death, singing freedom songs: "Woke Up This Morning With My Mind on Freedom" and "Ain't Gonna Let Nobody Turn Me 'Round" (303). The cops go wild, arrest them, and put them into paddy wagons and garbage trucks. They take them to the fairgrounds, roll up the windows, turn on the heater, and themselves go out, closing the door. Everyone starts sweating, and the girls start fainting. The cops rejoice at seeing their condition. The cops hit the demonstrators with sticks and arrest even those Negroes who were just looking on from their porches. They are all put in compounds with two large buildings used to auction off cattle during the annual state fair. The opening is closed up with wire, like a concentration camp. It is hot and sticky there, and four policemen with rifles guard them and keep an eye on them. As she looks through the wire at them, she imagines herself in Nazi Germany, the policemen as Nazi soldiers: "They couldn't have been any rougher than these cops. Yet this was America, the land of the free and the home of the brave" (305). As they march out of the compound in a single line to have dinner, they see the cook, who is from the city jail, standing over a large garbage can, stirring something in it with a stick. No one feels like eating, and within a few days, many are taken from the fairgrounds sick with hunger.

The day before Medgar's funeral, they are out of jail, and for the first time Moody sees so many Negroes together. Medgar's death has really brought them to the movement. She thinks that maybe his death will strengthen the ties between the Negroes and the Negro organisations, and if this happens, his death will not go in vain. The expression on their faces is that of anger, bitterness, and dismay, and they give a look as though any moment they are going to start rioting.

After Medgar's death, every Negro leader and organization in Jackson receives threats that they are next on the hit list, and things begin to fall apart. Within a week, everything changes; even the rallies are not the same. "Without the framework of an organized civil rights or black resistance struggle, individual and collective efforts at black liberation that focus on the primacy of self-definition and self-determination often go unrecognized" (bell hooks, *Talking Back* 77).

On Sunday, an integrated church-visiting team is organized by Reverend Ed King, and five or six churches are hit the same day. When they are asked to leave, they do so and go to the church again the next Sunday. One lady asks the usher to let them sit in the church, who replies that the church has decided what is to be done, a resolution has been passed, and they are to abide by it. At this, the lady answers that they are no one to decide such a thing; it is the house of God, and all decisions are taken by Him. As the usher does not agree, they leave and go to an Episcopal church where the ushers allow them to sit and worship with them. Moody composes herself for a few minutes, as she had never prayed with white people in a white church before. The church service is completed without incident, and the minister invites them to visit again, which gives a little hope to Moody.

Hunter-Gault goes back to Wayne to complete her first year and then comes back again to Atlanta, as she and Hamilton have to go to the federal district court in Macon for a hearing on their application. Their lawyers try to get a temporary restraining order against the university. They had been turned down repeatedly for a year, always on the basis of there not being enough room for them in the dormitories. The university never makes the mistake of saying the truth — that they are turning them down because they are Black. They appear in court. Judge William Bootle refuses to order the university to accept them on the ground that they have not exhausted all their administrative remedies. At the same time, he orders them to go to Athens for admission interviews in November, and he schedules a trial in Athens to consider a motion for a permanent injunction against the university in December.

Throughout the summer of the 1960s, Hunter-Gault spends her time supporting the students. She offers to get herself arrested and go to jail with her friends, but their lawyer, Donald Hollowell, explains, "An arrest, even a 'good one,' was an arrest, and that for me to have an arrest record would play right into the hands of the state. They could then legitimately turn me down" (146). She has to fly back to Atlanta and go to Athens for an admission interview, which at the time she thinks "was a going-through-the-motions waste of time. The university was wedded to intransigence" (150–151). It is a pretty routine interview for Hunter-Gault, but the three-man panel is rough on Hamp. They ask him things like whether he has ever been to a house of prostitution or a "tea parlor" or "beatnik places" (151). It is plainly absurd to ask such questions of "Mr. Clean" of Turner High School.

At the trial on 13th December, which Judge Bootle orders on their motion for admission to the university, the courtroom overflows with Black people, and white spectators are also present, who sit together in the morning and by the afternoon sit on separate sides.

Hamp's parents and Hunter-Gault's mother also come to Athens for the trial. Their legal team discovers the critical piece of evidence — a case identical to Hunter-Gault's, in which a white female student, attending a college on the same system as Wayne, has been admitted for the winter term. Asserting that there is no room, Georgia officials also project that even if they admit her, it will be too complicated to do so immediately because of the difficulty of reconciling the credits of Wayne's quarter system with Georgia's semester system. They argue that she will lose credits in the transfer, and therefore it will be best to delay her admission at least until she completes a whole year at Wayne. The university pretends that they are not discriminating against them. Hamp and Hunter-Gault testify in the presence of a crowd of two hundred spectators. After a few days, she returns to testify that she is not taking any courses at Wayne that she cannot get credit for if she does not continue with them in the second semester. Judge Bootle gives their lawyers five days to submit their briefs, and after five days sets a deadline of 4th January by which he wants to have everything in his hands.

After a few days, she goes back to Wayne, and on the afternoon of 6th January, 1961, she receives a call from a reporter of a New York newspaper who gives her the news that Federal Judge Bootle has ordered her and Hamp's admission to the University of Georgia. She shares the long-awaited news with her Delta sisters. She finds them quiet and serious instead of being happy, as they are afraid of what might be done to her; she asks them not to worry, assuring them that everything will be all right. Thirty-six hours later, she sits on a plane to Atlanta and arrives at the airport, where she is greeted by her happy, excited family members, reporters, and photographers. At the airport, she sees people reading newspapers that carry headlines about the decision and its immediate aftermath: "STATE ASKS U.S. JUDGE TO STAY NEGRO ENTRY. NEGRO BOY REGISTERS AT ATHENS. UNIVERSITY, STUDENT LEADERS PRESS FOR ORDER ON CAMPUS" (169). The Black people present at the airport have a brightness of pride and fill her with their power and confidence through the light in their eyes and the smiles on their faces. She recalls the saying of the University students marching on the streets, "*Our time has come*" (Italics original 169).

Hunter-Gault is disappointed to know that, before she left Wayne, Hamp had already gone to the campus on Saturday morning, but Donald Hollowell informs her that the Attorney General had gone to Macon to request Judge Bootle to grant a stay on his order to give more time to the state to prepare an answer for the integration order. The registrar is surprised to see them as they enter and lay a copy of the court order on his desk, and after securing the registration papers, they leave, promising to return on Monday morning. That day, the university is somewhat quiet, although some students burn crosses, and at the entrance of the campus "hung a Black effigy, which they called 'Hamilton Holmes'" (170). There are reports of Klan members visiting some fraternity houses—a social club for male undergraduates—and influencing members to revolt against the desegregation order. There is also great fear at the university that Governor Ernest Vandiver will "attempt to honour his campaign promise of closing down the university by letting 'not one, no, not one' Negro student ever attend classes with whites" (171). President Aderhold issues a statement expressing the "firm belief" that the university will continue its century and a half of service without interruption to the people of the state.

The Governor tells the Georgians that Judge Bootle's ruling has put the university at risk of closing, and if Hamp and Hunter-Gault enter, a cut-off of funds will go into effect because of the provision in the state law that states, "No further funds shall be used or expended on an integrated school" (171). On Sunday, they have a reunion at Hunter-Gault's house and decide that they will go to the campus early Monday morning, as there are no hotels for Blacks in Athens, and even if they find a Black home courageous enough to take them in, they have no security. They start for Athens early Monday morning, and Hunter-Gault plans how she is going to take her first steps on the campus as if she knows her place: "for the first time it would be I who would be defining my place on my terms, on territory that was their pride but was now mine, too," (172) and she walks onto the campus at Georgia, loving herself and demanding respect.

CORE (Congress of Racial Equality) opens an office in Canton, Mississippi, to start a voter registration campaign in Madison County. Moody is so fed up with the fighting and bickering among the organizations in Jackson that she is ready to go to Madison County—even where Negroes are frequently found dead. "Shortly before Christmas a man's headless corpse had been found on the road between Canton and Tougaloo with the genitals cut off and with K's cut into the flesh all over his body" (311). Everyone is concerned about

Moody, as they know she has agreed to work with CORE in that area, but as she had come from Wilkinson County, she does not think Madison will be worse than that.

Madison County is considered a place with a possible future for Negroes, in spite of all acts of violence. Records show that it has a population of twenty-nine thousand Negroes as against nine thousand whites, and the Negroes own over forty percent of the land in the county. Only about two hundred Negroes are registered to vote, out of which only half are actually voting. In Canton, the CORE office is in a small room adjoining a Negro café, which is owned by C.O. Chinn and his wife, a well-established Negro family. Mrs. Chinn's liquor license is taken away within a few weeks of the opening of the CORE office. She tells Moody that the place is broken into twice, and many Negroes are physically threatened. Only about fifty teenagers are involved in the movement from the area, as most of the Negroes do not want to be bothered. They are thoroughly brainwashed or are too insecure to work for the whites. In the case of distribution of allotments to the farmers, it always ends up with the white people getting most of the allotments. Regardless of how much land the Negroes have, they are never able to get more, and it seems to Moody "that the federal government was directly or indirectly responsible for most of the segregation, discrimination, and poverty in the South" (313). At night, there is a rally at the CORE office in which twenty teenagers participate and sing freedom songs, with Mrs. Chinn being the only adult among them.

George Raymond, the project director, introduces Moody to the teenagers and tells them all about her demonstrations and sit-ins. Moody addresses the teenagers and tells them that change is not possible with only a few believers. Everyone sits back and says they want freedom and believe that all men are created equal. Some of them believe that they are free just because their constitution guarantees them certain rights, but they are the ones who have to give meaning to those rights. They have to take certain positive actions to work on the problem, and for this, they have to join hands. After Moody ends her address, they sing three freedom songs, ending with "We Shall Overcome" (316), and then everyone goes home.

"We Shall Overcome" has been a civil rights song heard not just in the United States but in all parts of the world. It is not a marching song, not necessarily defiant; it is a promise. It is used as a folk song, a work song by slaves in the fields who would sing, "I'll be all right someday" (Adams, web. 28 Aug. 2013). It is known in the churches: "A Methodist minister, Charles Albert Tindley, published a version in 1901: 'I'll Overcome Someday'" (Adams, web. 28 Aug. 2013). Its first political use is by workers in a strike for a raise in pay against the American Tobacco Company in Charleston, S.C., in 1945. "They marched and sang together on the picket line, 'We will overcome, and we will win our rights someday'…." On 15th March, 1965, President Lyndon Johnson appeared before Congress and 70 million Americans watching on television, calling for legislation that would ensure every citizen the right to vote. "It is the effort of American Negroes to secure for themselves the full blessings of American life," Johnson declared in the speech. "Their cause must be our cause, too, because it's not just Negroes, but really, it's all of us who must overcome the crippling legacy of bigotry and injustice. And we shall overcome" (Adams, web. 28 Aug. 2013).

Saturday night is known as the "Nigger Night" (316) in Mississippi, as all the Negroes come to the town, sit in each other's car and talk, or move around, go to cafés or movies, or fight with others. Most whites do not even bother to come out on Saturdays; it seems like a completely black town. Moody thinks that they have to get some more adults involved one way or the other. If some of the Saturday night energy is used constructively or even directed at the right objects, it will make a tremendous difference in the life of the Negroes in Mississippi. She soon realizes that the Negroes in Madison County are the same as in other counties: "They were just as apathetic or indifferent about voting" (318). One day the teenagers are buckshot in a rally by Price Lewis, the white owner of the service station. After that, the teenagers stop going to the CORE office as their parents do not let them be part of the movement anymore. In between all this, Moody again receives a letter from her mother begging her to leave Mississippi, telling her that the white folks in Centreville have found out that she is in Canton and they intend to murder her. She asks her why she is wanting to get herself killed and what she is trying to prove. She adds, "Negroes are going to have troubles until they're dead, and after you are dead we'll still have the same problems" (343). Her mother tells her that even if she is dead, things will still be the same as they are now for the Negroes; her mother symbolizes the older generation's resistance to change.

Moody tries to register voters, but their applications are denied on a variety of grounds, among them useless voting tests and archaic requirements. They are only able to send a handful of Negroes to the courthouse to get them registered, and those few who go are fired from their jobs. The CORE workers are constantly threatened by the whites. Things turn worse when their money is cut off, as they are not producing registered voters. As a result, they starve for days without food. It soon becomes very frustrating and seems like a burden because of the threats, acts of violence, and fear of death. There is always so much work, so many problems, that Moody hardly ever thinks of anything except how to get the job done in the best way and survive on a daily basis.

In Hunter-Gault's life writing, "Most vivid of all is her recounting of the injustice and horror of her first days in the University of Georgia, when riots ignited around her" (Gale, "Hunter-Gault, Charlayne 1942 – Contemporary Black Biography," web. 15 Jan. 2017). She notes in the prologue, "That we were now daring to define our place irrespective of white wishes or demands sparked, among other things, the raucous greetings by mobs of white students and other forces of white resistance who within forty-eight hours would hurl epithets, burn crosses and black effigies, and finally stage a riot outside my dormitory while, nearby, state patrolmen ignored the call from university officials to come and intervene" (2). Reaching the campus, they walk through a noisy white crowd. The university has no security force and has not made any provision even for temporary protection on such a troublesome occasion. Hunter-Gault and Hamp register for classes amid shouts of protest; they can hear the rude protests of some of the louder students: "Nigger, go home" and "There goes the nigger" (173).

Everything goes smoothly till they get a distressing blow when they are informed that Judge Bootle has granted permission to the state "to halt the registration" (174). They gather their things and, wasting no time, leave the campus and get to know that their lawyers are already on their way to the Court of Appeals in Atlanta with a request to condone the stay. Judge Bootle avers that his stay is only for the purpose of allowing the state to "test the correctness" (175) of his integration order. Judge Elbert Tuttle, who condones the stay, declares that "the quickest disposition that can be made of this case, so far as granting these plaintiffs their right to an education in a state institution – as the trial court has clearly found that they are entitled to – is the best solution not only for them but for all others concerned" (175). At that moment, they have love for Judge Tuttle, and with warmth for him in their hearts, they rush back to the university to complete their registration.

They go to various departments, situated all over the vast, hilly campus, to sign up for their classes. The crowd follows them wherever they go, especially Hunter-Gault, thinking she will be more easily frightened. At the end of the day, they get into the car belonging to William Tate, the dean of men. The students move closer to stare into the car and start rocking the vehicle, giving a tense moment. Dean Tate gets down and starts grabbing the students, snatching their identity cards. The crowd gets back to allow the car to pass, uttering 'nigger thises' and 'nigger that's' (177), and they leave without any more interference.

.

Years after this day, Dean Tate tells Hunter-Gault that he and President Aderhold "felt that integration was inevitable; it would come. But we felt . . . that the longer we could delay it, the less possibility there was of violence" (176). They return to Atlanta that night with plans to come back to Athens for classes the next morning in the midst of rumours that the school is going to be closed for a "holiday"

session. Meanwhile, there is a lot of disturbance and agitation on the campus about the plans to close the university, and students respond by hoisting Confederate flags, exploding firecrackers, and roaming up and down the streets of Athens chanting and blowing horns.

Hamp and Hunter-Gault return for classes and go separate ways, he to the home of the Black restaurant owner, the Killians, who rents him a room in their house, and Hunter-Gault to Center Myers Hall, the central dorm of three adjoining buildings called North and South Myers. Had they been admitted as freshmen, Hamp too would have had to stay on campus, but now the on-campus requirement applies only to women. At the entrance of Center Myers, Hunter-Gault and her mother are welcomed by Mrs. Minnie Porter, the housemother, who shows them her two-room suite with a kitchen and a bathroom. She explains that the suite had been the office of the Women's Student Government Association, which has been moved somewhere else to make room for her. "The fiction of no-room-in-the-inn was still being maintained," (178) and during the course of conversation, Hunter-Gault learns that there are no other students living on the first floor with her.

No provision is made for Hunter-Gault to eat, and they do not know whether she will be allowed in the cafeteria or not, so after keeping her things in her suite she goes off to Killian's with her mother and Donald Hollowell. After dinner, she says goodbye to them and goes into her room to wait for her first night as a student at the University of Georgia. Within a few minutes, a few girls come to meet her, but they do not stay long, and soon Hunter-Gault is alone, thinking about what her life is going to be like in the coming days. As it gets dark, a crowd gathers outside, and Hunter-Gault hears them shouting:

Two, four, six, eight,
We don't want to integrate . . .
Eight, six, four, two,
We don't want no jigaboo.
(Italics original 178–179)

Hunter-Gault is too tired at this point to be tempted to look out of the window, so within a few minutes she goes off to sleep.

Wednesday morning, Hamp and Hunter-Gault attend their first class at the University of Georgia, officially ending nearly two hundred years of segregation, in the classroom in Meigs Hall, and no words are spoken to mark the event. This is a relief to Hunter-Gault, as at this point she just wants to get on with being a student as quickly as possible, and she thinks that the worst is over.

She attends her first journalism course, Ethics, and by the afternoon a college official brings her back to her ground-floor room at Center-Myers, where she is interviewed by newspaper women about her first day at the University of Georgia.

As it gets dark, she picks up a book and tries to study. Firecrackers begin popping outside like the previous night, and she decides to go to bed. Mrs. Porter comes in to suggest that she keep the curtains drawn and stay away from the windows, as they are expecting some trouble.

Later, as Hunter-Gault goes into the hall to drink water, she catches a glimpse of the faculty members, larger in number than the previous night, who volunteer to patrol the building. As she returns to her room, the noise outside gradually turns fierce. Suddenly, there is a crash in the bedroom and another crash as a Coca-Cola bottle follows the brick through the window. Hunter-Gault says, "Jagged splinters of window glass and fragments of the bottle had splattered across my dress, slippers, and the skirts and blouses that I had not yet had time to unpack" (182).

She goes out into the hall and meets a campus patrolman, to whom she tells all that happened, and who goes into her room to investigate. The crashing of the glass and the screams of one girl on the floor above, who is struck by a brick as she looks out of her window, bring most of the girls into the lobby.

Hunter-Gault realizes that it is time for the eleven o'clock news and that her mother in Atlanta will be waiting for it. She calls her to say that she is fine. The girls in the dorm begin to shout insults at Hunter-Gault and then at the schoolmates who had gone to her room to be friends with her. It is difficult for Hunter-Gault to sit and listen to some of the things they say about her without answering back. They say that she is about to become "a Black martyr, getting fifty dollars a day for this from the NAACP" (183).

After having waited in vain for help from the state patrol, the city police outside finally resort to tear gas. Thus, the entry of two Black students leads to racist riots.

Mrs. Porter informs Hunter-Gault that the dean desires her to leave for Atlanta for safety. On hearing this, Hunter-Gault feels totally sick and miserable, thinking, "I've failed, I've failed. I began to cry and, hard as I tried, I couldn't stop" (184). She packs quickly and leaves her room following Dean Williams. It is after midnight that the state troopers finally arrive, who are cool and impassive in their speech and manner.

They go to the house of Hamp, who is unaware of whatever happened until he receives a call from Attorney Hollowell, and they start back towards home together. Neither of them can get used to the idea that they have been "suspended" (185).

The violence witnessed on the University's campus is not the first, nor will it be the last. By the time Hunter-Gault and Holmes walk through the Arch, students had already attempted integration of other universities, often facing similar hostilities. "Autherine Lucy became the first black student to attend the University of Alabama in 1956. She was met by riots, which included a march to the university president's home, torched crosses and destroyed cars. As Lucy prepared herself for her first day of class, mobs had already formed around campus. 'Hey! Hey! Ho! Ho! Autherine has got to go!' filled the morning air as protestors threw rocks and eggs at her escort vehicle. The violence continued until Lucy was suspended 'for her own safety,' according to the University of Alabama website. Despite Lucy's failed attempt at desegregation, a tide of change had begun at Southern universities" (Demmitt, web. 13 Jan. 2011).

Hunter-Gault reaches Atlanta and turns into her block. Pulling up in front of the porch, she remembers that many months ago, only a local Black man had stood there telling her that she should give up the idea of trying to go to the University of Georgia. The news of their coming home reaches before them, and a few close friends gather at the house. Her mother welcomes both with open arms. Hollowell talks about the plan to go to Macon the next day to file a motion to get them readmitted, and it will depend on Judge Bootle's verdict whether they will go back immediately or get some rest through the weekend.

After everyone leaves, the only person left at Hunter-Gault's house is Carl Holman, the guru of the Student Movement, to whom she always looks up to talk. He is the guiding light of *The Inquirer*, which evolves from the early days of the movement and helps the students inform the community of their activities to gain local support. From the first day, Holman treats Hunter-Gault's journalistic aspirations with dead seriousness and helps nurture and encourage her at every step.

The next day, reporters come and interview her about her reaction to the riot. She first corrects their mistaken assumption that she cried because she was afraid. She tells them that she cried because she was disturbed, disappointed and hurt to know that she had been suspended. They ask if she will go back; she answers that she will go back if given a chance, whatever it may imply. Attorneys Hollowell and Motley go to Macon and ask Judge Bootle orally for an immediate reversal of the suspension, which he denies. Instead, he gives another ruling before the court that struck down the state law that would have cut off funds to any desegregated state institution. In Georgia newspapers, it is called

"A Killing Blow to Ga. School Segregation Laws" (191), which is not the victory their attorneys had gone after. However, it is a victory.

Later, on Friday afternoon, their attorneys again make the trip back to Macon to meet Judge Bootle, who, after giving the university time to readmit them voluntarily and following a discussion about whether rules will be changed or bent to allow Hunter-Gault to live off-campus, issues his next-to-last ruling in the case, ordering the university to admit them no later than 8 a.m. on Monday morning.

Back on campus, they find the place quietly recovering, with everybody trying to do the best they can. Hamp and Hunter-Gault go separate ways with armed government escorts in plainclothes, who they feel make them stand out at a time when they need to try to blend in. The efforts made by campus leaders and others over the weekend seem to be paying off, and they write friendly notes for both of them. The university announces that any student "attending or taking part" (194) in future riots or demonstrations will be suspended or expelled from school.

The FBI conducts an investigation into the causes of the riots, and eighteen male students leave the university, "including ten who were suspended, three who refused to attend school with Negroes, and five others who 'wanted to drop out until the crisis was over,' according to the *Atlanta Journal-Constitution*" (195). Two students publicly admit taking part in the riot, and the man carrying a gun and walking in the dorm asking for Hunter-Gault is arrested and sent to the mental asylum. A majority of faculty members sign a petition criticizing the violence and calling for their return to the campus. Carl Holman encourages her to write a piece about her first week back at the University of Georgia for the upcoming edition of *The Inquirer.* She writes that on her first night back in Athens, she receives flowers, cards, letters, telegrams, postcards, and gifts from all parts of the world with prayers and words of encouragement.

There is relief to see the crowd getting thinner while moving from one class to another. The few friends they make are there when they return, as firm as before, and the classes progress at a normal pace. A classmate provides her with notes for the classes missed. Along the corridors of the dorm, there are whispers, "She's back" (198), but nothing more is said. They walk alone to the classes with no officers accompanying them, and an occasional 'Hi' from other students helps relieve whatever tension they experience: "The University of Georgia is beginning to seem more and more like 'my' school and I think both Hamp and I are developing a sense of pride in being a part of it" (199). She ends by saying that she hopes and trusts that things will continue as they have been and that nothing will change this. Over the next two and a half years, Hunter-Gault works to have the usual college experience, "if not only through 'self-hypnosis,'" she joked. "'I didn't think of myself as a symbol or historic figure,' she said. 'The attitude I had was one that not only enabled me to take a walk into history, but be a relatively normal college student as well … I got what I came for.'" There have been changes since the early pioneers; however, Hunter-Gault said the work isn't finished. "'We've had progress,' she said. 'But I guess those of us on the frontlines in those days might like to see more … I think it's been an amazing 50 years, and let's hope in the next 50 we'll see giant steps beyond anything we've seen until today'" (Demmitt, web. 13 Jan. 2011).

Moody has been planning to be a part of "the August 28 March on Washington" (333) since the announcement. She joins the march to the Lincoln Memorial with Reverend King, various celebrities, and the Negroes. They sing freedom songs, and Martin Luther King talks about his dream of freedom for the Negroes. She says, "By the time we got to Lincoln Memorial, there were already thousands of people there. I sat on the grass and listened to the speakers, to discover we had 'dreamers' instead of leaders leading us. Just about every one of them stood up there dreaming. Martin Luther King went on and on talking about his dream. I sat there thinking that in Canton we never had time to sleep, much less dream" (334–335). Her doubts, frustration, and discontent with the movement and its leaders are brought forth. On their way back, they decide to spend the night in Tennessee and travel through Alabama during the day for fear of being killed by someone after the march. Moody is the only Negro in the car with Reverend King and other white activists of the movement. They sleep in a Federal Park, and Moody feels bad thinking that her white friends have to sleep in the park because she is Black and cannot sleep in the same hotel with them. The next morning, the drive through Alabama goes without incident; Reverend King drops Moody at the Freedom House in Canton and drives on to Tougaloo.

With the opening of school in Canton for the next session, Moody becomes more aware of the terrible poverty in the area. The teenagers who have worked with them are not able to return to school because their parents have been fired from their jobs and cannot afford to buy school clothes for their children. These teenagers have worked to keep themselves in school but, because of the voter registration drive, have not been able to find jobs. Moody feels guilty to see these kids out of school and job, standing hungry all day, as if she is responsible for their predicament. A lady lives in a two-room house with her five children across the street from Moody's office. She supports them and her sick father on the five dollars she earns doing domestic work. Moody notices that the school is open for two weeks, but the two girls are at home every day. She gets to know that their grandfather is terribly sick, and after buying medicine for him, their mother has no money left to buy school clothes for them. Their eldest brother is able to buy clothes for himself and the two brothers, but not for the sisters.

After hearing this, Moody's childhood gets revived again: "All that I had vowed to forget and overcome came back to me. The life these kids were leading was a replica of my own past" (339). She remembers how her mother had suffered with them when their father had left them, and how they went hungry all the time, never having anything to eat but bread or, at times, beans. The next day, she receives her first cheque of twenty-five dollars from CORE, as she is on the payroll now and is finally being paid. She takes the two girls living across the street for shopping and is very happy to see them going to school the next day. In these girls, she sees the echoes of her own life. She has grown from someone scraping to clothe herself and her own family to someone who can provide clothing for others.

On 15th September 1963, Moody's twenty-third birthday, she hears the news of the church bombing in Birmingham, Alabama. She is disheartened and describes her passionate outburst against the whites and against God. "As long as I live, I'll never be beaten by a white man again. Not like in Woolworth's. Not anymore. That's out. You know something else, God? Nonviolence is out. I have a good idea Martin Luther King is talking to you, too. If he is, tell him that nonviolence has served its purpose. Tell him that for me, God, and for a lot of other Negroes who must be thinking it today. If you don't believe that, then I know you must be white, too. And if I ever find out you are white, then I'm through with you. And if I find out you are black, I'll try my best to kill you when I get to heaven" (347). She believes that this bombing is Birmingham's answer to the march on Washington. She expresses her frustration as she had spent years protesting, staging, taking part in sit-ins, getting arrested, being beaten and publicly humiliated, and in an instant, all her efforts seem to be in vain. "For the oppressed, the exploited, the dominated, domination is not just a subject for radical discourse, for books. It is about pain, the pain of hunger, the pain of overwork, the pain of degradation and dehumanization, the pain of loneliness, the pain of loss, the pain of isolation, the pain of exile, spiritual and physical. Even before the words, we remember the pain" (bell hooks, *Talking Back* 3–4).

COFO (Council of Federated Organizations), a statewide coalition of all the national civil rights groups in Mississippi, organizes a meeting to decide about running Aaron Henry, the state NAACP president and chairman of COFO, and Ed King of Tougaloo on a freedom ballot in the upcoming election for Governor and Lieutenant Governor of Mississippi. They believe that more Negroes will cast their votes in the freedom election than are already registered, and they plan to have enough support so that thousands of Negroes in various counties might participate. They think that this will prove to the nation that Negroes want to vote and will vote if they are not afraid to do so. Moody opposes the whole idea as she thinks that poverty relief is more important for the poor rural blacks in Mississippi than voting rights, but as she is the only person on the committee opposing the freedom election, she agrees to try to get votes.

It is hard to explain the freedom election to the local Negroes. They make special leaflets to pass out to the Negroes, advertising the freedom vote in the county fair in Canton. The fair is also segregated, a week for whites and a few days for the Negroes. The first day the fair is open to Negroes, they go there to distribute the leaflets but are disheartened to see that the Negroes don't even take the leaflets offered to them. Moody goes to Jackson for a weekend where she meets Bobbie, one of the high school girls who had worked in Canton with her for some time, who shows her a Klan leaflet that she had got from a friend of hers who lived near a white neighbourhood. Moody cannot believe her eyes to see her picture on the Klan blacklist. There were pictures of Medgar Evers, John Salter, Joan Trumpauer, Reverend Ed King, Emmett Till, of ministers and Negroes who had been killed, with a cross marked on their faces. She does not ever bother about daily threats, but being on a Klan blacklist is the most horrible scare of her life.

Back in Canton, there is plenty of work to be done for the freedom vote and they spend their days pushing and begging people to participate in the election. There is so much work, confusion, and too many threats; Moody feels so tired and burdened as if she is carrying the weight of the world on her shoulders. In 1985, when asked in an interview whether many people who worked in the movement had suffered 'battle fatigue,' Moody answered in what is transcribed as halting speech: "Yeah – you know you got that I think from my reading last night, but actually when I – I think a lot of people – you don't know the effect that it has on – on you, I mean mentally. It wears, it tears at the root of your heart" (Gwin 105).

On the first day of the freedom vote, only a few Negroes come, while some prefer casting their vote on the street rather than going to the office. Moody is very depressed to see the poor result of their working hard for three weeks and realizes that the freedom vote cannot help. They need to solve the immediate problems of the Negroes—of food and jobs—so that they can fight against the whites rather than being their slaves till death. She believes that economic security will give blacks the power and inclination to demand their other rights, so they should focus on economic issues, such as helping black farmers buy their own land, rather than on the freedom vote. She makes sure that the movement distributes clothing to needy blacks in the area.

For three days of the polls, they plead with the Negroes to demonstrate their desire to vote, but in the end, the total number of votes cast does not impress Moody after putting in so much hard work. The blacks refuse to band together to improve their situation, and she is repeatedly frustrated to see how willing blacks are to accept injustice. bell hooks avers, "It often troubles me that black people in the United States have not risen en masse to declare solidarity with our black sisters and brothers in South Africa. Perhaps one day soon – say Martin Luther King's birthday – we will enter the streets at a certain hour, wherever we are, to stand for a moment, naming and affirming the primacy of black liberation" (*Talking Back* 112). Moody concludes that the movement has not improved the lives of people in Mississippi. She believes that the leaders of the Civil Rights Movement, such as Martin Luther King Jr., "relied too heavily upon nonviolent demonstrations and rallies that were proving largely ineffective. The closing chapters of *Coming of Age* stress the need to reinvigorate the movement" ("*Coming of Age in Mississippi: Context*," web. 18 Jan. 2017).

On the last eve of the freedom vote, she tells her co-workers that she plans to leave the project for some time. Due to lack of sleep and nervousness, she is on the verge of a breakdown brought on by finding herself on the Klan's blacklist. She says, "I had gotten so tired of seeing people suffering, naked and hungry. It just seemed as if there was no end to it, or at least 'the Vote' was not the way to end it" (376). It becomes increasingly obvious that these political rights will not mean an end to the poverty and suffering of the blacks, and the movement should focus more on bread-and-butter issues. Her co-workers try to persuade her to stay, telling her what a good worker she is, but soon they realize that Moody has made up her mind to leave, so they do not pressurize her. On reaching the station, she finds herself sitting in the white waiting room with a white civil rights worker who is a fundraiser for CORE. Sitting there in the station, she gets the same feeling she had in all the other sit-ins she had participated in: "I remember getting up once, and going to the Negro section to ask the Negroes there if they knew the white section was desegregated," (377) and she realizes that she will never be leaving the movement for good. "Moody had already sacrificed at least a quarter of her life to the movement. Along with hundreds of other female students, she risked everything on a daily basis, hoping that blacks would someday be treated like first-class citizens of the United States" (Ezra 151).

The public schools in the South are not desegregated, and every case the NAACP takes on is challenged by massive resistance. Still, the new mood and energy among the South begin to steer in changes so rapidly that not their hearts, but their minds start to accept the inevitability of desegregation. Georgia abandons "its massive-resistance laws, which had been designed to keep schools segregated 'for a thousand years,' and court-orders desegregation of public schools to begin in the fall of 1961" (Hunter-Gault, *In My Place* 202). The Student Movement triumphs; in exchange for an end to the sit-ins and other demonstrations, merchants agree to desegregate their lunch counters and other facilities after the schools are desegregated in the fall. Hunter-Gault tells that they are not there in the University of Georgia because they want people to love them: "We were there because we were entitled to get the education that our parents' taxes paid for as citizens of the state of Georgia" (203). Hamp and Hunter-Gault go home every Friday after their last class in his car, and when their schedules do not match, she takes a bus from "the still-segregated tiny bus station to Atlanta" (200). On weekends, when they go home, she often goes on speaking trips as far as New York or as close by as some small Georgia town. Unlike Hamp, she loves public speaking, which is "like a lifeline to a different world" (203) for her. They also go to various places to receive awards given to them by different organizations that are proud of them for the role they play in desegregation.

Though the university is now officially desegregated, there is some confusion in the mind of the administration over just how much is required under the court order. The trouble arises when Hunter-Gault presses the issue of eating in the cafeteria, as she believes she has a right to eat there and she always has stomach problems because of her irregular eating schedules. She presses the issue of the cafeteria with her lawyer, who takes the matter to Judge Bootle, who proclaims that the desegregation order includes all the university facilities, including the swimming pool. She is not allowed to take modern dance as some of the students object to her being in the class. She selects swimming as her first choice and bowling as her second choice; some of the students say that they do not want to get in the water with the "nigger," (206). The bowling alley used by the university belongs to the town of Athens, and the desegregation order does not extend to town facilities. The result of her choice is that there are no physical education courses for that quarter.

The day Judge Bootle gives his ruling on the facilities, Hunter-Gault walks the short distance from her dorm to the dining hall; with all eyes focused on her, she holds her plate for one of the black cooks to fill with food of the South that surpasses race. She walks over to an empty table and takes a seat, but soon she is joined by Marcia Powell, who had been there at every critical stage of the desegregation of the university, and now again she is there to be with her. She is a human being who does not see any conflict between her basic humanity and her capacity to be a good journalist. She is hated as the "white-girl traitor" and "nigger lover" (207) by those eating in the cafeteria for giving company to Hunter-Gault. Both of them are aspiring journalists and remain friends throughout life. Brian Lanker, in his 1989 book, *I Dream a World: Portraits of Black Women Who Changed America*, quoted Hunter-Gault saying, "You have to assess every situation that you're in and have to decide, is this happening because I'm black? Is this happening because I'm a woman? Or is this happening because this is how it happens?" (62).

Her mother buys her a car so that she can go safely from the dormitory to the main campus. Both Hamp and Hunter-Gault have problems with their cars; students take out the air of the tires, at times from all four tires in the parking lot, and sometimes they take a sharp object and scratch "NIGGER" (214) on the driver's door. By the time they complete their first year, she has an offer of internship at the *Louisville Times*, the afternoon paper belonging to the Bingham family. She gets a letter from the editor, Norman Isaacs, and she discusses the prospect with Carl because she wants to work on *The Inquirer* for the summer. He encourages her to go to Louisville, saying that the experience of working on a "real" (215) daily newspaper will make her even more valuable to *The Inquirer*, and she will have plenty of time to make her contribution to the paper after she gets back. At the time she takes the job, she is not aware that she will be "the first Negro ever to be hired." She learns a lot from her experience at *The Times*, and after two months, when she is leaving, Norman Isaacs tells her that she can come back the next summer even, and probably as a reporter when she graduates. She goes back to Atlanta, and all that she learns at *The Times*, she applies to her work at *The Inquirer.*

No other Black student joins Hamp and Hunter-Gault in their first full year, and each of them develops different ideas about how they want to approach the next year and a half at Georgia. All along, Hamp feels that he has something to prove at Georgia; he wants to show the whites that they are wrong in their attitude that Blacks are inferior. He is a brilliant student, and he has no desire to get involved in anything beyond his studies. Hunter-Gault does not feel that she has to prove anything to anybody, and she realises that this is the only college experience she is going to have, so she wants to get the most out of everything by getting personally involved. Hamp always scores the highest on most of the tests in all his classes. That may have convinced the students that he is not inferior, but it also causes them to dislike him more, as his grades raise a normally modest curve to a level that is beyond the reach of many of them; on the other hand, Hunter-Gault scores different grades in different courses and even flunks with other students. In the fall term of her senior year, a few Black students join the University of Georgia who do not have to face the hatred and anger that the two faced in their first year. In this semester, she decides to get some experience working on the student newspaper, *The Red and Black*. The editor keeps asking people to do things, but he never speaks to Hunter-Gault, so after working there for some time, she leaves and never goes back, for, "It wasn't my place" (235). Hunter-Gault crafts her narrative around a "spatial metaphor, underscoring both the depth of her solitude on UGA's all-white campus and the haunting realisation that Blacks have always had a clearly defined place in white society, and that stepping out of that place often carried a steep, sometimes deadly price" (Pratt 156).

Moody goes to New Orleans to stay with her grandmother Winnie, who does not even let her enter her house as she is scared of her because of her civil rights work. Then she goes to her uncle George Lee, who is living with his wife, who welcomes her gladly and asks her to stay as long as she wants. She decides to go to Maple Hill Restaurant for a job. They all welcome her and tell her how proud they are of her after the sit-ins and all her civil rights activities. Mr. Steve, the owner of the restaurant, speaks to her about the movement and is happy to give her a job. With a week's salary, she and Adline are able to find an apartment for themselves. Junior, who is living with Winnie and working as a short-order cook, often comes to meet them in their new apartment, and Adline and he plan the birthday party they are going to give their mother when she comes to town. Moody dreads thinking about the party, as she had not seen her mother in two years and had even stopped answering her letters.

Junior brings Toosweet to their apartment. Moody tries to appear cheerful and speak to her mother and little sister, Jennie Ann, who is also with her mother. After Moody had left the house, her mother had two more babies and is carrying a three-month-old baby. She is happy to meet them all after a long time, and she has so much to talk to her mother, who remains busy talking to Adline. Her mother asks her when she is coming back to Mississippi, to which she replies that she does not know if she will come back or not. Her mother tells her to get a job and settle down. Moody answers that she has a job and is settled. Her mother asks her to get a teaching job in New Orleans rather than working in a restaurant and washing dishes after spending four years in college. Moody replies that she is not the teaching kind, and she will not teach in New Orleans or in Mississippi even if they pay her a million a year, for she feels that it is better to wash dishes than teach in "awful, segregated, inferior Uncle Tom schools" (381). She does not like her mother telling her what to do with her education, as when she was sick and starving in college, she could not take money from Raymond and send her to buy some food. She is able to finish her college only because of her own desire to do so, without any encouragement from anyone, so now she will do whatever she intends to do.

Toosweet's birthday is celebrated at George Lee's place, and when Moody reaches his house, she feels like a stranger there as no one speaks to her. She feels like she has committed a crime and everyone is punishing her by not talking to her. Her family thinks she is selfish for endangering their lives by getting involved in the movement. She wishes to go back to Canton and work with the people who understand her. Here among her people, she seems crazy as she grieves over problems they do not even think about. Her family, as well as numerous other Blacks, accept injustice and work to perpetuate racial inequalities despite being Black themselves. She has nothing in common with the people around her except the colour of her skin, and she hates to see the Negroes so content with their life. She sees how complacent they are with their situation, and this frustrates her. One day, as she is working in the restaurant, Julian, the new cashier, informs

Moody that President Kennedy is shot dead. Hearing this, everything around her goes black, as to most of the Negroes, and especially to her, the President had made "Real Freedom" (389) a hope. The Negroes had lost their best friend, who was in a position to help determine their destiny; he had been considered the saviour and ultimate supporter of the Civil Rights Movement, and his death is a huge setback. She is changed by the violence she experiences, by learning to channel it into a rock-hard exterior, one that cannot be broken down by hateful words or hateful actions.

Moody sits there in shock, staring at everyone and not seeing anyone, thinking, "So much killing. And when will it end? When?" (387). She somehow pulls herself together and walks through the dining room to the customers who are waiting for her. She gets enraged to see all those white faces and feels like racing up and down the table, breaking dishes, smashing food into their faces, and shouting and yelling at them, calling them "MURDERERS!" (388). She wonders what she is doing in this segregated restaurant, serving all of these "evil-minded murderers" (388). Mr. Steve sees her crying and thinks she is fainting, so he asks her to take the day off. As she changes her uniform, she feels afraid to go out into the cruel, evil world and thinks that as she walks on the street, everything will be pitch black. "A world this evil, should be black, blind, and deaf, and without any feelings at all. Then there won't be any colour to be seen, no hatred to be heard, and no pain to be felt" (389). She realises that coming back to New Orleans is even worse than staying in Canton.

Anne Moody thinks of getting involved in the movement again and attends her first meeting of the CORE chapter in New Orleans within a week. There, the CORE has a voter registration drive going on in Orleans Parish, and Moody volunteers to be a part of the teams that are being organised to canvass on Saturdays and Sundays. Moody finds it as hard to persuade Negroes to register in New Orleans as it was in Mississippi. According to her, the only big difference about canvassing in New Orleans is that there, the Negro and white civil rights workers can canvass together without being openly threatened with assault. Junior goes to Centreville and brings back the sad news of Emma's brother Clift's death by being shot in the face.

Moody is disheartened to hear about a death in her family and thinks herself responsible for this. She writes a letter to Emma and receives her reply after a long time. She feels so helpless to read that Emma hopes that she will be able to help uncover the mystery behind Clift's death. Moody thinks that Negroes are not even considered humans and are just shot and butchered like hogs. She meets Bob Moses, the SNCC director in Jackson, Mississippi, where she goes for her graduation ceremony from Tougaloo College. She talks to him about Clift's murder and the death of other Negroes in Woodville. He tells her that they were just "terror killings," (404) they were murdered to keep Negroes in their place and to keep civil rights workers out of the southwest. "In her autobiography, Ida B. Wells-Barnett describes how the lynching of her friends had such an impact on her worldview that she subsequently devoted much of her life to [the] anti-lynching cause" (Collins 27).

The last gathering Hunter-Gault attends in Atlanta is the Emancipation Proclamation Services at Union Baptist Church. It is one of the exciting events of the year for blacks, where she is asked to introduce the speaker, Donald Hollowell. She knows that it is the last civil rights event she is going to participate in for a long time. She finds the things they say to be racially insensitive and totally at odds with the movement's position expressed by Dr. King: "that people should be judged not by the color of their skin but by the content of their character" (239). Carl Holman tries his best to see that the organizations and members of the community keep the promises of financial support, but that does not help her pay her increased expenses. Sometimes she earns a few dollars when she goes somewhere to speak, but now she is tired of travelling.

She just wants to finish her last year and "live for a while in blissful obscurity, preparing myself for the next phase of struggle; for what I now regarded as a near-sacred calling – providing the kind of information that would help people understand one another as human beings, acknowledging but affirming their differences, in the hope that never again would a black child of the South have to cross the kind of burning sands that Hamp and I had at Georgia, to take our rightful place" (240). By now, the movement gives her a sense of mission that is bigger than herself, and she feels that she has to lose her public self in order to find her place in the new world, where the lives of other people will be the central point, rather than their colour or status. She wants to be known to the world through the efforts of her own ability rather than through something that has been an ordinary routine occurrence for the time and the place. She does not want to be a symbol. As quoted in *Essence* magazine, she pronounces, "To become a historic symbol was not the point of what I did. The point of what I did was to have access to the best education I could in the state to become a journalist" (Fraser 41–42). She desires to be famous one day, but not simply for going to college; she wants to be valued for her abilities rather than for some moment in history which any other black student would have also done if given the chance.

By this time, preparation for graduation is going on, and Hunter-Gault and her mother send invitations to everybody who played a meaningful role in her life. Her father, her grandmother, her brothers, and the black people of Atlanta come to be a part of her graduation on 1st June, 1963.

Hunter-Gault states in *Southern Living*, "I think it was the result of having a goal and having support for that and being supported by a lot of really good people who made sacrifices for us" (qtd. in Young 78–83). She is nervous about what will happen when Hamp and her names are called out for their diplomas, but by the time it happens, the only sounds to be heard are the cheers and applause emanating from their family members and close friends. She thinks, "This is how it ought to be, as I sat there in my place" (246), as no one else seems to notice.

Likewise, Patricia Hill Collins shares her experience: "In 1978 I offered a seminar as part of a national summer institute for teachers and other school personnel. After my Chicago workshop, an older Black woman participant whispered to me, 'Honey, I'm real proud of you. Some folks don't want to see you up there [in the front of the classroom], but you belong there. Go back to school and get your Ph.D., and then they won't be able to tell you nothing!' To this day, I thank her and try to do the same for others. In talking with other African-American women, I have discovered that many of us have had similar experiences" (Collins 113–114).

Moody goes to Canton to be a part of the big "Freedom Day" (405). Everyone at the Freedom House hugs her as if she has come home to her family after a while. Within an hour, she makes three hundred posters with freedom slogans for the march. Mrs. Devine tells her that they are expecting about five hundred adults and eight hundred high school students ready to demonstrate at the courthouse, and Moody cannot believe it when she sees three hundred adults pile out of the church for the march. The entire street is lined up with cops, and as the adults enter the church, they sing freedom songs:

Oh, Freedom, Oh, Freedom,
Oh, Freedom over me.
And before I'll be a slave
I'll be buried in my grave
And go home to my Lord and be free.
No more lynchings, no more lynchings,
No more lynchings over me.
And before I'll be a slave
I'll be buried in my grave
And go home to my Lord and be free.
(*Italics original* 407)

To the adults, heaven will end their problems, but the teenagers believe that the power to change things is within them. Their way of thinking seems to be, "God helps those that help themselves" instead of "When we get to heaven things will be different, there won't be no black or white" (408). They know that things will remain the same unless they participate in the movement and fight for the change themselves. Moody can see them as men and women living a normal life, as a real part of this world, "as a group of people that belonged – belonged because they had fought the battle and won" (408).

All hopes for the future come to life again. Looking at the teenagers on the canvassing teams, Moody realises that the future of the movement is in the youth, and the movement must focus on practical affairs: the younger generation is the hope of the struggle for equality. Aretha Franklin, in the song *"A Change Is Gonna Come,"* expresses "this feeling of enduring despite the odds. She sings that there were times that she thought that she would not last for long. She sings of how it has been an 'uphill journey all the way' to find the strength to carry on. But despite the difficulties, Aretha 'knows' that 'a change is gonna come'" (qtd. in Collins 132).

One of the cops in the street asks the teenagers why they are marching, calling them "niggers" (410). A teenager replies that they are marching because they are aiming to taste a bit of the freedom that the white people are enjoying. They are going to eat in the white restaurants, drive their police cars, vote, and do everything else that the whites do. The cops get angry and pull a young man, McKinley Hamilton, hit him with sticks on his head, and almost kill him. They go to the church to discuss the matter with Reverend Cox, CORE field secretary, and eighty volunteers go for a march with an eighty-six-year-old man leading it. All the marchers are stopped by the cops and taken to jail. The Negroes are angry because of the cops beating McKinley, and the whites are mad because the Negroes are trying to get together finally.

Moody returns to Tougaloo to attend her graduation ceremony from the college; she feels sad to see that neither her parents nor any other family member is there for the ceremony. She is happy to receive her diploma, and when she is back in New Orleans, Adline gifts her a very pretty green dress, which symbolises her attainment of a college degree and Adline's acceptance of Moody's goals. Adline is happy to see her diploma, as she is the first person in the family to graduate from college.

Moody goes back to Canton after a few days and feels worse than she had ever felt before. She plans to go to Jackson, and the moment she reaches the COFO headquarters, she finds a bus going to Washington and joins them. The bus is filled with volunteers who all seem far more exuberant and younger than her. As the bus starts moving, everybody sings, and Moody leans back in the seat and listens:

We shall overcome, We shall overcome
We shall overcome some day.
Oh, deep in my heart I do believe
We shall overcome some day.
The truth will make us free,
The truth will make us free,
The truth will make us free some day.
Oh, deep in my heart I do believe
The truth will make us free some day.
(*Italics original* 423)

Images of earlier happenings keep crossing her mind – the Taplin burning, the Birmingham church bombing, Medgar Evers' murder, the blood gushing out of McKinley's head, and all the other murders. With tears welling up in her eyes, she wonders whether they will really overcome racism and all other problems someday; she wonders if things will change and the Negroes will ever be free. It reflects her grievous frustration with the movement.

Moody later reflects, "I realized that the universal fight for human rights, dignity, justice, equality and freedom is not and should not be just the fight of the American Negro or the Indians or the Chicanos. It's the fight of every ethnic and racial minority, every suppressed and exploited person, everyone of the millions who daily suffer one or another of the indignities of the powerless and voiceless masses" (Opatrny PDF). She dedicates her life to the cause of fighting for civil rights. She says that, "we made a few visible little gains; yet at the root, things always remained the same; and that the movement was not in control of her destiny, nor did we have any means of gaining control of it. We were like an angry dog on a leash that had turned on its master. It could bark and howl and snap, and sometimes even bite, but the master was always in control" (Wynn, web. 20 Jan. 2017).

In My Place is a resonant success story, a story of triumph over obstacles, of recognition and empowerment. Hunter-Gault's story is about the universal adolescent search for one's place in family, among one's peers, in community, and eventually in the world. *The New Yorker* exhibits, "This book is a vivid retelling of history, and should take its place as one of the informal literary classics of the civil rights movement" (135). As a nineteen-year-old, Hunter-Gault challenged

Southern law and Southern violence to become the first Black woman to attend the University of Georgia, and thus her life writing is a powerful act of witness to the brutal realities of segregation. It is the biography of her generation, as it epitomises the experiences of many courageous Black students who led the Civil Rights Movement in the 1960s.

Throughout her successful career, she has never lost sight of herself as a Black journalist, and in a piece for *Fortune*, she emphasizes the need for the media to present African Americans "as whole people" (qtd. in Gale, "Hunter-Gault, Charlayne 1942 – *Contemporary Black Biography*," web. 15 Jan. 2017). In 1968, she accepted a position with the metropolitan staff of *The New York Times*, and during this tenure, she wrote a critical note to top editors objecting to their practice of using the term "Negro." She attacks the presumptions her white bosses had about people of colour. Her points are taken into consideration, and *The New York Times* adopts the word "Black" as standard usage. She asserts in *People* magazine, "Nowadays it seems almost silly. But it was one of those defining moments in the history of Black journalism in major white institutions" (73–76).

Anne Moody's life writing helps one understand what life was like in the South before and during the Civil Rights Movement. Senator Edward M. Kennedy, the spokesperson for *The New York Times*, in his 1969 review, declares that *Coming of Age in Mississippi* is "a history of our time, seen from the bottom up, through the eyes of someone who decided for herself that things had to be changed" (5). Her personal story manifests that the Civil Rights Movement was a slow and difficult process, and it was hard to persuade people to join the movement. It talks about the struggles and hardships in securing even basic rights. It is also a reflection of how a hopeless cry from a downtrodden segment of society gets transformed into an organized outcry of resilience and empowerment. It is true that the nature of racist oppression and exploitation has changed, as slavery has ended and the apartheid structure of Jim Crow has legally changed, but "white supremacy continues to shape perspectives on reality and to inform the social status of Black people and all people of color" (bell hooks, *Talking Back* 114).

The Civil Rights Movement in the United States has been a primarily nonviolent struggle to secure full civil rights and equality under the law for all Americans. The movement has had a lasting impact on United States society by increasing social and legal acceptance of civil rights, and in its exposé of prevalent racism. The Civil Rights Movement of the 1950s and 1960s witnessed great changes in American society. From *Brown vs. Board of Education* to the Montgomery Bus Boycott, March on Washington, Freedom Rides, the Black Power Movement, and the Civil Rights Act of 1964, the era guaranteed basic civil rights for all Americans, irrespective of race. Key Civil Rights Organizations such as the NAACP, SCLC, SNCC, and CORE played vital roles during the period defined by race, violence, and democracy.

The history of Black civil rights is the story of America's caste system; it is the story of how, for centuries, upper-class whites treated African Americans as slaves, easily identifiable because of their dark skin. To all mainstream civil rights leaders, with the current social conditions, many African Americans and poor people must remember the names Malcolm X, Martin Luther King Jr., and Medgar Evers as constant reminders of past struggles. In 2014, America marked the fiftieth anniversary of the March on Washington, the Civil Rights Act of 1964, and Freedom Summer. In 2015, it recognized the fiftieth anniversary of the Voting Rights Act of 1965. As they move into the twenty-first century, America finds itself at the beginning of a new era defined by its own set of civil rights struggles:

"The battles of 2015 are in some ways markedly different from those of the 1950s and 1960s, as 'whites only' signs and overt displays of condoned racism are mostly relegated to history. However, what remains is a country full of disparately impacted populations, with people of color facing disadvantages at home, at work, at school, and in the justice system, all in the context of a society that prides itself on its imagined march towards post-racial colorblindness" (*The Present and Future of Civil Rights Movements: Race and Reform in 21st Century America*, web. 16 Jan. 2018).

The African American women writers powerfully manifest their confrontation with and triumph over a racist, sexist society by giving the reader true success stories which can be the guiding light for many.

Chapter 5

From Closed Doors to Open Roads: Conclusion

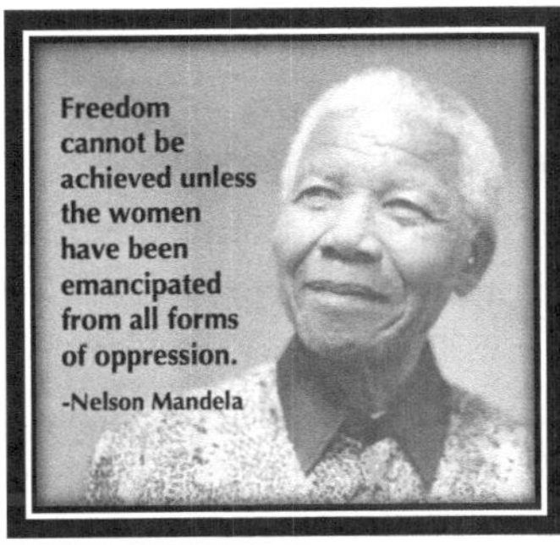

She had been getting ready for her great journey to the horizons in search of people; it was important to all the world that she should find them and they find her.

–Hurston,
Their Eyes Were Watching God 108

Literary representation is a complex phenomenon, for it is substantially influenced by ideological and political stances; it is an ideological tool that reinforces the system of inequality and subordination. Literature is a representation of the pulses and vibrations that reverberate in society. Through the representation of events, it reflects multiple socio-cultural realities, including ideologies, cultural ethos, and power politics inherent in the dynamics of presenting reality. Representation is of substantial significance in literary analysis, for it plays a decisive role in solving the conflicts owing to the racio-cultural patterns of different communities. In representation, the marginal/oppressed group is rendered voiceless largely due to structural domination, for representation comes from a privileged position of power, supported by educational opportunity, citizenship, class, race, gender, and location.

The binary dialectic of centre/margin has been largely the creation of representation and the relationship between the haves and have-nots, and in the historical past, subaltern representation was completely sidelined and ignored. Literature has emerged as a safety valve for the social consciousness of the oppressed. The representation of subalterns highlights their unique cultural features, their tragic exploitation, as well as their fight for rightful claims. The representation of subaltern subjects is based on the argument that the focus should now be shifted to the marginalized in society, and this transition must centralize subalterns' marginal position in society.

There are oppressive mechanisms of silencing, suppressing, and censoring; therefore, finding a voice is a pertinent determinant to move in the direction of freedom. A shift in focus from core to periphery is one of the most recent developments in literature at the national and international level. It is a fact that the dominant ones have used literature as a potential instrument for misrepresenting the oppressed, and literary representation is the only empowering site for the victims to contest oppressive hegemonies. Literature as a discipline necessarily involves representation, and this new trend questions the elitism and exclusiveness of literature to represent the powerful elite that advocates the voice of the formerly oppressed 'Other.' The inaudible and marginalized voice is brought to the forefront so that the earlier erasure and deliberate hegemonic mindset are subverted.

The subordination of the subaltern is strengthened by socio-economic, racio-cultural, and linguistic dominance. The dominant power structure controls the concepts of national identity, social reforms, and developmental parameters, and the subaltern discourse seeks to reconsider and re-examine them with a fresh perspective. There is a need to dislodge dominant modes of representation so as to subvert and challenge hegemonic ideologies. The suppression of subaltern experiences into silence and absolute devaluation in national historiography is contested, and the focus is now towards the reconstruction of subaltern history. Current critical discourses are incorporating the marginalized, the minorities, and the sub-cultural groups.

Subaltern denotes marginalized and oppressed sections of society who are the victims of hegemonic dominance, largely due to their marginal place or no place at all in cultural history. Now the marginalized are gaining centre stage because they refuse to be subjected to misrepresentation and are creating new discourses. Subaltern studies attempt an authentic, consistent, and interpretative version of history, which is contradictory to the mainstream discourses or official documentation of history. Audre Lorde, in the poem "Litany for Survival," addresses the fear of speech among the marginal group and urges them to speak, "… and when we speak we are afraid our words will not be heard nor welcomed but when we are silent we are still afraid. So it is better to speak remembering we were never meant to survive" (qtd. in bell hooks, *Talking Back* 17).

Marginalization is the powerlessness and exclusion experienced by a group; to be marginalized is to be forced to occupy the sides or fringes and thus not be at the centre of things. It is a process wherein individuals or entire communities are denied various rights, opportunities, and resources that are normally available to the members of other groups. This has a substantial effect on a person, for he is made to stand out and be different from the rest. The Third World nations, developing nations, and women comprise various minority groups. American society has triply disempowered and disenfranchised African American women on the basis of race, gender, and class. Among these three oppressions, racism is the most powerful one. They are hated and degraded because of their skin colour. She is Black and also a woman, and thus she is in a doubly disadvantaged position in white American patriarchal society. Sexism and racism started simultaneously for Black women when they were enslaved. They were made to work along with Black men in plantations and were sexually abused by their white masters. Besides hard labour during the day, they became sex objects for white slave masters at night, rampantly raped and forced to procreate a new breed of slaves. Even after freedom, African American women are often raped, and their modesty is outraged by white men.

Though Black men have always been fighting against oppression, they themselves have been tyrannical towards their own women. They have been abused, hated, mutilated, and raped by African men as well as by white men. She finds herself pushed to the brink, being affected by racism and crippled by sexism. They also suffer from classicism, as they are the least privileged ones as compared to white males, white women, and African American males. They are positioned on the lowest rung of the socio-economic ladder. Right from the days of slavery, she is considered the least deserving one, though she has been working alongside Black males. She has been taking care of the children, their family, and is an integral part of the social milieu, but she is an invisible citizen in the most vulnerable position. African American women writers aim to break down traditional structures and dislocate narrative strategies in order to re-examine subject identity and demonstrate the complexity of female experience. The ethos represented by the Black woman can be associated with the situation of those women who occupy the margins of society in terms of race, culture, and social positioning. Women writers go through a potentially challenging pilgrimage of self-discovery and finally ascertain a voice and space of their own. By writing about their lives, the marginalized are valorized, and their oppression is transformed into empowerment. In their life writings, they recount the mistreatment and marginalization that they experience as Black women in a hostile society.

Life writing is an extension in the field of literature, and it covers what used to be called an autobiography or biography, and the different ways of inscribing the 'self' in literature. It enables a writer or a reader to understand himself better and his relationship with the world. It is a site of struggle in the representation of life and self. The term life writing suggests different ways of writing and can be seen as a new strategy for giving ownership and validation to the individual, a reclamation of agency, particularly for the marginalized. It facilitates females to explore subjectivity by reflecting on the self and the world; such openness posits life writing as a relevant point of departure for a multitude of contemporary ideological issues. Life writing raises consciousness, gives space to the uninhibited expression of the female point of view, and is a vehicle for deciphering or decoding the female self. It appropriates feminism, as it is a way of telling women's stories, of re-making a female story, creating a new tradition and mode of interpretation of writing for women silenced by institutionalized, monologic discourse. It emphatically exhorts women to break the silence, to claim language, and validate their unique subjective experience.

Life writing is the African American way of preserving cultural memory; at the same time, it challenges their marginalization and oppression by the socio-eco-politico-literary establishments. This act of penning one's own story is a way for African American women to create their own identities, rather than those formally created and promoted by the whites. Black women are marginalized, considered dark and ugly, rather than dark and lovely. They write to express what life has been to them, as well as to release their mental agony. It opens the doors to greater understanding of the culture and how she forges her identity despite travails.

The twentieth century has been a period of intense literary activity for African American women writers. It was a time when, for the first time, these talented writers started to write and exhibit their creative genius. They finally come out of the shadows of racism and sexism and create works without inhibitions, portraying their growth, struggle, and accomplishments. African American women writers are the mouthpieces for Black women. They have embraced the reality and created the truth in their own way. They spread self-awareness by actively pinpointing the multiple oppressions and learn to rely and depend on themselves, and also learn to fight for themselves, because if they don't, who will?

The twentieth-century African American women writers have achieved a rare literary feat. They have debunked the falsified myths about a Black woman, shattered the racist and sexist iconoclasts, and reconstructed and revisioned new canons in African American literature. Being both Black and female, these writers write from a vantage point. They project the vision of the world through the eyes of Black female characters. Their vision allows them to see what white people, especially males, fail to see. With a penetrating glance, they cut through the layers of institutionalized racism and sexism so as to uncover social contradictions and dilemmas which plague everyone, regardless of race and gender.

For the oppressed and the exploited, finding a voice is a pertinent determinant of liberation to move in the direction of freedom. In the process of learning to speak as subjects, they participate in the global struggle to end domination. Coming to voice is a gesture of resistance, an affirmation of struggle for women within oppressed groups who have suffered anguish, despair, and rage. The shift from silence to speech leads to self-transformation, especially for women who previously never had a public voice. Maya Angelou, in the foreword to Zora Neale Hurston's *Dust Tracks on a Road*, maintains, "There is an eerie, sometimes pathetic, ofttimes beautiful urge that prevails in Black American lore, lyrics and literature. The impulse, simply put, is to tell the story … to tell one's own story … as one has known it, and lived it, and even died it" (vii). Speaking is a way to engage in active self-transformation. It is important for women who resist and rebel, survive and succeed, to speak openly and honestly about their lives and the nature of their personal struggles so as to resolve and reconcile contradictions.

Black feminism is a necessary step to end racism and sexism in view of the nature of gender oppression and the magnitude of resistance to racial justice. The feminist thinkers strive to assert their social identity both individually and collectively. With one penetrating glance, they cut through layers of institutionalised racism and sexism and uncover the core of social contradictions and dilemmas. The feminist struggle to end patriarchal domination is of primary importance to women and men globally because it is the domination that is encountered in everyday life. Black feminism, as an activist response to oppression, will be needed as long as Black women's subordination within intersecting oppressions of race, class, gender, sexuality, and nation persists.

Within the context of social injustice sustained by intersecting oppressions, Black feminist thought, as a critical social theory, aims to empower African American women. Black feminism is a theoretical concept developed to focalise attention on the multiple oppressions experienced by Black women, reflecting and defining their everyday experiences in their own terms, in search of self-awareness and self-empowerment. It is a necessary step towards ending racism and sexism, given the nature of gender oppression and the magnitude of society's resistance to racial justice. Unless intersecting oppressions themselves are eliminated, Black women cannot be fully empowered. Maria Stewart's 1831 speech advises the "daughters of Africa" to "Awake!

Arise! No longer sleep nor slumber, but distinguish yourselves. Show forth to the world that ye are endowed with noble and exalted faculties" (qtd. in Richardson 30).

Twentieth-century African American women's literature is that of growing up Black in a hostile environment. These writers show how African American girls develop a self-resilient spirit in order to cope with an adverse environment. The accounts of the lives of these writers chronicle their frequent encounters with racism, sexism, and classism as they describe the people, events, and personal qualities that helped them to survive the devastating effects of their environment. They highlight the role models and family members who sustained and nurtured them, and the events that contributed to their development into strong, independent young women.

Dust Tracks on a Road by Zora Neale Hurston, written at the age of fifty, poignantly describes what it is like to grow up poor, Black, and female. She is one of eight children in a Black family with small prospects of making a name for herself. As an energetic woman, she overcomes odds to achieve a liberated and rewarding life. Hurston is born in Eatonville, Florida, America's first incorporated Black community; her father is a driving force in the community, being a powerful preacher. Her mother, who inspires her children "to jump at de sun," dies when she is nine. The liberating force for Hurston is her love for knowledge; at the Black grammar school she wins a reading contest and receives books that ignite her imagination. She learns about real life at Joe Clarke's store, the meeting place of the men in town. After her mother's death, she moves from one place to another in search of a job and education. It is her own initiative that helps her rise above her circumstances. She gives an account of her rise from childhood poverty in the rural South to a prominent place among the leading artists and intellectuals.

Once she learns that an actress in a travelling Gilbert and Sullivan troupe is looking for a maid, she approaches the woman and, in her service, gets a marvellous education in humanity and the arts. With her fighting spirit, she struggles to achieve the education she considers a must. She learns that if one wants to go to school, the thing to do is to go to school, so she goes back to night high school, then to Howard University and Barnard College, where she works under anthropologist

Franz Boas and studies the folklore of her people in Polk County, Florida. She makes her way in research on fellowships, and this leads to a lifelong interest in the roots of her people. Consequently, she becomes an outstanding anthropologist in the field of Black folklore and culture. She surveys everything from African American songs to voodoo and leaves a mark on modern American music.

With inborn talent and hard work, Hurston faces multiple hues of life. Some of Hurston's greatest friends and confidants are the upper-class whites who have been kind to her. Race consciousness is completely absent from her work as she explains that there are white niggers and Black niggers; being a nigger is a matter of character rather than colour among the Blacks. She does not refer to the race riots and other atrocities of her times, and there is little discussion of the issues of race and segregation. Hurston presents a balanced view of the effects of racism on Black life not because she is unaware of the seriousness of racial politics, but simply because she refuses to accept the oppression of Blacks as the definition of her life. Her life is a dramatic adventure, and she proves herself to be essentially a survivor.

I Know Why the Caged Bird Sings by Maya Angelou covers her life from childhood to adulthood and describes the way she is raised in segregated rural Arkansas until the birth of her son when she is seventeen. She focuses on the inner spaces of her emotional and personal life; she recalls the sins of the past and the rituals of healing and reconciliation, and thus creates a work of poignant realism and hope. Angelou inscribes resistance to racism, sexism, and poverty within the imagery, language, and meaning of her text, with her truth-telling vision and perspectives. As a young girl, she struggles growing up, gains knowledge, develops a positive self-image, and realises that she can control her life by her strong intellect. She takes the chaos of her life and creates her own order. Being a lover of literature from a very young age, she appreciates it, looks for answers in it, and finds it to be an anchor.

The popularity of *I Know Why the Caged Bird Sings* rests on the achieved pathos as it accomplishes a controlled poignancy in representing the portrait of the artist as a young Black woman. The pertinent point of her struggle is to find her own way of handling white oppression. With positive encouragement and full support from her mother, she confidently challenges the racist order and fights with an invincible spirit to become the first Black female streetcar conductor in San Francisco at the age of fifteen. The moral stance of the text challenges the audience to confront the contradictions of life, to create positive change in one's self and community. Angelou emerges miraculously from violence, sexual abuse at the age of eight, and neglect, evoking awareness through the agency of memory.

Angelou faces the dual injustice of racial hostility and male exploitation and describes her quest for physical and psychological survival. She decides to write *I Know Why the Caged Bird Sings* because not enough had been written for young Black girls in the United States. She wants to remind her fellow African Americans that despite the obstacles and pain they endure, there is much love and humour to be found in the African American community. The text has definite appeal for young Black girls, as Oprah Winfrey describes in an interview with Angelou in 1993 that the work is important to her because it is the first book she has read that reflects her own experiences. It is a universal tale of survival and continues to be instructive on matters of race and gender. Angelou's life is a struggle of an individual at a personal level, and in the larger context, it exemplifies the marginalised sections of society.

Triangular Road: A Memoir, written by Paule Marshall at the age of eighty, recounts powerful first-hand stories of her family and travels. She is best known as a novelist who explores issues of Caribbean and African American identity. She focuses on the three water bodies that made up the triangular slave-trade route: the James River, the Caribbean Sea, and the Atlantic Ocean. She mingles the history of each with her development as a writer. Her parents are from Barbados, a principal way station in the slave trade. They move to Brooklyn, where Marshall grows up in a close-knit West Indian community and first discovers her passion for books. She poignantly writes of the slave trade that came through Richmond. She narrates a centuries-long history of human atrocities, historically locating Barbados, Virginia, and Grenada in the context of the slave trade and African presence.

Marshall pays homage to Langston Hughes, who with great goodwill provides her the opportunity to accompany him on the cultural tour of Europe. His acts of kindness and encouragement inspire her throughout her career. She portrays her imposing grandmother, M'Da-duh, whom she meets once when she is seven and immortalises in one guise or another in every work she pens down. She gets her first lesson in the art and craft of writing by hearing her mother and friends talk in the kitchen, with their Bajan proverbs and colourful stories. She briefly talks about her first marriage, her only child, and eventual divorce. Once, she suffers from writer's block, and by packing prized notebooks full of factual research, she finally understands that she is a storyteller first and is responsible for the story, and that historical truth will come in automatically if she crafts her tale honestly.

At the very end, she pays homage to Black African creativity and comradeship. *Triangular Road* ends in Africa, where the journey of her ancestors had begun. She describes FESTAC, the Second World Festival of Black and African Arts in Lagos, Nigeria in 1977. It highlights the chaotic nature of the African American struggle for civil rights, in which she got involved as early as the 1940s. The journey sparks a passion to rediscover her African heritage. Retrospectively, she embraces important lessons that include mentoring and encouraging young writers, nurturing and making room for one's passion, and, through a literal or spiritual return, pays homage to her heritage and lineage. *Triangular Road* is of great significance as a literary text as well as a socio-historical-cultural document that celebrates womanhood and affirms liberation.

Coming of Age in Mississippi by Anne Moody, written at the age of twenty-eight, delineates what it was to grow up Black in the era of Jim Crow. It narrates her life from her early childhood through her involvement in the civil rights movement as a young Black woman. A daughter of poor sharecroppers, she starts working for white families at the early age of nine. She endures a tumultuous childhood, bearing the triple burden of poverty, racism, and discrimination; fearing the depths of hate as seen in the murder of Emmett Till, with rising racial tensions in the community. Though undergoing emotional distress, Moody is a devoted and popular student. After attending Natchez Junior College on a basketball scholarship, she receives a bachelor's degree in 1964 from Tougaloo College, a historically Black institution near Jackson.

During these years, she is active in civil rights activities in Mississippi, working with the NAACP (National Association for the Advancement of Coloured People), CORE (Congress of Racial Equality), and SNCC (Student Nonviolent Coordinating Committee). Moody is a principal participant in the sit-in to desegregate Woolworth's lunch counter. Along with other demonstrations in Jackson, she takes part in the historic 1963 March on Washington and spearheads voter registration efforts. Being a dedicated worker, going to jail is a common occurrence in her life, though she is always concerned about the safety of her family. She organises groups of teenagers to register Black voters in Canton. The threats and violence against the student activists continue, and Moody finds herself on the Ku Klux Klan's blacklist at the age of twenty-three.

After graduating from Tougaloo in 1964, she works as the civil rights project coordinator until 1965 at Cornell University in Ithaca, New York. Eventually, she becomes disenchanted with the civil rights movement and moves to New York, where she writes *Coming of Age in Mississippi.* This is an eloquent and poignant account of Moody's impoverished childhood, her personal and political struggle against the pervasive racism of the Deep South, and her association with the civil rights movement. It received high acclaim both as a historical and personal document and is considered substantially important in the study of the civil rights movement. *Coming of Age in Mississippi* is an amazing story of Anne Moody's unbreakable spirit and character throughout the first twenty-three years of her life. Time and again, she speaks of unthinkable odds and conditions and how she attains success eventually.

In My Place by Charlayne Hunter-Gault dwells on her family history and descriptions of the southern towns where she spends her childhood. She possesses the felicity of a woman confident of her abilities and certain of her place in history. She identifies strong teachers, good friends, and a dignified father struggling as a chaplain in a racist regime who shape her and encourage her to be herself. It is also the story of a girl who dreams of being a reporter like the comic-strip character Brenda Starr, at a time when realising such a dream was beyond reach. She manifests how her upbringing prepares her for a long walk across America's racial divide and achieves what once seemed virtually impossible. After attending a largely white school in Alaska, she spends her high school years in the supportive Black environment of Atlanta. Being self-confident and ambitious, she willingly offers herself as a test case in the struggle for equality in education. In 1961, Charlayne Hunter-Gault, at the age of nineteen, becomes the first Black woman to desegregate the University of Georgia. She takes the first step in a massive realignment of American society when she walks the Athens campus past a jeering mob of white students.

The 1961 desegregation of the University of Georgia by Hamilton Holmes and Charlayne Hunter is considered a defining moment in civil rights history, leading to the desegregation of other institutions of higher education in Georgia and throughout the Deep South. Holmes and Hunter had attended all-Black Turner High School in Atlanta, where Holmes had been valedictorian, senior class president, and co-captain of the football team. Hunter was ranked third in her graduating class, edited the school paper, and was crowned Miss Turner. Nevertheless, for a year and a half, university officials gave a variety of reasons for denying their applications. On 6th January 1961, federal judge William Bootle handed down his verdict that the two were fully qualified for admission and would already have been admitted had it not been for their race and colour. Even after facing agitation and riots, Holmes and Hunter graduated from the desegregated University of Georgia in 1963.

Hunter-Gault speaks of harassment and support in those dramatic years, as well as of her growth as a journalist, her public speaking tours, and even her romance with a white Southerner. She concludes with *In My Place* – the title of the stirring speech that she delivers to the 1988 graduating class at the University of Georgia. The speech includes a number of challenging thoughts about education, prejudice, marriage, and the need for more Black faculty members and students. Between the lines of her speech, there is her journey from reading the adventures of Brenda Starr to Charlayne Hunter-Gault, who travels a long way from the racist insults that first greeted her on campus to become a role model for journalists. *In My Place* is a book about sit-ins, marches, court battles, and riots; a story of a young girl's entry into the civil rights movement – a movement that permanently changed the status of Blacks in America and altered the very structure of society. It is a powerful act of witness to the brutal realities of segregation; the universal fight for human rights, dignity, justice, equality, and freedom. It is not just the fight of the American Blacks or the Indians; it is the fight of every ethnic and racial minority, every suppressed and exploited person, every one of the millions who daily suffer indignities as the powerless and voiceless entities.

The twentieth-century African American women writers are integral to African American women's literature and have enriched the American literary tradition with their unique perspectives, causing a paradigm shift in African American literature. Fighting against white supremacy and their own men's abuse, they have carved their own niche. They have played a vital role in knitting together the rich, vibrant yarns of folk culture, race, and tradition to produce the multi-coloured fabric of African American literature. They have brought a change in the way of thinking of African Americans, especially that of African American women. Their impact can be felt not only in the field of literature but in every aspect of African American life.

Even now, women in society are faced with numerous challenges and problems; the major challenges are gender discrimination and marginalisation. Racial segregation remains deeply entrenched in housing, schooling, and employment, despite important strides to desegregate U.S. society since 1970. For many African American women, racism is not something that exists in the distance; they encounter racism in everyday situations, in workplaces, stores, schools, homes, and everyday social interactions. While they no longer live within the rigid structures of racial apartheid that characterised earlier history, they live within a culture of domination, surrounded by religious and educational institutions which reinforce the values, beliefs, and underlying assumptions of white supremacy. Despite various calls by human rights activists and non-governmental organisations to abolish and eliminate discrimination and marginalisation of women, the fact is that their condition is still not praiseworthy.

Through marginalisation, society sets the limits to what an individual can achieve. For example, in the workplace, women have been marginalised from top managerial or executive positions. Society believes that only men can serve well as senior managers or chief executives. Due to this assumption, women who are better qualified than their male counterparts are sidelined for executive positions because they are viewed as poor managers or inferior beings. In February 2010, Oprah Winfrey stated in her television talk show – *The Oprah Winfrey Show* – that approximately one hundred thousand women in the United States of America have been marginalised from various white-collar jobs and executive positions in most organisations, including state corporations. The marginalisation of women in the workplace has resulted in increased discrimination against women and has also resulted in the dominance of men in the workplace.

Race, class, and gender still constitute intersecting oppressions, but the ways in which they are now organised differ from prior eras. Women are abused by their husbands, young girls are exploited by sex tourism and trafficking, and girls in many countries are forced into arranged marriages at early ages. The marginalisation results from various stereotypes and other preconceived notions. Therefore, the dire need is to avoid such destructive stereotypes and assumptions to create a healthy, balanced society. As per African American writers, the power to save the self lies within the self, no matter how oppressed an individual is. In this journey towards personal empowerment, other Black women may assist a Black woman, but the ultimate responsibility for self-definitions and self-valuations lies within the individual only. Black women's persistence is fostered by the strong belief that to be Black and female is valuable and worthy of respect. Her beliefs in self-definition, self-valuation, and self-reliance that stem from her struggles to survive apprise the world of her worldview.

Oprah Winfrey emphatically states that the marginalisation of women depicts serious flaws in assumptions towards women. She suggests that society should take the sole responsibility to ensure that women are not marginalised in any way. It is the responsibility of society to guarantee and provide women with the adequate support they require in relation to employment, education, policy formulation, and other roles. Society should ensure that the needs and concerns of women are fully addressed. Gender discrimination and maltreatment of women should be highly discouraged, condemned, and stopped so that women can breathe freely.

What needs to be done is what women and girls have been desperately striving for throughout – to ensure full equality. By equality, one means equal access to food, shelter, healthcare, education, employment, and the right to live. By promoting the rights of girls around the world, instances of many other abuses due to cultural and religious stereotypes that continue to remain unchallenged or blatantly ignored will decrease. One must be aware that gender inequality is an enormous contributor to poverty around the world, and if poverty is to be eradicated, the starting point is to end the abuse against women. Though girls do suffer more than boys, all children suffer when their mothers face inequality. Women around the world have been striving for independence. It is a wake-up call that by marginalising girls, society itself is crippled. Women should be given the freedom to live, to speak, and to work as per their choice, and men should respect them for what they are.

Black women's struggle is part of a wider struggle for human dignity, empowerment, and social justice. Black women intellectuals' commitment to women's empowerment advances the strikingly similar theme of the oneness of all humans. The select African American women writers have broken new ground, created new literary canons, and paved the way for twenty-first-century writers. Today, young and dynamic writers who are creating an upsurge in the literary world are, in one way or another, indebted to these twentieth-century African American women writers.

There is a need for the solidarity of humanity, the oneness of life, and the injustice of all favouritisms—whether of sex, race, country, or condition—must be done away with. The black woman feels that woman's cause is one and universal; and until race, colour, sex, and condition are seen as accidents and not the substance of life, not till humanity and happiness are conceded to all, not till then is woman's lesson taught and woman's cause won—not the white woman's, nor the black woman's, not the red woman's, but the cause of every man and woman who has writhed silently under a mighty wrong. The select writers are spokespersons for the blacks, especially the black women; they leave all barriers apart, reach the stars, and turn seemingly impossible fantasy into reality. The black women are singing their own songs, and they are singing them bravely, boldly, and remarkably.

MAYA
ANGELOU
“A bird doesn’t sing
because it has an
answer, it sings because
it has a song.”

Works Cited

Primary Sources

1. Angelou, Maya. *I Know Why the Caged Bird Sings.* New York: Random House, 1969. Print.
2. Hunter-Gault, Charlayne. *In My Place.* New York: Vintage, 1992. Print.
3. Hurston, Zora Neale. *Dust Tracks on a Road.* 1942. New York: Harper Perennial, 1996. Print.
4. Marshall, Paule. *Triangular Road: A Memoir.* New York: Basic Civitas, 2009. Print.
5. Moody, Anne. *Coming of Age in Mississippi.* New York: Dell, 1968. Print.

Secondary Sources:

Books:

1. Abrams, M. H. "Postcolonial Studies." *A Glossary of Literary Terms.* 7th ed. 3rd rpt. Bangalore: Prism, 1999. 237. Print.
2. Agins, Donna Brown. *Maya Angelou: A Biography of an Award-Winning Poet and Civil Rights Activist.* New Jersey: Enslow, 2013. Print.
3. Anand, Tarlochan Singh, ed. *Perspectives on the Afro-American Novel.* Jalandhar: ABS, 1994. Print.

4. Anderson, Linda. *Autobiography*. London: Routledge, 2001. Print.
5. Andrews, William L., ed. *African American Autobiography: A Collection of Critical Essays*. Englewood Cliffs: Prentice Hall, 1993. Print.
6. Angelou, Maya. *The Complete Collected Poems of Maya Angelou*. New York: Random House, 1994. Print.
7. Beaulieu, Elizabeth Ann. *Writing African American Women (Two Volumes): An Encyclopedia of Literature by and about Women of Color*. U.S.A.: Greenwood Press, 2006. Print.
8. Beauvoir, Simone de. *The Second Sex*. 1952. New York: Vintage, 1989. Print.
9. bell, hooks. *Ain't I a Woman: Black Women and Feminism*. Boston: South End Press, 1981. Print.
10. ---. *Feminist Theory: From Margin to Center*. London: Pluto Press, 2000. Print.
11. ---. *Outlaw Culture: Resisting Representations*. New York: Routledge, 1994. Print.
12. ---. *Talking Back: Thinking Feminist, Thinking Black*. Boston: South End Press, 1989. Print
13. Bell-Scott, Patricia. *Life Notes: Personal Writings by Contemporary Black Women*. New York: Norton, 1994. Print.
14. Bennett, Michael and Vanessa D. Dickerson, ed. *Recovering the Black Female Body: Self-Representations by African American Women*. U.S.A.: Rutgers UP, 2001. Print.
15. Berlin, Ira et.al, eds. *Slaves No More: Three Essays on Emancipation and the Civil War*. UK: Cambridge UP, 1992. Print.
16. Bhabha, Homi K., ed. *Nation and Narration*. New York: Routledge, 1990. Print.
17. Bloom, Harold, ed. *Zora Neale Hurston's Their Eyes Were Watching God*. New York: Infobase, 2009. Print.
18. Bottaro, Jean and John Stanley. *History for the IB Diploma: Democratic States*. UK: Cambridge UP, 2011. Print.
19. Boynton, Victoria and Jo Malin. *Encyclopedia of Women's Autobiography*. Westport: Greenwood Press, 2005. Print.

20. Braxton, Joanne M. *Black Women Writing Autobiography: A Tradition Within a Tradition.* Philadelphia: Temple UP, 1989. Print.
21. Braxton, Joanne M., ed. *Maya Angelou's I Know Why the Caged Bird Sings: A Casebook.* New York: OUP, 1999. Print.
22. Brignano, Russell C. *Black Americans in Autobiography: An Annotated Bibliography of Autobiographies and Autobiographical Works Written since the Civil War.* Durham: Duke UP, 1984. Print.
23. Brockmeier, Jens and Donal A. Carbaugh. *Narrative and Identity: Studies in Autobiography, Self and Culture.* Amsterdam: John Benjamins, 2001. Print.
24. Brownley, Martine Watson and Allison B. Kimmich, ed. *Women and Autobiography.* U.S.A.: Rowman and Littlefield, 1999. Print.
25. Butterfield, Stephen. *Black Autobiography in America.* Amherst: Massachusetts UP, 1974. Print.
26. Byerly, Victoria. *Hard Times Cotton Mill Girls: Personal Histories of Womanhood and Poverty in the South.* U.S.A.: ILR Press, 1986. Print.
27. Cannon, Katie. *Black Womanist Ethics.* Atlanta: Scholars Press, 1988. Print.
28. Carby, Hazel. *Reconstructing Womanhood: The Emergence of the Afro-American Woman Novelist.* New York: OUP, 1987. Print.
29. Carson, Clayborne and Kris Shepard, ed. *A Call to Conscience: The Landmark Speeches of Dr. Martin Luther King, Jr.* New York: Hachette, 2001. Print.
30. Chand, Neerja Jayal. "Moving the Centre: Black Canadian and Dalit Literature." *WRITING BLACK AND WRITING DALIT: Essays in Black African and Dalit Indian Writings.* Ed. Harish Narang. Shimla: IIAS, 2002. 71. Print.
31. Chong, Dennis. *Collective Action and the Civil Rights Movement.* U.S.A: Chicago UP, 1991. Print.
32. Christian, Barbara. *Black Feminist Criticism: Perspectives on Black Women Writers.* New York: Pergamon, 1985. Print.

33. Collins, Patricia Hills. *Black Feminist Thought: Knowledge, Consciousness, and the Politics of Empowerment.* New York: Routledge, 2000. Print.
34. Conway, Jill Ker, ed. *Written by Herself: Autobiographies of American Women: An Anthology.* New York: Vintage, 1992. Print.
35. Cox, Vicki. *Maya Angelou: Poet.* New York: Infobase, 2006. Print.
36. Davies, Carole Boyce. *Black Women, Writing and Identity: Migrations of the Subject.* London: Routledge, 1994. Print.
37. Davies, Charlotte Aull. *Reflexive Ethnography: A Guide to Researching Selves and Others.* London: Routledge, 1999. Print.
38. Davis, Angela Y. *Blues Legacies and Black Feminism.* New York: Vintage, 1998. Print.
39. Davis, Anita. *Max Notes for Maya Angelou's I Know Why the Caged Bird Sings.* U.S.A.: Research & Education Association, 1994. Print.
40. Day, Keri. *Unfinished Business: Black Women, the Black Church, and the Struggle to Thrive in America.* New York: Orbis Books, 2012. Print.
41. Dimri, Jaiwanti. *Images and Representation of the Rural Woman: A Study of the Selected Novels of Indian Women Writers.* Shimla: IIAS, 2012. Print.
42. Eakin, Paul John. *How Our Lives Become Stories: Making Selves.* New York: Cornell UP, 1999. Print.
43. Edelman, Hope. *Motherless Daughters: The Legacy of Loss.* 20th Anniversary ed. U.S.A.: Da Capo Press, 2014. Print.
44. Els, Mandi. *Mandi's Story.* Singapore: Genesis Books, 2010. Print.
45. Ezra, Michael, ed. *Civil Rights Movement: People and Perspectives.* U.S.A.: ABC-CLIO, 2009. Print.
46. Featherston, Elena, ed. *Skin Deep: Women Writing on Color, Culture and Identity.* Freedom, CA: The Crossing Press, 1994. Print.
47. Ferguson, Moira. *A Human Necklace: The African Diaspora and Paule Marshall's Fiction.* U.S.A.: New York State UP, 2013. Print.

48. Ferguson, Russell et.al, ed. *Out There: Marginalisation and Contemporary Cultures.* New York: MIT Press, 1992. Print.

49. Fergusson, Mary Ann. *Images of Women in Literature.* Boston: Houghton, 1973. Print.

50. Gale. *A Study Guide for Anne Moody's Coming of Age in Mississippi.* U.S.A.: Cengage Learning, 2002. Print.

51. ---. *A Study Guide for Maya Angelou's I Know Why the Caged Bird Sings.* U.S.A.: Cengage Learning, 2015. Print.

52. Garcia, Marito, and Jean Fares, eds. *Youth in Africa's Labor Market.* Washington: World Bank Publications, 2008. Print.

53. Gillespie, Marcia Ann, Rosa Johnson Butler and Richard A. Long. *Maya Angelou: A Glorious Celebration.* New York: Knopf Doubleday, 2008. Print.

54. Gramsci, Antonio. *Prison Notebooks.* New York: Columbia UP, 1992. Print.

55. Gwin, Minrose. *Remembering Medgar Evers: Writing the Long Civil Rights Movement.* U.S.A.: Georgia UP, 2013. Print.

56. Haas, Michaela. *Bouncing Forward: Transforming Bad Breaks Into Breakthroughs.* New York: Enliven, 2015. Print.

57. Harley, Sharon, and by Rosalyn Terborg-Penn, ed. *The Afro-American Woman: Struggles and Images.* Baltimore: Black Classic Press, 1978. Print.

58. Heilbrun, Carolyn G. *Writing a Woman's Life.* New York: Norton, 1988. Print.

59. Hemenway, Robert E. *Zora Neale Hurston: A Literary Biography.* U.S.A.: Illinois UP, 1980. Print.

60. Henry, C. Michael, ed. *Race, Poverty, and Domestic Policy.* U.S.A.: Yale UP, 2004. Print.

61. Herman, A.L. *Community, Violence, and Peace: Aldo Leopold, Mohandas K. Gandhi, Martin Luther King Jr., and Gautama the Buddha in the Twenty-First Century.* New York: New York State UP, 1999. Print.

62. Hill, Lynda Marion. *Social Ritual and the Verbal Art of Zora Neale Hurston.* Washington: Howard UP, 1996. Print.

63. .Hurston, Zora Neale. *Their Eyes Were Watching God.* U.S.A.: Illinois UP, 1937. Print.

64. Jackson, Stevi, ed. *Women's Studies: Essential Readings*. New York: New York UP, 1993. Print.
65. Johnson, James Weldon. *Along This Way: The Autobiography of James Weldon Johnson*. New York: Viking Press, 1933. Print.
66. Jones, Alethia and Virginia Eubanks, eds. *Ain't Gonna Let Nobody Turn Me Around: Forty Years of Movement Building with Barbara Smith*. U.S.A.: SUNY Press, 2014. Print.
67. Jones, Sharon L. *A Critical Companion to Zora Neale Hurston: A Literary Reference to her Life and Work*. New York: Infobase, 2009. Print.
68. Jule, Allyson. *A Beginner's Guide to Language and Gender*. Great Britain: Cromwell Press, 2008. Print.
69. Kadar, Marlene, ed. *Essays on Life Writing: From Genre to Critical Practice*. Canada: Toronto UP, 1992. Print.
70. Katz, Phyllis A, and Dalmas A. Taylor. *Eliminating Racism: Profiles in Controversy*. New York: Plenum Press, 1988. Print.
71. King, Martin L, and Clayborne Carson. *The Autobiography of Martin Luther King, Jr.* New York: Intellectual Properties Management in association with Warner Books, 1998. Print.
72. King, Martin Luther, Jr., Clayborne Carson, and Kris Shephard. *A Call to Conscience: The Landmark Speeches of Dr. Martin Luther King, Jr.* New York: Warner Books, 2001. Print.
73. Kulkarni, Harihar. *Black Feminist Fiction: A March Towards Liberation*. New Delhi: Creative Books, 1999. Print.
74. Lanker, Brian. *I Dream a World: Portraits of Black Women Who Changed America*. New York: Stewart, Tabori and Chang, 1989. Print.
75. Lentricchia, Frank and Thomas McLaughlin, ed. *Critical Terms for Literary Study*. 2nd ed. U.S.A.: Chicago UP, 1995. Print.
76. Lerner, Gerda, ed. *Black Women in White America: A Documentary History*. New York: Vintage, 1972. Print.
77. Loewenberg, Bert J, and Ruth Bogin. *Black Women in Nineteenth-Century American Life: Their Words, Their Thoughts, Their Feelings*. University Park: Pennsylvania State UP, 1976. Print.
78. Lorde, Audre. *Sister Outsider: Essays and Speeches*. U.S.A.: Crossing Press, 1984. Print.

79. ---. *The Cancer Journals.* San Francisco: Aunt Lute Books, 1997. Print.

80. Luthra, H.L. *A Textbook of General Studies.* 12th ed. New Delhi: Pitambar Publishing Company, 2006. Print.

81. Markandaya, Kamala. *Nectar in a Sieve.* New Delhi: Penguin Books, 2009. Print.

82. Martin, Lori Latrice, Hayward Derrick Horton and Teresa A. Booker. *Lessons from the Black Working Class: Foreshadowing America's Economic Health.* U.S.A.: Praeger, 2015. Print.

83. Megna-Wallace, Joanne. *Understanding I Know Why the Caged Bird Sings: A Student Casebook to Issues, Sources and Historical Documents.* U.S.A.: Greenwood Press, 1998. Print.

84. Mitchell, Juliet. *Psychoanalysis and Feminism: A Radical Reassessment of Freudian Psychoanalysis.* U.S.A.: Penguin Books, 2000. Print.

85. Morrison, Toni. *Race-ing Justice, En-gendering Power.* New York: Pantheon, 1992. Print.

86. ---. *Sula.* New York: Random House, 1974. Print.

87. Murray, Pauli. *Song in a Weary Throat: An American Pilgrimage.* New York: Harper & Row, 1987. Print.

88. Neisser, Ulric and Robyn Fivush, ed. *The Remembering Self: Construction and Accuracy in the Self-Narrative.* UK: Cambridge UP, 1994. Print.

89. Nelson, Emmanuel Sampath, ed. *African American Autobiographers: A Sourcebook.* U.S.A.: Greenwood Press, 2002. Print.

90. Perry, Ruth and Martine Watson Brownley, ed. Mothering the Mind*: Twelve Studies of Writers and Their Silent Partners.* New York: Lynne Rienner, 1984. Print.

91. Porter, A.P. *Jump at de Sun: The Story of Zora Neale Hurston.* U.S.A.: Lerner Publishing Group, 1992. Print.

92. Prasad, G. J. V. *Journal of School of Language, Literature and Cultural Studies.* New Delhi: Pencraft, 2007. Print.

93. Pratt, Robert A. *We Shall Not Be Moved: The Desegregation of the University of Georgia.* U.S.A.: Georgia UP, 2005. Print.

94. Richardson, Marilyn, ed. *Maria W. Stewart, America's First Black Woman Political Writer: Essays and Speeches.* Bloomington: Indiana UP, 1987. Print.

95. Rodriguez, Barbara. *Autobiographical Inscriptions: Form, Personhood, and the American Woman Writer of Color.* New York: OUP, 1999. Print.

96. Sanders, Cheryl. *Empowerment Ethics for a Liberated People.* Minneapolis: Fortress Press, 1995. Print.

97. Schweninger, Loren. *Black Property Owners in the South, 1790-1915.* U.S.A.: Illinois UP, 1997. Print.

98. Showalter, Elaine. *Literature of their Own: British Women Novelists from Bronte to Lessing.* Princeton: Pinceton UP, 1977. Print.

99. Smith, Sidonie, and Julia Watson, eds. *Women, Autobiography, Theory: A Reader.* Madison: Wisconsin UP, 1998. Print.

100. ---. *Reading Autobiography: A Guide for Interpreting Life Narratives.* Minneapolis: Minnesota UP, 2010. Print.

101. Smith, Sidonie. *Where I'm Bound: Patterns of Slavery and Freedom in Black American Autobiography.* U.S.A.: Greenwood Press, 1974. Print.

102. Smith, Valerie. *Self-Discovery and Authority in Afro-American Narrative.* Cambridge: Harvard UP, 1987. Print.

103. Stover, Johnnie M. *Rhetoric and Resistance in Black Women's Autobiography.* Gainesville: Florida UP, 2003. Print.

104. Tate, Claudia, ed. *Black Women Writers at Work.* New York: The Continuum P, 1983. Print.

105. Tomm, Winnie. *Bodied Mindfulness: Women's Spirits, Bodies and Places.* Canada: Wilfrid Laurier UP, 1995. Print.

106. Thurman, Howard. *The Search for Common Ground: An Inquiry Into the Basis of Man's Experience of Community.* New York: Harper & Row, 1971. Print.

107. Vagnerova, Marie, Ladislav Csemy, and Jakub Marek. *Homelessness among young people in Prague.* Charles University Prague: Karolinum Press, 2014. Print.

108. Varghese, Lata Marina. *A Land of One's Own: Women and Land Rights in Literature and Society.* U.K.: Cambridge Scholars Publishing, 2015. Print.

109. Wade-Gayles, Gloria. *No Crystal Stair: Visions of Race and Sex in Black Women's Fiction.* New York: The Pilgrim Press, 1971. Print.
110. Walker, Alice. *In Search of Our Mothers' Gardens: Womanist Prose.* Florida: Harcourt, 1983. Print.
111. ---. *Living by the Word.* U.S.A.: Harcourt Brace Jovanovich, 1988. Print.
112. Wall, Cheryl. *Changing Our Own Words: Essays on Criticism, Theory and Writing by Black Women.* New Brunswick: Rutgers UP, 1991. Print.
113. Washington, Mary Helen, ed. *Black-Eyed Susan's and Midnight Birds: Stories by and About Black Women.* New York: Anchor Press, 1975. Print.
114. ---. *Invented Lives: Narratives of Black Women, 1860-1960.* New York: Anchor Press, 1987. Print.
115. West, Dorothy. *The Living is Easy.* U.S.A.: The Feminist Press, 1948. Print.
116. Witcover, Paul. *Zora Neale Hurston.* U.S.A.: Holloway House, 1994. Print.
117. Woolf, Virginia. *A Room of One's Own.* Canada: Broadview Press, 2001. Print.

Journals and Reviews:

1. Adell, Sandra. "Mystic Sisterhood." *Transition* 55 (1992): 185-90. Print.
2. Anderson, Jace. "Re-writing Race: Subverting Language in Anne Moody's *Coming of Age in Mississippi* and Alice Walker's *Meridian.*" *A/B Auto/Biography Studies* 8.1 (1993): 33. Print.
3. Bell, Derrick. Rev. of *In My Place* by Charlayne Hunter-Gault. *Book Review* 2 November 1993: 3-4. Print.
4. Cannon, Katie Geneva. "Resources for a Constructive Ethic in the Life and Work of Zora Neale Hurston." *Journal of Feminist Studies in Religion* 1.1 (1985): 37-51. Print.
5. Cobb-Moore, Geneva. "Rev. of Order Out of Chaos: The Autobiographical Works of Maya Angelou by Dolly A. McPherson." *A/B Auto/Biography Studies* 7.1 (1992): 140. Print.

6. Couser, Thomas G. "Autopathography: Women, Illness, and Lifewriting." *A/B Auto/Biography Studies* 6.1 (1991): 65-75. Print.
7. DuCille, Ann. "The Occult of True Black Womanhood: Critical Demeanor and Black Feminist Studies." *Signs* 19.3 (1994): 591-629. Print.
8. Fraser, C., Gerald. "Charlayne Hunter-Gault: From Front Line to Firing Line." *Essence* March 1987: 41-42. Print.
9. Georgoudaki, Ekaterini. "Contemporary Women's Autobiography: Maya Angelou, Gwendolyn Brooks, Nikki Giovanni, Lillian Hellman, and Audre Lorde." *Diavazo* 237 (1990): 62-69. Print.
10. hooks, bell. "Writing Autobiography." *Feminisms: An Anthology of Literary Theory and Criticism*. Ed. Robyn R. Warhol and Diane Price Herndl. New Jersey: Rutgers UP, 1993. 1036-39. Print.
11. Kennedy, Edward M. "Rev. of *Coming of Age in Mississippi* by Anne Moody." *New York Times Book Review* 6 January 1969: 5. Print.
12. Kerr, Audrey. "What Becomes of the Colored Girl?: Black Women, Autobiography and Womanist Theology." *Quodilbet* 2.3 (2000): 30-35. Print.
13. Krasner, James. "The Life of Women: Zora Neale Hurston and Female Autobiography." *Black American Literature Forum* 23.1 (1989): 113-26. Print.
14. Lee, Felicia R. "Voyage of a Girl Moored in Brooklyn." *New York Times* 12 March 2009: C1. Print.
15. Louai, El Habib. "Retracing the Concept of the Subaltern from Gramsci to Spivak: Historical Developments and New Applications." *African Journal of History and Culture* 4.1 (2012): 5. Print.
16. Mackethan, Lucinda H. "Mother Wit: Humor in Afro-American Women's Autobiography." *Studies in American Humor* 4.1-2 (1985): 51-61. Print.
17. Monroe, Arthur. "Festac 77 - The Second World Black and African Festival of Arts and Culture: Lagos, Nigeria." *Black Scholar: Journal of Black Studies and Research* 9.1 (1977): 34-37. Print.

18. Rev. of *In My Place* by Charlayne Hunter-Gault. *Atlantic* December 1992: 151. Print.
19. ---. *People* 7 December 1992: 73-76. Print.
20. ---. *New Yorker* 21 December 1992: 135. Print.
21. Rev. of *Dust Tracks on a Road* by Zora Neale Hurston. *New Yorker* 14 November 1942: 79. Print.
22. Singh, Krishna. "Postcolonial Subalternization in the Plays of Girish Karnad." *Criterion: An International Journal in English* 2.1 (2011): 1. Print.
23. Sharma, Rekha, ed. *Conifers Call: Shimla Journal of Poetry and Criticism* 8.1 (2016): 1-16. Print.
24. Smedley, Audrey. ""Race" and the Construction of Human Identity." *American Anthropologist* 100.3 (1998): 690-702. Print.
25. Smith, Sidonie. "The Song of a Caged Bird: Maya Angelou's Quest after Self Acceptance." *Southern Humanities Review* 1973: 365 – 75. Print.
26. Thomas, Karen M. Rev. of *Triangular Road* by Paule Marshall. *Dallas Morning News Book Review* 2009: 5. Print.
27. Troester, Rosalie. "Turbulence and Tenderness: Mothers, Daughters, and 'Othermothers' in Paule Marshall's *Brown Girl, Brownstones.*" *Sage: A Scholarly Journal on Black Women* 1.2 (1984): 13-16. Print.
28. Wade-Gayles, Gloria. "The Truths of Our Mothers' Lives: Mother-Daughter Relationships in Black Women's Fiction." *Sage: A Scholarly Journal on Black Women* 1.2 (1984): 8-12. Print.
29. Walker, Alice. "The Black Woman's Story." *New York Times* 12 February 1984: 94. Print.
30. Wilson, Blake. Rev. of *Triangular Road: A Memoir* by Paule Marshall. *New York Times Book Review* 17 April 2009: BR21. Print.
31. Yardley, Jonathan. "A Memoir from Paule Marshall, Author of *Brown Girl, Brownstones.*" Rev. of *Triangular Road* by Paule Marshall. *Washington Post Book Review* 1 March 2009: 165. Print.
32. Young, Dianne. "Their Southern Way With Words: Charlayne Hunter-Gault." *Southern Living* June 1990: 78-83. Print.

Essays:

1. Lupton, Mary Jane. "Singing the Black Mother: Maya Angelou and Autobiographical Continuity." *Maya Angelou's I Know Why the Caged Bird Sings: A Casebook*. Ed. Joanne M. Braxton. New York: OUP, 1999. 129-148. Print.
2. McPherson, Dolly A. "Initiation and Self-Discovery." *Maya Angelou's I Know Why the Caged Bird Sings: A Casebook*. Ed. Joanne M. Braxton. New York: OUP, 1999. 21-48. Print.
3. Moore, Opal. "Learning to Live: When the Bird Breaks from the Cage." *Maya Angelou's I Know Why the Caged Bird Sings: A Casebook*. Ed. Joanne M. Braxton. New York: OUP, 1999. 49-58. Print.
4. Walker, Alice. "The Black Writer and the Southern Experience." *In Search of Our Mothers' Gardens*. By Alice Walker. New York: Harcourt, 1983. 15-21. Print.

Internet Sources:

1. "A Celebration of the Life of Maya Angelou." 12 Sept. 2014. Web. 20 Jan. 2017. <www.wbai.org/articles.php?article=2256>.
2. Adams, Noah. "The Inspiring Force of 'We Shall Overcome.'" 28 Aug. 2013. Web. 2 Feb. 2018. <https://www.npr.org/2013/08/28/216482943/the-inspiring-force-of-we-shallovercome>.
3. "African American Literature." 6 Sept. 2008. Web. 10 Jan. 2016. <http://www.britannica.com/EBchecked/topic/926640/African-American-literature>.
4. "African American Literature: The Civil War and Reconstruction." Web. 12 Jan. 2017. <kids.britannica.com/blackhistory/article-232349>.
5. Andrews, William L. "African American Literature." 20 Sept. 2013. Web. 12 Jan. 2017. <https://www.britannica.com/art/African-American-literature/The-Black-Arts movement>.
6. "Anne Moody." Biography. Web. 14 Aug. 2016. <http://www.biography.com/people/anne-moody-37999>.

7. "Aunt Moody and *Coming of Age in Mississippi*: Analysis." Web. 20 Jan. 2017. <schoolworkhelper.net › English>.
8. Austin, Curtis J. "On Violence and Nonviolence: The Civil Rights Movement in Mississippi." Web. 2 Feb. 2018. <http://www.mshistorynow.mdah.ms.gov/articles/ 62/the-civil-rights-movement-in-mississippi-on-violence-and-nonviolence>.
9. "Black History and Women: People and Events in African American and African Women's History." Web. 23 Dec. 2016. <womenshistory.about.com › ... › African American Women: General Resources>.
10. Chappell, Bill. "Integrating a Southern Giant: A Pioneer Looks Back." 7 Jan. 2011. Web. 2 Feb. 2018. <www.wbur.org/npr/132712913/a-pioneer-looks-back-50-years-after-making-history>.
11. "*Coming of Age in Mississippi*: Context." Web. 18 Jan. 2017. <www.sparknotes.com › ... › Literature Study Guides › Coming of Age in Mississippi>.
12. "*Coming of Age in Mississippi*: Popular Essays." Web. 18 Jan. 2017. <newyorkessays.com/essay-coming-of-age-in-mississippi-2/>.
13. "*Coming of Age in Mississippi*: Researchomatic." March 2012. Web. 19 Jan. 2017. <www.researchomatic.com/Coming-Of-Age-In-Mississippi-115796.html>.
14. "*Coming of Age in Mississippi*: Themes, Motifs, and Symbols." Web. 6 Feb. 2017. <www.sparknotes.com › ... › Literature Study Guides › Coming of Age in Mississippi>.
15. Creech, James. "What Represents in a Representation? A Question Concerning Michael Foucault's Age Classique." *Man and Nature/L' home et al nature* 2 (1984). Web. 10 Dec. 2015. <http:idreading/ideridit/1011807/>.
16. Danto, Erzulie. "Black Feminism in the US." Web. 21 Aug. 2004. <http://www.rastafarispeaks.com/cgibin/forum/archive1/config.pl?read=43728>.
17. Demmitt, Jacob. "Charlayne Hunter-Gault Remembers Negativity, Protesting." 13 Jan. 2011. Web. 3 Feb. 2018.

<https://www.redandblack.com/news/...hunter-gault.../article_ af6a56a4-3386-5554-8d3.

18. "*Dust Tracks on a Road* Analysis: Form and Content (Masterpieces of Women's Literature)." Web. 17 Jan. 2017. <https://www.enotes.com › Study Guides>.
19. "*Dust Tracks on a Road* – Zora Neale Hurston." Web. 14 Sept. 2016. <www.zoranealehurston.com/books/dust-tracks-on-a-road.html>.
20. Emancipation Proclamation. Web. 10 Aug. 2016. <https://www.archives.gov/exhibits/ featured_documents/emancipation_proclamation/>.
21. Gale, Thomson. "Marshall, Paule 1929 – Contemporary Black Biography." Web. 14 Jan. 2017. <www.encyclopedia.com › People › History › Historians, Miscellaneous: Biographies>.
22. ---. "Hunter-Gault, Charlayne 1942 – Contemporary Black Biography." Web. 15 Jan. 2017. <www.encyclopedia.com › ... › Journalism and Publishing: Biographies>.
23. ---. "To Da-duh, in Memoriam" 1997. Web. 5 June 2017. <www.encyclopedia.com/education/news-wires-white-papers.../da-duh-memoriam>.
24. Gibson, Julie. "An Analysis of Maya Angelou's *I Know Why the Caged Bird Sings.*" 17 Oct. 2016. Web. 21 Jan. 2017. <https://academiclibrary.com › English>.
25. "Go There To Know There: Phillis Wheatley: African American Foremother of Poetry." Web. 13 Sept. 2016. <gotheretoknowthere.blogspot.com/2010/09/phillis-wheatley-and-david-walker.html>.
26. "Great Migration." 2010. Web. 5 June 2017. <www.history.com/topics/black-history/great-migration>.
27. Grisso, Selma. "Feminism As A Theory." Web. 16 Jan. 2016. <https://prezi.com/ qdnofarmtsdz/feminism-as-a-theory/>.
28. "Harlem Renaissance Women: African American Women Dreaming in Color." Web. 27 Dec. 2016. <womenshistory.about.com › ... › Harlem Renaissance Women>.
29. Huff, Christopher Allen. "Student Movements of the 1960s." 28 March 2017. Web. 2 Feb. 2018.

<www.georgiaencyclopedia.org/articles/history-archaeology/student-movements-1960s>.

30. "*I Know Why the Caged Bird Sings* by Maya Angelou: Key Facts." Web. 20 Jan. 2017. <www.sparknotes.com › ... › I Know Why the Caged Bird Sings>.
31. "*In My Place*." Web. 16 Jan. 2017. <https://www.buffalolib.org/vufind/Record/698964/Reviews>.
32. "*In My Place* by Charlayne Hunter-Gault." Web. 12 Sept. 2016. <https://www.kirkusreviews.com/book-reviews/charlayne-hunter...2/in-my-place-2/>.
33. "*In My Place* Summary." Web. 16 Jan. 2017. <https://www.enotes.com › Study Guides>.
34. Juris, Carolyn. "*Triangular Road: A Memoir* by Paule Marshall." May 2009. Web. 15 Jan. 2017. <www.bookslut.com/nonfiction/2009_05_014419.php>.
35. "Marginalization of Women in the Society." Web. 14 Jan. 2018. <https://essayswriters.com/essays/Review/marginalization-of-women-in-the-society. html>.
36. "Maya Angelou." Anti Essays. Web. 28 Nov. 2012. <http://www.antiessays.com/free-essays/306322.html>.
37. "Maya Angelou." Anti Essays. Web. 28 Nov. 2012. <http://www.antiessays.com/free-essays/210946.html>.
38. "Maya Angelou Leadership and Legacy." Web. 20 Jan. 2017. <61477672.weebly.com/ legacy.html>.
39. "Maya Angelou Poems: Reception and Legacy." Web. 21 Jan. 2017. <www.gradesaver.com/maya-angelou-poems/wikipedia/reception-and-legacy>.
40. "Maya Angelou - Poet, Civil Rights Activist, Author, Activist – Biography." 5 June 2017. Web. 20 July 2017. <https://www.biography.com/people/maya-angelou-9185388>.
41. Millar, Patti. "Life Writing Definitions." Web. 29 Aug. 2016. <http://maivish058.qwriting.qc. cuny.edu/life-writing/>.

42. Nolan, Hamilton. "Poverty and Racism Aren't the Same, But Black People Are Getting Screwed by Both." 25 Jan. 2016. Web. 8 June 2017. <gawker.com/poverty-and-racism-arent-the-same-but-black-people-are-1754950415>.
43. Penrice, Ronda Racha. "Sit-ins and their impact on the Civil Rights Movement." Web. 2 Feb. 2018. <http://www.dummies.com/education/history/american-history/sit-ins-and-their-impact-on-the-civil-rights-movement>.
44. "Portrayal of Women in Literature." Web. 15 April 2012. <http://www.crossref-it.info/articles/322/Portrayal-of-women-in-literature>.
45. "Racial Prejudice." Web. 8 Sept. 2017. <www.allaboutpopularissues.org/racial-prejudice. htm>.
46. Taylor, Steve. "Why Men Oppress Women: The psychology of male domination." 30 Aug. 2012. Web. 10 Feb. 2017. <https://www.psychologytoday.com/blog/out-the-darkness/.../why-men-oppress-women>.
47. Tekinay, Asli, Ana Friale, Ahmed Saber. "Contemporary African American Autobiography." Web. 10 Nov. 2012. <http://www.salzburgglobal.org/asc/csacl/progs/lit98/group5/>.
48. "The Present and Future of Civil Rights Movements: Race and Reform in 21st century America." Web. 16 Jan. 2018. <https://law.duke.edu/clrp/conference/civilrights/>.
49. "Toni Morrison: African American Women's Writing." Web. 13 Jan. 2017. <vle.du.ac.in/mod/book/print.php?id=11856&chapterid=23436>.
50. Trachtenberg, Peter. "*In My Place* by Charlayne Hunter-Gault: Teacher's Guide." Web. 16 Jan. 2017. <www.randomhouse.com/highschool/catalog/display.pperl?isbn=9780679748182>.
51. "Voting Rights Act." 2009. Web. 31 May 2017. <www.history.com/topics/black-history/voting-rights-act>.

52. Wynn, Meshay. "Anne Moody: A Biography." Web. 20 Jan. 2017. <www.mswritersandmusicians.com› Mississippi Writers>.
53. Yardley, Jonathan. "A Memoir from Paule Marshall, Author of 'Brown Girl, Brownstones.'" Web. 1 March 2009. <http://www.washingtonpost.com/wp-dyn/content/article/2009/ 02/26/AR2009022602576.html>.
54. "Zora Neale Hurston and the Post-Modern Self in *Dust Tracks on a Road*." The Free Library. 1998 African American Review. Web. 15 Sep. 2016. <http://www.thefreelibrary.com/ Zora+Neale+Hurston+and+the+post-modern+self +in+%27Dust+Tracks+on+a...-a0 21232160>.

PDF File:

1. "African American Woman Writer: Zora Neale Hurston – Author, Anthropologist And Folklorist." 1997. PDF file. Web. 5 Jan. 2017. <https://www.palmbeachschools.org/ sc/wp-content/uploads/sites/85/.../Unit20.pdf>.
2. Ampadu, Lena M. "Black Women Writers as Dynamic Agents of Change: Empowering Women from Africa to America." 2006. PDF file. Web. 30 Dec. 2016. <forumonpublicpolicy.com/archive07/ampadu.pdf>.
3. Carby, Hazel. "White Woman Listen! Black Feminism and the Boundaries of Sisterhood." Web. 11 Sept. 2016. <jan.ucc.nau.edu/~sj6/carby%20white%20woman%20listen.pdf>.
4. Carvalho, De. "Beauty Matters, Family Matters: The Experience of Growing Up an African-American Girl." 2006. PDF file. Web. 1 Feb. 2017. <livros01.livrosgratis.com.br/ cp046860.pdf>.
5. Chakraborty, Chandrima. "Subaltern Studies, Bollywood and *Lagaan*." Web. 11 Sept. 2016. <jan.ucc.nau.edu/~sj6/chakrabortylagaan.pdf>.
6. Karthikeyani, G. "Double Marginalisation." 2012. PDF file. Web. 1 June 2017. <shodhganga.inflibnet.ac.in/bitstream/10603/37255/3/chapter3.pdf>.

7. Scott, Robin Patricia. "Being Black and Female: An Analysis of Literature by Zora Neale Hurston and Jessie Redmon Fauset." 1986. PDF file. Web. 2 Jan. 2017. <https://dspace.mit.edu/bitstream/handle/1721.1/33806/17940803-MIT.pdf>.
8. Sickels, Amy. "*I Know Why the Caged Bird Sings*: African American Literary Tradition and the Civil Rights Era." 2010. PDF File. Web. 27 Jan. 2017. <salempress.com/store/pdfs/caged_critical_insights.pdf>.
9. "The Status of Black Women in the United States." 7 June 2017. PDF File. Web. 14 Jan. 2018. <https://iwpr.org/wp-content/uploads/2017/06/The-Status-of-Black-Women-6.26.17.pdf>.
10. Opatrny, K. "Voices From the Gaps: Anne Moody." 1998. PDF file. Web. 9 Feb. 2017. <conservancy.umn.edu/bitstream/handle/11299/166276/Moody,%20Anne.pdf>.

Dissertation:

1. Harris, Meta Y. "Black Women Writing Autobiography: Marginalisation, Migration, and Self-Identity." Diss. of Manchester Univ, 2003. Print.
2. Roy, Mantra. "Speaking Subalterns: A Comparative Study of African American and Dalit/Indian Literatures." Diss. of South Florida Univ, 2010. Print.